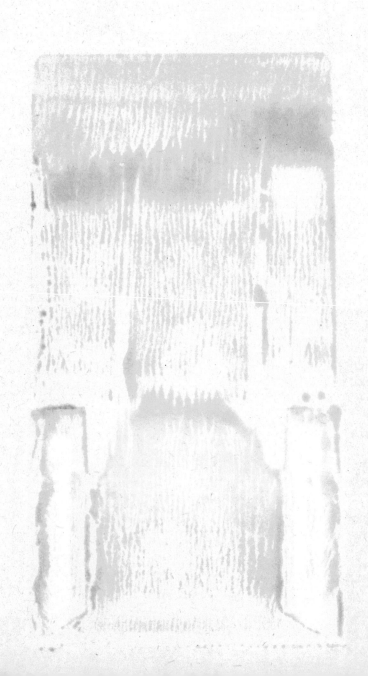

OXFORD MONOGRAPHS ON
SOCIAL ANTHROPOLOGY

General Editors
MAURICE FREEDMAN B. E. B. FAGG
A. C. MAYER E. ARDENER

PORTRAIT OF A
GREEK MOUNTAIN
VILLAGE

JULIET DU BOULAY

CLARENDON PRESS · OXFORD
1974

Oxford University Press, Ely House, London W.1

GLASGOW NEW YORK TORONTO MELBOURNE WELLINGTON
CAPE TOWN IBADAN NAIROBI DAR ES SALAAM LUSAKA ADDIS ABABA
DELHI BOMBAY CALCUTTA MADRAS KARACHI LAHORE DACCA
KUALA LUMPUR SINGAPORE HONG KONG TOKYO

ISBN 0 19 823186 5

© OXFORD UNIVERSITY PRESS 1974

PRINTED IN GREAT BRITAIN BY
BUTLER AND TANNER LTD
FROME AND LONDON

TO
My Mother
AND TO
The People of Ambéli

PREFACE

IT will quickly be evident to readers of this book that what insight I have gained into the life and ways of thinking of the people of Ambéli is largely through the world of the women. As a woman myself the only possible course of action was to go where I was invited and where I was least an anomaly, and this was into the houses. Although I was quite often invited to the cafés and always accepted, these occasions were normally used by the villagers to ply me with questions about England or occasionally to embark on heated metaphysical arguments, and when interest in me regarding these topics was beginning to wane and the men to return to their normal conversation, I would become aware that it was time for me to leave, and left. In this way I never grew conversant with the men's world of politics (while these were still being discussed) or economics, quarrels, or litigation, at first hand, although naturally I observed some of these things in action during the day-to-day life of the village. However, my position as one of the women of the village did not debar me totally from getting to know the men—rather it gave me a knowledge of the men in their houses and fields as opposed to a knowledge of them in the wider social scene: as hosts and fathers rather than as the protagonists of their families in the competitive and often highly charged atmosphere of the outside world. In this way my study is inevitably one-sided, but since the society itself invests the house and family with key significance, I hope that in concentrating my study on these things I may fairly claim to be, in part at least, representing these people truly.

My relationship with the villagers was entirely personal, never formal. They knew from the beginning that I was writing about them, though found it hard to believe that my reason for being there was because I valued their way of life and wanted to get to know it more deeply. Linked to notions of advancement, great salary, and world renown, my presence there became more understandable, though never entirely so. However, with their strange and wonderful acceptance of the foreigner and of foreign ways, they did receive me into their society and trust me with a part of their lives. I have tried not to betray their trust, but rather to relate what I learned in such a way as to reveal something of the un-selfconscious depth at which they live. But even so, because any such writing about a society must involve a degree of revelation which the people concerned might find uncomfortable, the village has been given a pseudonym and all the names of the villagers changed.

My deepest thanks go to Dr. John Campbell for his continual and patient support during the long process of writing this book, and for his invaluable advice on many vital issues. For help of a different kind my thanks also are due to Dr. Philip Sherrard who was endlessly ready to discuss with me the ideas and problems that arose out of my association with the villages. I am indebted to Dr. Rodney Needham who first took me on as a student of anthropology; to Dr. Rory Williams for reading the text and helping with numerous difficulties; to Mr. Kevin Andrews for detailed assistance with the last chapter; and to Dr. John Peristiany for his continual encouragement at all times. I thank also Miss Elizabeth Marden who took a great deal of trouble going over the text and cutting out grammatical howlers, and Mrs. Sue Henny whose work on typing this book in its original form was whole-hearted and invaluable. The Principal and Fellows of Linacre College were a source of support during my first writing up of this research, as were the Warden and Fellows of St. Antony's College during the last stage of the work; the Director and Staff of the British School of Archaeology at Athens provided me unfailingly with a much-needed oasis from time to time when life in the mountains got too difficult; and Mrs. Anna Sherrard, above all, gave me over many years in Greece a refuge and a home. To the villagers of Ambéli I owe an unrepayable debt, for they gave me their friendship and their hospitality in one of the most vivid and happy periods of my life.

St. Antony's College
 Oxford   J. du B.
October 1973

CONTENTS

A*

LIST OF PLATES

LIST OF TABLES

PART I

I
THE VILLAGE

THIS book is a study of a phenomenon which is becoming all too frequent in the present day—a dying village community. However, since it is concerned mainly with the values and attitudes which are derived from a long tradition and which even in the present times sustain the villagers in a sense of purpose and destiny, it is concerned more with life than with death.

I went there in 1966, making my first tentative exploration one morning in late August. It was hot, even at seven o'clock, and the sun flooded the stubble fields with a bleak yellow radiance which cast long shadows but yet promised no shelter—burning inevitably out of a cloudless sky. Rising slowly at first, the path skirted some gardens and wound its way upwards through increasingly abandoned fields brittle with tangled meadow grasses and parched flowers, and into the first fringes of the pine forest where the air was pungent with resin, and the shiny leaves of the mountain shrubs—myrtle, smoke plant, arbutus, holm-oak, and juniper—began to form the thick forest undergrowth. The valley sides grew steeper and the stillness more dense and sibilant with just the croak of a hooded crow or the cheep of a sleepy bird heard over the murmuring of the forest. At one point I crossed a water-course, now in summer merely a tumble of boulders, a damp trickle seeping out of the side of a mossy rock, shadowed by plane and oak.

After this the way changed from its easy undulations along the valley side and climbed steeply between high banks where the feet of countless animals had scored the path deep into the earth, and began to rise rapidly through the forest slopes. Half-way up the mountainside the path emerged from the pines on to the shallower once-terraced fields where a few olive trees grew and where crops had recently been harvested, until finally, about two hours after I had set out, the presence of the village was heralded by little garden plots green with runner beans, courgettes, melons, and the path itself altered from trampled earth and polished rock to a stone cobbled surface built by past generations but now falling away at the edges into endless disrepair. At the approach of the shoulder of the mountain the path levelled out, heaps of chaff left over from the threshing appeared, and threshing-floors and stone barns; and suddenly the path turned and dipped down over the crest and the village in a cluster of russet roofs and whitewashed walls appeared below me, held in a protecting semi-circle of the mountainside. Here and there between the houses and among the compact irregularity of outbuildings and woodstacks and tiny gardens, the green of fruit-trees was welcoming, and over everything stirred a cool northerly air which blew over ranges of brown foothills from a broad stretch of distant sea.

This was Ambéli, a small village in Euboea—thirty-three houses, 144 inhabitants—but big enough if I was to get to know, as I hoped, every person there. I was lucky on this first visit to make the acquaintance of the community secretary, a woman who, even though completely ignorant of who I was or what my intentions were, received with no apparent surprise my eventual confession that I hoped to find a room and come to live in her village. 'You can stay with the widow', she said, and promptly arranged it. Thus I was let into the life of one of the most fascinating and dramatic people in the village, the young widow whose husband had been murdered by a fellow villager seven years before, when she was twenty-five, leaving her with a son of just over a year old, and a daughter of fourteen days. The daughter, neglected in the grief and despair engendered by the catastrophe, had died soon afterwards, so now the widow, at thirty-two still young, lived alone with her son and was apparently willing to take me in.

The village itself turned out to be, in its main characteristics, exactly what I had been looking for. It had a priest and a local council; it was remote, high (600 metres), and had snow in the winter; it was small, airy, and very beautiful. Since my interest in making this study lay largely in the more traditional aspects of village society, I had been looking for a village without regular transport, and thus without too constant communication with the more urban-oriented world. In Ambéli I found such a village, for although it possessed a road, one which led north-east out of the village and linked it with the market town of Kateríni, this road had such a bad surface and approached the village at such an impossible gradient that even then few vehicles ever came up, and six months later, in January 1967, its use was terminated

abruptly by the collapse in a gale of the bridge which spanned
the ravine over which all traffic from Ambéli to Kateríni had to
pass. It turned out that the constructors of the bridge had used no
iron in the span and had put in cement only for show on the
pointing of the blocks. Inside, the bridge was filled up with a mass
of stones and earth, the contractors having 'eaten', as the villagers
said, the larger part of the money allocated for its building. After
this, the villagers were forced to use in summer, when the water
was low, the rapidly decomposing old road, and in winter the old
mountain track which joins the river at a point more easily forded,
and which is spanned by a precarious pine bridge for use when the
river is in spate. The fortunes of the road were to provide a constant theme during my stay in Ambéli, for of all the modern conveniences which the villagers, lacking piped water, regular transport, and electricity, feel themselves most to need, it is quick and
convenient communication with the outside world. The time taken
from Ambéli to Kateríni on foot or with an animal is, at the very
least, one and a half hours.

This situation makes Ambéli an anomaly in the surrounding
district where all the other villages have roads and many of them
regular means of transport, and the result has been that while
within the village much of the traditional way of life and thought
has been preserved, the desire to remain in such a way of life has
been, among the younger people at any rate, almost entirely
eradicated. When I went to live in Ambéli, the village had by no
means been untouched by change, yet many aspects of this change
had not been assimilated into the way of life within the village,
and had remained still as half-accepted ideas and unfulfilled
ambitions. The fact that no machinery could get into the village
and no produce out of it, without being transported by a mule
whose maximum load should not be more than 100 kilos, had meant
that methods of farming and therefore the way of life in general
had remained in many important respects exactly as they had been
for hundreds of years; and along with these inherited activities
had necessarily been preserved to a considerable degree the system
of ideas which had traditionally validated them. Yet concurrent
with this high degree of traditionalism, almost as a result of it,
there had been for the previous six years a movement towards
emigration so intense that the days of the village were already
numbered. As things stand at the moment it is virtually certain

that long before the end of the century this community will have ceased to exist.

In 1966, for instance, Ambéli possessed, together with a number of young married couples, two young men and seven girls who were all of an age for marriage. Within the next two years all had married, and all of them out of the village. All the other young men of a similar age group had already left, either to enlist in the Merchant Navy or to emigrate overseas—chiefly to Germany and Canada. In the two and a half years that elapsed between my departure from the village in the spring of 1968 and my return to it in the autumn of 1970, five more houses had been abandoned as age had compelled, or opportunity encouraged, the inhabitants to lead a 'better' life elsewhere. By then, every one of the village children over thirteen had been sent to a grammar school, and even if they fail in their examinations and are compelled to come back to the village for a stretch, there is not the remotest possibility —saving a national disaster—of any of these children marrying and settling in the village, or of any of the *émigrés* returning permanently to it.[1]

The main elements in the process of change may be seen in communities all over Greece, and in this respect the difference between the communities lies less in what is happening—that is to say the change from traditional and symbolic thinking to modern and secular thinking—than in the way in which it happens. In certain senses, therefore, Ambéli was no different from a thousand other Greek villages. However, in the degree of traditionalism which still survived even while this coexisted with a considerable pressure towards modernity, it provided a good example of contemporary village society in which nevertheless the old and the new had not become so fused as to be indistinguishable. The focus of this book is primarily on the traditional and static aspects of this society, for it is these which embody the fundamental social and metaphysical presuppositions on which the value system and consequently much of social action are traditionally based. These presuppositions find their chief expression in the people's understanding of the house and of the principal masculine and feminine roles within it, and are based on an inherited tradition concerning the nature of good and evil. To this central body of attitudes

---

[1] For a further discussion of this question see Appendix I on Emigration and Demography.

and beliefs I then attempt to relate other and often contradictory dynamics of social life as observed nowadays. These dynamics can be seen in two main areas of village life—in the competitive character of social relations, and in the phenomena of social change as these occur throughout all levels of the community as a result of the impact of new and often alien values.

This book, then, is an attempt to identify the values that unify the community, and to trace the related strains which these values none the less impose on village life. It is an attempt also to show that, although quarrels and hostility, jealousy and suspicion, are inseparable from the particular way in which the villagers live out their priorities, these conflicts are not basic to village life, but rather contingent and derivative. Two village sayings illustrate this scheme of relative importance—'Χριστὸς Νικάει' (Christ Conquers), and 'ὁ Δαίμονας προχωράει' (the Devil is making progress). The difference in the translation of the present tense in either case is intentional, for whereas the saying referring to the Devil is used by the villagers to describe the origin of the incidents in which evil is seen to occur, that relating to Christ is one which they use as a prayer, or an axiom, for it defines a characteristic of Christ which is part of the immutable order of reality. Evil, while being accepted as real enough on its own level, is seen as a temporary interference in the natural course of things where Christ is already victorious. The basis is assured, even though the battle needs continually to be engaged.

The village has not always been in the position in which it now lies, and every villager will tell one how its old site was originally about a kilometre down the mountain slope which lies directly behind the village and to the south. The story goes that in the seventeenth century this original village had a population of over 1,000, although towards the end of the eighteenth century this had diminished considerably. It had a certain amount of traffic through it, because lying as it did in a long valley leading north-west–south-east through the island it was on a central communications route. This village was destroyed by the Turks in April or May, c. 1804.[1] The reason for this is not known, but as it is told now, the

---

[1] This date is calculated from conversations with an old woman in Ambéli who was born in 1894, and remembers her grandfather talking of the destruction of the old village. He was 8 when it occurred, and he died at the age of 110,

Turks killed and burned indiscriminately for seven days, after which, as their custom is said to have been, they declared an amnesty for any who had escaped. Many of the survivors fled to a nearby island, others dispersed in various parts of the country, but a few remained in the area, or returned to it, to found a new village on the present site of Ambéli.

The choice of the site is said to have been due to a herd of pigs rooting around and discovering the water which the people of Ambéli claim, and with truth, is better than any in the surrounding district. At all events, the remaining survivors of the destruction settled there, living at first in huts made of branches, and then building themselves houses. This village also was later discovered by the Turks, and an *Agá* took possession of it.

Ambéli was then, as now, largely forest, with some arable land, and on the advent of the *Agá* it became a *tsiftlík*, the owner of which had all rights over the land, and various rights over the peasants who were his unwilling tenants.[1] The situation of the villagers at that time is described by the present villagers in the following words: 'They had to beg their bread, and that with economy.' So, naturally enough, they took to harvesting and threshing the grain secretly. The story that follows is one of true Odyssean cunning.

In the course of time the *Agá* inquired the reason for the poor yield of the harvests, and was told, 'There's a fearful beast ravaging the crops and eating the corn. We go every day in peril of our lives.' So he set out himself, with a few of the villagers, down the valley in the direction of the old village to see about this story.

---

when his grand-daughter was 12 or 13. The season is known because the little boy, who was lost during the destruction and found only when his parents returned weeks later, kept himself alive by eating sweet grasses known as βρίζες which only grow in the spring.

[1] During the earlier stages of Turkish domination, *tsiftlíks* were land grants made by the Sultan to Muslim settlers in Turkish-occupied land. These *tsiftlíks* varied in size from 6 to 15 hectares, and were sufficient to ensure the livelihood of one family. With the degeneration of the Turkish feudal order at the end of the seventeenth century, the *tsiftlíks* developed into much larger properties where the landlord held rights over whole villages whose inhabitants thus became his enforced tenants. These villagers had no legal protection against his demands, among the most serious of which was his claim of the land as his full heritable property, and thus of the right to evict the peasants at will; and his exaction from the villagers of a rent which amounted to between one-fourth and one-half of the gross product of the land. J. Tomasević, *Peasants, Politics and Economic Change in Yugoslavia*, California, London, 1955.

The valley is wide just behind Ambéli, narrowing as it drops down to the south-east, past the site of the old village, to a gorge enclosed by two towering cliffs. On each of these cliffs had been stationed a man, with a long horn and a flint-lock. As the *Agá* approached, he heard the regular thump-thump of the villagers threshing the forbidden grain secretly on a hidden threshing-floor between the two cliffs.

'What is that?' he inquired.

'That's the beast, listen to what a noise he makes! We're not going any further—you can go on your own if you like,' his companions answered.

Just then a dreadful noise, 'Oooooh, Oooooh', broke out from one cliff, and was answered by another from the opposite one, and as the two hidden men blew on their horns sparks flew from their flint-locks. The *Agá* was so frightened at this fearful manifestation that he fled back up to the village and away, selling the whole *tsiftlík* cheap to the inhabitants, before, it is said, the neighbouring *Agás* had departed from their properties in the surrounding district.

Part of this story is true, at least. The *tsiftlík* of Ambéli was in fact sold, in 1853,[1] to the nineteen heads of families in the village. The property thus acquired by the whole village amounted to 12,500 *strémmata* or 3,125 acres,[2] and the better part of it was shared out between the various heads of households according to which each obtained a property of approximately 75 acres,[3] good land consisting of both arable and forest. It was not, however, the earliest instance of the departure of a Turkish ruler from the area, for Kateríni bought its independence in 1827. The result of these two transactions was that Kateríni (pop. 1,408),[4] being the first relatively large village of the area to gain its independence, became the first centre in the area for regional government; and Ambéli, privately owned by the inhabitants as well as being of large extent, acquired the reputation in the neighbourhood of

[1] This date is taken from records in the Public Notary's office in Kateríni.

[2] For convenience in the text, English terminology is used wherever practicable. The Greek unit of land measurement is a στρέμμα. 1 στρέμμα = 0·2471 acres, or 0·10 hectares.

[3] For a fuller description of this situation see Appendix II on Land Tenure.

[4] This figure is taken from the Population Census of 1961, Ἐθνικὴ στατιστικὴ ὑπηρεσία τῆς Ἑλλάδος, 1962. 'Πληθυσμὸς τῆς Ἑλλάδος κατὰ τὴν ἀπογραφὴν τῆς 19ης Μαρτίου 1961', Athens.

being wealthy. It is only in recent days that those advantages held by Ambéli have become as little prized as they have, both by the villagers themselves and by the world outside.

The village lies just below the crest of the mountain ridge, lapped on one side by the pine forests, on others by gardens, fields, and vineyards, backed by the hilltops, and facing over the steep valley to the foothills and the sea. In appearance it is typical of the traditional, closely knit, mountain village of Greece, built as much for protection against foreign occupiers and local brigands as for the attempt to get all the houses at the periphery of the village equally near the one source of water which has to serve for all. In the latter certainly they were successful, and the furthest house is not more than three minutes' walk away from this fountain—very clear, very cold water which collects around the roots of an ancient plane tree and has been tapped by the villagers into three channels. The phenomenon of the farmstead, distant from a village by some miles and set on its own among the fields, is rare in rural Greece, and gregariousness in Ambéli is such that one of the criteria of a desirable house is that it should not be, as they call it, 'on the edge' of the village, that is to say with nothing behind it but the open country, and no houses immediately beside or in front. One such house which is thought to be 'on the edge' and to 'have no neighbours' is a house which is screened by trees at the back, and at the side which looks over the main village, but to have two houses in sight about twenty yards away, and several others within reach of a two- or three-minute walk.

The village has at first sight no one specific focal point, but appears simply as a random cluster of houses. The main path runs transversely through the centre of the village, and if one traces it as it comes from the south over the shoulder of the mountain from the fields in the valley behind the village, one follows it past the foot of the church, which it leaves to the right, through the upper half of the village, past two cafés which it leaves on either side, and into the main square where a third café is situated, whereupon it dips east and runs out of the village, becoming the old road to Kateríni. North and south run two steep, once-cobbled paths, one leading to a different set of valleys and fields to the south and east of the village, and the other into the fertile valley bottom in front of it. Various subsidiary paths lead to the different neighbourhoods of the village, and from any one point there is a generally accepted route to any other point, deviation from which will invariably elicit the question, 'Why don't you go *that* way?'

The orientation of the houses, seen in relation to the placing of their front doors and of the yards which are invariably in front of these doors, seems to have been influenced by a sort of gravitational pull exercised by the main square, for all the houses, if they do not actually face the square, face on to the path that most quickly leads to it. It could be argued that since the same main path that leads to the square leads also to the fountain, the orientation is rather to the fountain than the square. But this seems to be disproved by the placing of the two houses nearest the fountain, for while these could easily face this fountain in preference to the square, they do not, in fact, do so. At all events, it is apparent from the general construction of the village that it was built as an introverted community whose houses are organized exclusively around its own population and the activities taking place by the fountain, on the main path, and in the square, rather than according to any conception of independent preferences or with reference to any other centre outside the village; for not one house faces out of the village or looks towards the incomparable view which stretches away below.

The result of this is that the front yard, where so much of the activity of the household is carried on, is usually on the most public side of the house, and therefore that concealment from the public eye of any activity which takes place in that yard is a lost cause. In the yard the baking and washing are done, wood is chopped, animals are tethered, dishes washed; and in the summer months, looms may also be set up in the shade of some tree or of the overhanging veranda, or maize rubbed from the cob, tomatoes cut up and salted for tomato paste, haricot beans dried and sorted, and so on. None of these activities is secret in itself, but the garnering of information about as many people as possible is vital to the life of a villager, both from the point of view of simple enjoyment of the knowledge of what is going on around him, and because it might just become relevant in a certain situation to know what a particular person was doing at a certain time on a certain day. To the extent therefore that this curiosity is indulged, a type of secrecy becomes correspondingly valued.

However, while this particular orientation of the houses acts

against the degree of possible privacy for activities taking place
in the yards, there is another factor involved in the general layout
of the houses and stables in the village which to some extent com-
pensates for this. This layout is one which has been described by
Friedl in her book on Vasilika,[1] and which is typical of very many
Greek villages. It gives the appearance of being completely random, and makes the village seem more like a natural growth on
the mountainside rather than a man-made imposition. The paths
wind around now the corner of a house, now the fence of a garden
or the edge of a yard or stable, and the setting of the village on the
mountainside increases this lack of order by causing the houses to
occur here and there as the slope of the hill dictates. Every house
therefore is surrounded by its own little oasis of semi-privacy: the
pile of wood for the winter protects one end of the yard, the little
shelter for the mud oven, or a hen-house, may interrupt the view
from other directions. The result of this is that to obtain a direct
view of what is happening in another person's yard it is often
necessary to go to a specific vantage point, or to pass directly on
the path leading by that yard. Although people will do what they
can to find out what is happening in other people's lives, they have
not the time or the shamelessness to indulge in obvious spying,
and so knowledge of these activities tends to be limited to what can
be observed and passed on by close neighbours, deduced by tan-
talizing glimpses from far off, or noticed by those who have cause—
or excuse—to use the particular path concerned. This, so to speak,
fortuitous privacy, is reinforced by the general orientation of the
houses towards the main square, for because of this many of the
houses face the side or the back of their neighbour's house, rather
than its front yard.

The village therefore falls naturally into various separate areas,
the activities of which are to some extent protected from the
public gaze while at the same time not being essentially private.
Within these areas, neighbours are plainly in the best position for
noticing closely what goes on in each other's houses, but even then
such an arrangement is not always reciprocal. The fact that
Christina can see into Drosoula's yard easily does not necessarily
mean that Drosoula can see into Christina's. There is likely,
however, to be an alternative yard into which Drosoula can see,
so the *status quo* is maintained. These groups are the bases of

[1] E. Friedl, *Vasilika: A Village in Modern Greece*, New York, 1962.

'neighbourhoods' which give rise to a precisely termed but un-
certainly defined relationship between, particularly, the women of
the houses concerned. It is, however, a relationship so fluid as not
to provide any real stability for those who are thus defined 'neighbours', and so while the neighbourhood is a type of grouping
which has a relevance in the life of the villager, it does not override
the fundamental concept of the village as a single community.
Divisions and loyalties between various collections of houses do
exist, and may coincide with separation and with proximity, but
they do not exist as the direct result of a system of formal neighbourhoods.

The physical layout of the village thus reveals a way of thinking
according to which, after his own individual house, the villager
looks to the community rather than to selected components within
it for his final *raison d'être*. The family is seen to exist in the context of the community, and since it is to the village that the villager
looks to confirm his identity, it is to the village that the right be-
longs to know and to pass judgement on what goes on in every
individual's front yard. Nevertheless, since in the case of a conflict
of interests it is the family rather than the village which commands
the villager's first loyalty and gives him his basic stability, it is only
as far as the front yard that the curiosity of the community gains
easy access. The house itself is more impregnable.

The village is defined clearly by the ending of the houses and
the beginning of open country—the area of the village being 'from
threshing-floor to threshing-floor'—and those barns where the
straw is kept for the animals which lie on the further edge of these
threshing-floors are thought of as being 'beyond the village'. At
two of the entrances to the village, east and west, are placed little
shrines with icons in them, and a sanctuary lamp (καντήλι)—a
little glass holding a wick floating in oil—and anyone who wishes or
who happens to think of it may go in the evening to renew the oil
and relight the flame. These shrines indicate and invoke the presence in the village of the holy people of the Orthodox world—
Christ, the Mother of God, and the Saints—and define the
sanctuary of the village where people pass and where the spirits of
evil are kept at bay, from the wild world of field and forest and
mountain where the demons live and where no help is at hand in
the event of danger. Over the village presides the particular
presence of the saint to whom the church is dedicated—in Ambéli

the Mother of God—and it is the festival of this church which
once a year provides, so to speak, the 'name-day'[1] of the village,
the festival (ἑορτή) of the church. At this time each family invites
its relations from other villages for two or three days of eating and
drinking and dancing, and in this situation particularly the identity
of the village as such over the separate identities of the individual
families within it becomes especially apparent, and the whole
community unites in a rare burst of communal activity 'To show',
as they say, 'our village to the world' (νὰ δείξουμε τὸ χωριό μας
στὸν κόσμο).

[1] These are days which in the village are known as 'ὀνόματα' or 'names'. In
Ambéli the men celebrate their name-day in accordance with the festival of the
particular saint after whom they are named. Women do not have similar
celebrations.

2. The House

II
THE HOUSE

BEFORE 1950, all except for a few of the houses of Ambéli were long single-storey buildings, comprising one large room. One end of this room would usually be raised as a low platform where the family lived; at the other end all the farm implements would be kept and the animals housed. Lighting was often from one source only, a sloping window in the roof (φεγγίτης), and many of these houses had no chimney but would have a fire in the middle of the room whose smoke eddied around the rafters and finally drifted out between the tiles.

After 1950, however, new ideas began to make themselves felt. People began to partition their houses to keep the animals out of the living quarters, and little by little most of the owners built an extra storey on to the ground floor, which was reached by an outside staircase and a wooden veranda. All the houses built then, and earlier, had solidly constructed stone walls about 1 ft. 6 in. thick, whitewashed both outside and in, with rafters and ceilings of pine. The house in the village to be most recently enlarged had a first floor in brick added to it in 1958. Since then no new houses have been built in the village, although several people have replaced the wooden verandas, as they rotted, with cement ones edged with iron railings.

Plainly the first principle according to which the old houses were built was that they should shelter those who lived in them; but there is another principle which they expressed which goes beyond the mere idea of physical shelter and involves the unity of the family group understood in its very widest definition. Within the house not only the family would collect at the end of the day, but also all the creatures and articles involved in that family's way of life. Under the same roof, in the same large room, the men, like the animals, slept on the floor, while the plough lay against the wall, the hens roosted on the beams, and the pig grunted in the corner. Membership of this group and right to this shelter were obtained not only by those who by blood or marriage were related to the central family, but also by those who contributed by their work or their produce to its life. These four walls, therefore, housed an exclusive group in which everything, down to the least chicken, was a full member, bound together by mutual obligations according to which the animals were entitled to protection, and the men, service. The simplicity of the inhabitants' way of life and the design of the house allowed for considerable expansion of this group, especially in its human aspect, whenever that was necessary—for there was under normal conditions no question of there 'not being enough room' when all the room needed by the guest was the space he would take up, rolled in a blanket, on the floor. To lack such space, and still more, food, for the guest, was a matter crucially touching the honour of the family, and a guest whether relative, friend, or stranger was, once received into the house, entitled to honorary membership of the group for as long as he remained.

In the present day, even though the houses have on the whole many fewer members, partitions have been erected between the people and the animals, and people sleep not only in beds but often in separate rooms as well, this principle still obtains, and may be seen in the attitudes to guests and to animals even though it is no longer so evident in the present construction of the houses.

By far the greater number of these houses have their first-floor rooms used for living in, while the two downstairs rooms are used as a stable and a store room. In five of the houses, however, one of the ground-floor rooms is used as a living-room while the opposite room is a store room which combines as a stable if there is no other outbuilding for the animals, or which is used solely for housing such things as farm implements, bins of corn, oats, lentils and other cereals, cheeses, tins of oil, paraffin, fleeces, hanks of wool, and so on. Three houses only have remained as single-storey buildings, having a stable and other outhouses built on to their two living-rooms.

In addition to the houses with their adjacent outbuildings—a hen-house made of resin tins and perched in the fork of a tree, a place for the pig, the little shelter which protects the mud oven, the stable—nearly every house will have a building known as a hut, or, in this context, a barn, in which the hay and straw are kept, which is a single-roomed, windowless building made of the same materials as the houses and situated somewhere on the edge of the village.

The family then still lives, as in the older days, in close contact with the animals—the horse or mules, the household goats, and perhaps a sheep—which are in almost every case either below or opposite the rooms in which the family sleeps; and in most cases the plough-animals are capable, if their feed at 2 a.m. and again at 6 a.m. is forgotten, of waking up the family by banging against the manger and making sleep impossible. The house is still thought of as a unit enclosing a group which includes animals and inanimate property as well as the family in the centre, and the only difference between past and present times lies in the greater sophistication with which these various components are now disposed. The range of outbuildings has increased, but these buildings are still clustered close to the house around the yard—the yard itself being effectively the house's external dimension of which every square inch is highly prized, and bitterly fought for in the event of threatened annexation.

In this context, the house can be described merely as a particular arrangement of property which defines quite simply an area of ownership which is passionately defended in an environment where resources are few. But this is only a partial description and does not give due value to the significance of property, which is that it is not only an economic asset, but is also involved with the owner's personality, and with the particular nature of his identity in society. This is to say more than that property takes on the nature of a status symbol, which is of course the case; it is to say that the nature of the owner's relationship to what he owns is such that any action against any part of his property, from theft, however slight, down to the maltreatment by another of one of his animals, is bitterly resented not only because of the financial or economic loss that might be involved, but also because such action against anything belonging to him constitutes an action against himself and against the other members of his household. Where the house is concerned, this attitude is intensified.

The house as a physical structure is deeply linked with the identity of the family, for as the family is the principal and irreducible group of this society, so the house in which the family lives is the chief stronghold of those values which are basic to that society. The house therefore takes on many of the connotations of the family—the two words often being used interchangeably—and there are crucial respects in which it is membership of the house rather than the fact of blood relationship which defines the area within which these intra-familial values are most fully practised. This distinction between the actual structure of the family itself, and the house which contains the family, must be treated with care, for of course it is for the family that the house is built, and around the family that all its activities are organized. Yet it is still true to say that the practical terms within which village life is lived cause it to be the house and its permanent members, rather than the entire family unit (whose members may be dispersed in different houses or different countries), which provide the effective focus for the total loyalty and mutual support that is the chief feature of the relations between members of the same family.

One of the chief reasons for this is the sheer physical labour and the amount of time which are involved in running the house and farming land in a largely unmechanized society. Once a married couple is committed to its own house and farm, there is inevitably little energy to spare to help their respective families of origin, and less time left in which to see them. In these circumstances, the physical distance even of one house from another is enough to invalidate the continual practical reciprocity which characterizes family life in this community. It is for this reason, therefore, that the tightest group of society is to be found not in a special category of blood relations—whether married or unmarried—but in the members of a house, for outside that house lies the outside world, and the outside world represents always different loyalties and opposing interests.

It is plain therefore that it is very difficult to separate in popular Greek thought the house from the family, a fact which is illustrated in the frequent reference in Ambéli to the family by using the word 'house'—σπίτι. And it is interesting in this context that the word for family, οἰκογένεια, is a compound from οἶκος, the word in Katharévousa for house, and -γένεια, the stock, i.e. people who originate from the same house.

It must not, however, be supposed from this that all the members of a family living in the same house are always in a state of perfect amity, for naturally there occur quarrels and disagreements between husbands and wives, and where there are in-laws living in the same house there can be a great deal of bad feeling. There are many tales of autocratic mothers-in-law, of bickering and squabbling between the various wives, of quarrels between the sons of the family who thought that their own wives or children were not being treated fairly. From the moment of marriage, and especially from the moment of the birth of the first child, the new family becomes firmly established as a separate entity even in the parental home, and the seeds of division lie unequivocally in the formation of this new group before any move has been made into a different establishment. Because of this, many of the stories of the separation of the extended family into separate households rest on the assumption of the impossibility of several families with growing children all being able to get on well together, and of how the independence of one's own family group is a prerequisite for a harmonious life.

However, it is at the same time true that the normative values of this society all contribute to the house being a sanctuary from the troubles which its members find in the outer community, and it is one of the characteristics of the society that the solidarity of the house rests not so much on everyone within that house behaving well to each other, as on the united front that they all present to the outside world. Illustrating this I quote a comment regarding someone who had got drunk at the annual festival, had threatened to shoot a café owner with whom he was not on good terms, and to cut out his liver, and had had a fight in another café with a visitor from Athens in the course of which he had broken a window and some glasses. For this he was being taken to court, and the expectation of all was that he would be heavily fined. Of this event a villager said, 'What business had he got to go and beat up a stranger? If he gets drunk, let him come back and beat his wife or his child. *They* won't take him to court. . . .' The speaker's wife, and the others in the room, endorsed this statement.

Thus, whatever the relations within the house, the members of it do their best to conceal their differences and to close their ranks in the face of the wider community, and this solidarity is recognized in the fact that the 'house' or 'family' is treated by that community as a single social reality. It is to the house, rather than to individuals within the house, that invitations for weddings, remembrance meals, and funerals are sent, and the 'house' that is represented by one or more of its members in church, on name-days, and at other social events. The inhabitants of a house are implicated more easily in a quarrel contracted by one of its members than are similarly related members who have moved to

separate houses. Tales of feuds or of great misfortune, resulting in
the ending of a family line or in the evacuation of the whole
family from the village, are invariably summed up with the words,
'The house was scattered' (σκρόπησε τὸ σπίτι), or, in the case of a
more inclusive disaster, 'Three houses were utterly destroyed'
(τρία σπίτια καταστράφηκαν).

The house in Ambéli is traditionally handed down through the
male line to the youngest son, who brings his bride into the house
to look after his parents while they are alive, and to become mistress of the house after they are dead. This custom has lapsed
since 1964 with the increase of emigration and depopulation, but
in 1966–8, village experience was still close enough to its traditional
practice for the extended family to be thought of as the norm. In
earlier times a common though not universal practice was to
incorporate several married sons and their families into the parental home, even though they later separated into their own estab-
lishments, leaving the youngest son, most recently married, to
remain with the ageing couple. More recently, since 1940, the
extended family has come to consist of the old parents and the
family of one married son. Thus, even though, by now, no more
sons or daughters are marrying into the village, there are six
houses in which the senior couple live together with their married
son, his wife, and the children of that union, while of all the other
houses there are only two cases in which the older generation,
living alone, also has a married son living in the village. Of these,
one son lives in the house adjoining that of his widowed mother,
and their two households co-operate in many ways; in the other
case, while the old parents live in one house and their married son
in another, in every other respect they live, eat, work, and organize
their finances as a single unit.

Land is divided equally among the sons as and when they need
it[1]—usually on their marriage—but because village properties
have traditionally been unable to stand too great sub-division, the
custom developed for the son remaining in the house with his

---

[1] Daughters were often included in equal partition of the land, but this was
usually because of the father dying without having made a will. The intention
was nearly always to give dowries to the daughters in the form of some goats
or sheep, perhaps a cow, a sum of money, a field or garden consisting of up to
half an acre—any one or all of these things—and then legally to exclude them
from any further right to inherit. The effect of this was that forest land and the
greater part of the arable land were, in the main, left to the sons.

parents to buy the shares of those brothers who could not be accommodated on the land, while the latter went as *esógambroi* (ἐσώγαμπροι, s. ἐσώγαμπρος—men who go to live uxorilocally, 'grooms' who are 'in' their wives' houses) to other villages, or emigrated abroad. Because of this, therefore, and because of the 'old people's portion' (γεροντομοίρ'), which is a few extra acres given to the son who looks after his parents in their declining days—the house in Ambéli is also closely associated with the land.

The inheritance of the house and land is explicitly connected by the villagers with the good behaviour of the son and his bride to the old people while they are alive, and with their proper celebration of the memorial services after they are dead. While they are alive, the bride is sometimes said to think, 'Let them die, and I'll be on my own', but at the same time to be intelligent enough to realize that it is only by her good behaviour to her husband's parents that she will ensure her inheritance. After they are dead, she looks at the house and farm which is now hers, and remembers them with gratitude for what they have passed on to her. Conversely, the parents have a responsibility to deal fairly with those who look after them. This natural sequence according to which the care of an old person results in inheritance by the one who cares for them was expressed succinctly in a comment referring to a widow who had inherited a house and a large property from her mother-in-law, even though this mother-in-law had three sisters, one brother, and several nephews and nieces living in the village. When I asked about this I was told: 'She looked after the old woman, fed her, washed her, and she inherited.'

It is with the house and land, then, and those who live in the house, rather than with any blood relations who may have gone to live elsewhere, that responsibilities both to the living and to the dead are connected; and in the form of children the living aspect of the family takes on particular significance, for in the individual lives of the children born to the house the continuity of the family and its victory over death are ensured, and 'the name is heard again' (ἀκούγεται τὸ ὄνομα πάλι).

In the house the family gathers in a mutual affection and trust which are in many respects the antithesis of its external relations. Within the house secrets are kept, while a son or daughter who marries out of the house, whether or not they continue to live in the same village, will both keep some secrets from their family of origin and likewise be kept out. I was present when a man tried to conceal from his married daughter the amount of the dowry his son was expecting to get from his fiancée; and I was entrusted, by the young widow in whose house I was living, with a secret which she would not tell her brother or father because they were 'in another house'. Only 'within the house' does complete confidence or mutual trust exist, and this is expressed in so many words: 'Confidence does not exist outside the house' (δὲν ὑπάρχει ἐμπιστοσύνη ἔξ᾽ ἀπ᾽ τὸ σπίτι). However, simply because confidence is not found outside the house, it is all the more essential within it, and within the house members of the family are at one in their interests and ambitions, and in their assessment of the other families making up the community outside. In this environment of common toil and mutual relaxation, affection, and trust, even small children are expected to understand and to support their families in their perpetual need to defend themselves from the curiosity and enmity of others.

The house, therefore, in terms of village thought, is indissolubly linked with the history of the family, and with the practical observance of a high code of honour and a pattern of responsibility which bind members in a close and positive relation to each other during their lives, and which continue after death. The affection and sense of security, which are felt by the villager, particularly by the old, in their own house, are very great; and it is noticeable that all the old people of Ambéli prefer to stay in their own houses as long as they can possibly manage to look after themselves, rather than move to another house in another village to stay with one of their married children. This is due partly to a disinclination to move from the place where they have lived for sixty years or so, but it is also related to the fact that parents, or parents-in-law, have in their own house an authority which they lose the moment they go into the house belonging to another, even that of their own son. The house, representing the continuity of the generations as well as the years of their own toil, is involved with their lives in a way that is deeper than that resulting in mere affection, and invests them with the dignity of a status within the ancestral hierarchy which they are stripped of when they move, mere helpless old people, into a house which to them is nothing but a place to live.

Throughout the village the interior design of the houses is guided by a single principle—one room is used for living in, another is kept as the best room, and any other rooms are used for bedrooms or occasionally as stabling. Several houses, however, have only two rooms for the family, and in this case, or if the family is large, the best room also is used for sleeping in.

In the winter the floor of the living-room will be covered with rugs—coarse goat-hair carpets which used to be an essential item in the girls' dowries (though they are so no longer), or rag rugs which the women make on the looms with strips of old clothes which they cut up when they are past wearing. The bed in the corner is covered with a different type of woven rug (μπατανία), and smaller rugs (πάντες) of this sort are hung on the walls either side of the fire-place. Other than the bed, the furniture consists of a hard chair or two, a number of low wooden stools, and a low table about 2 feet high, which usually stands on end in a corner, to be pulled out when it is needed for some household task, or at meal times. In this room there will be a tall pile of folded rugs built up against the wall and covered with a dark rug, or with a cream-coloured cotton sheet edged with hand-made lace. Sieves, pans, and cooking implements are hung from nails in the wall, or kept in the store room, while the few plates and knives, forks, and spoons, and perhaps odd medicaments are kept in a little glass-fronted cupboard set into the wall. Beams, and often a plank slung from the ceiling, provide extra shelf space.

It is in this room that the fire burns all winter, lapsing only at night or if the house is left empty, and not only does it provide heat for cooking, and warmth, but it gives light in the evening when, to save paraffin, pieces of resinous wood are laid one by one on the fire and burn with a bright golden flare. There is little need for economy over wood since there is a great deal of dead wood in the forests, and only the labour needed for cutting and carrying it puts a limit on how much a house uses. This is the room in which all the work in the day-time is normally carried on, and it is here also, because it is the warmest, that the oldest couple in the house sleep.

The best room is quite different. This is the room kept for the formal visiting on a name-day, or for a meal on a special occasion when guests are invited for the midday or evening meal on feasts such as Christmas, New Year's Day, the Carnival (᾽Απόκρεω, the festival before the beginning of Lent), Easter, the village festival in August, and so on. This is the room where most of the photographs are kept, piled on the mantelpiece or the table. The rugs pinned to the wall are usually printed cloths with garish designs bought from some town, or from a travelling tinker, and the table-cloth is usually of the same variety. Plastic flowers in a heavy cut-glass vase are sometimes on the table. The large bed kept in this room is covered with a bought counterpane and with cushions which, if not bought, will have been worked by the daughter of the house according to a modern design. Pictures of ladies being serenaded in gondolas, of castles perched amid Gothic scenery, or of huntsmen with dogs shooting ducks or deer are very frequent in these best rooms. Here, even in winter, a fire is very seldom lit, and on these formal visits one freezes amid chilly splendour, longing for the smoky cosiness of the lowly living-room.

It is usually in this room that the spare clothes are kept, hanging from hooks on the wall and covered with nylon sheeting, or in a large wooden trunk, which also holds any dowry coverings which are still unused. The daughter's *trousseau* is usually kept in this room since inevitably it is cleaner than the living-room, and every one of these things must go to her future home in perfect condition.

In one of these two rooms, or perhaps in the little hall outside, the icons will be kept on a shelf high up in the eastern corner, with the sanctuary lamp hanging in front. This is lit every Saturday evening, on the evening before a saint's day, and during the saint's day itself.

Any other room, or rooms, are used as bedrooms, and are sparsely furnished with a bed, possibly a table and a hard chair, and any other articles not easily accommodated in the other rooms. The process of going to bed and getting up being the simple business that it is, requiring no more than the removal of the top garments, these rooms are thought of as purely functional, for sleeping and storing, and are not designed round ease, beauty, or comfort.

It is the living-room, therefore, that is the effective centre of the house, and only for a few months in the summer is its function partially usurped by the yard. During the hot months, from June to early September, the cooking is often done outside on a little mud shelf which is built as an extension of the oven, many of the household tasks will be carried on outside, and people sit in their doorways or on their verandas, chatting and gossiping with each other. However, for three parts of the year the cooking and all the other household tasks are done in the living-room, and the yard reverts to its normal function where only those jobs are done that cannot be done inside—the washing, baking, chopping wood, tethering animals, and so on. Winter and summer, discussions which demand any degree of privacy are carried on inside the house, and meals are always eaten inside.[1]

If the living-room is the centre of the house, the hearth is the centre of the living-room, and members of the family gather around it not only at meal times, but at any other time of day when they are in the house, for all activities which take place in the house take place around the one source of warmth in it. From mid-October to mid-April a fire is lit every morning for heat as well as for cooking, and is kept alight all day. The fire-places are large, and the fire is built by propping some logs, about 3 feet long and often very heavy, fan-wise up the chimney. Smaller branches laid up against the bottom of the logs are essential, and the fire is lit initially with a little pile of pine-shavings—resinous crescents of wood which are sliced away from the trees when they are being tapped. Once the fire is burning well it is kept going easily by knocking away the burnt ends of wood and drawing the unconsumed ends together again. This means that the fire needs continual attention, but has the advantage not only of reducing the time that would otherwise be spent chopping wood, but also of bringing it about that if the fire is left unattended for any length of time and the logs are securely placed, they will, as they burn away, simply fall apart, and the fire will slowly go out.

The household uses three main types of cooking implements. One is a broad-based, narrow-mouthed pot made of aluminium or enamel with a long handle (μπρίκι), which is heated by being pushed in among the embers. These are of various sizes ranging from about 3 to 5 inches high, and are used for making coffee, heating milk or rice for the children, for making mountain-tea in winter, and heating small amounts of soup if anyone is sick. The normal meals for the household are prepared in a large aluminium or copper pot without a handle (κατσαρόλα or, locally, τέντζερ), which is placed on an iron tripod over the fire. Food which is cooked in the oven, such as roast meat, or 'pie' (πίττα—a dish made of thin sheets of φύλλο or leaf pastry, and filled with cheese and eggs, or occasionally with wild spinach), is cooked in a large round dish of copper or aluminium, without a lid (ταψί). Bread is

---

[1] There are some very rare exceptions to this, see p. 55.

set to rise in a long wooden trough divided into compartments, and is then shaped into large round loaves and baked on the floor of the oven. The oven itself is always in the yard and is large and shaped like an upside-down bee skep. It is made of mud and straw, with a round mouth, and is sheltered from the wind and weather by a rough shed made of wooden planks and sheets of corrugated iron or beaten-out resin tins. It is usually kept scrupulously clean and whitewashed frequently, and is heated by burning in it a lot of dry sticks—usually the old branches left over from the winter feeding for the goats—and then by raking out the embers which are left at the mouth of the oven to keep the heat in.

In nearly every house the meals are eaten at a low wooden table which is pulled out when it is needed from its resting place against a wall, and put away again after the meal is finished. A piece of sacking is spread on the floor under the table to catch the crumbs, and the eaters sit around on the little stools which are the normal fireside furniture.

When the meal is served and the bread cut up, and everyone seated at the table, each person will cross himself and begin to eat. In only one household that I was ever in for a meal did anyone begin his food before the whole family was collected at the table, and this was a boy of twelve who was reprimanded by his mother for being a pig—a judgement which implies in this society not merely a person who behaves badly, but one whose behaviour is not fitting for an intelligent creature, for a human being. On one occasion we waited for a quarter of an hour with the spaghetti congealing on the table until the husband was able to come up from the café in which he was serving. People talk during meals, and at the end each one will cross himself as he finishes, before the table is cleared away and the family draw close on their stools around the fire. The meal is a traditional ritual chiefly observed in the evening; but whether the meal is eaten inside the house or out in the fields, the eater will cross himself before and after it, and, especially if it is in the house, the ceremony of waiting until everyone is collected is observed even if it is a hurried meal with only the women present.

Except for the great festivals and periods when they co-operate over the farms, the villagers very rarely eat in one another's houses. However, there is a form of visiting which is slightly more formal than the casual dropping in which forms the normal day-time pattern, while being less formal than the institutionalized visiting on a name-day or on the acceptance of an invitation to a meal. This is the 'evening visiting' (νυχτέρεμα). From October to April, when, as the villagers say, 'the night is long' and work outside is completed by 5 or 6 o'clock in the evening, the family will gather for the evening meal and then when the table has been cleared away they will sit and talk until they go to bed at about 9 o'clock. This is the time at which those who can leave young children with a grandmother or aunt, or whose children are grown up, go to the houses of relatives or friends and chat for two or three hours. This type of visit can be carried out on the spur of the moment, or can be in accordance with a casual invitation—'Come and spend the evening with us tonight'; but there is a definite pattern to this visiting, and every family has a large range of families to whom they will never go in this way, even though they may be on perfectly good terms with many of them. To visit someone's house purely for the sake of company, a 'relationship' of some sort is required. Evening visiting is informal and always takes place comfortably in front of the fire in the living-room.

Formal receptions, however—occasioned by the advent of a total stranger to the house, or an engagement, a name-day, or other festival—are invariably in the best room. In this room the visitor will sit at the table on a hard chair instead of crowding with the family on their little stools around the fire-place, and immediately on arrival a little plate of sweet preserve and a glass of water will be served (κέρασμα), usually also with a tiny glass of ouzo or liqueur, by the hostess who stands with the tray waiting to receive the plate and glass after the guest has finished. This ritual is inseparable from entertainment in the best room, while it is a matter of inclination if the visitor is being received informally. It is customary for the guest to take up the drink first, and as he does so the traditional phrases of good wishes, thanks, and welcome are exchanged; just as at a formal meal the host, as he crosses himself before beginning, will say to the guest, 'Welcome' (καλῶς ὥρισες), to which the guest responds, 'I am fortunate to be with you' (καλῶς σὲ βρῆκα).

Even in the present day, the food which the guest is given to eat is for the most part produced by the family's own work on its own land,[1] and the villagers' way of life depends primarily on subsistence agriculture. Cash gained through the sale of resin from the pines is an important though secondary resource which every family possesses to a greater or lesser extent, except for those consisting only of the very old.

The fields around the village consist either of natural patches of fertile ground along the valley bottoms, or of terraced fields made by the present inhabitants' forefathers along the shallower valley sides. Each householder's land is seriously fragmented, no one owns a field of more than five acres, and there are no single stretches of forest belonging to one person larger than seventeen acres. Some of the fields are fragmented into pieces as small as a quarter of an acre and in certain patches of forest where inheritance has been by groups of brothers or cousins, a single person may own only two or three trees. The main crop grown in these fields is wheat, and this, with oats, barley, hay, vetch, broad beans, lentils, various kinds of haricot beans, and chickpeas, makes up the staple diet on which the villagers live and feed their animals.[2] Maize is grown on particularly fertile ground, and green beans,

[1] See Appendix II on Land Tenure. The land surrounding Ambéli is composed roughly of two geological types—a small proportion of rocky limestone outcrops which are almost totally infertile and support nothing but wild flowers, thick mountain grasses, and herbs; and a heterogeneous soil containing clays and marls. The total property (12,500 *strémmata*) covers a mountainous area varying from a height of 250 m to 750 m, and is divided up in the following proportions:

Fields, olive groves, and barren areas	3,200 *str.*
Pine forests (*Pinus halepensis*), evergreen and broad-leaved shrubs	8,350 *str.*
Fir forests	950 *str.*

Plane trees grow in the valleys, and there are some rare occurrences of walnut, chestnut, and oak. The average mean gradient of the forest is 40% in which the greater proportion consists of moderate gradients but which includes sections among the higher levels of fir and especially around the ravine dividing the village territory from that of Kateríni, which are extremely steep.

The figures for the property are taken from two surveys of the area which were presented by K. B. Dhamianou, Forester, for the administration of the forests of Ambéli over the five-year periods following the years 1941 and 1947. *Κ. Β. Δαμιανοῦ,‘ Ἔκθεσις περὶ προσωρινῆς διαχειρίσεως τοῦ συνιδιοκτήτου δάσους —, Εὐβοίας, διὰ τὴν περίοδον 1940–1941 ἕως 1944–1945,'* 1941. '*Περὶ προσωρινῆς διαχειρίσεως τοῦ συνιδιοκτήτου δάσους —, Εὐβοίας, διὰ τὴν πενταετίαν 1/9/1947–31/8/1952,'* 1947.

[2] The following figures are given as an average for the land under cultivation by a normal working family consisting of the husband and wife with one or

haricots, tomatoes, courgettes, onions, and other vegetables in the two areas of land which have a good water-supply and have been made into gardens. Tiny gardens within the village and watered by hand supplement these resources.

In addition to subsistence farming and harvesting the resin from the pine forests, the villagers have a variety of occupations: several of them keep bees, two have shops, and three own cafés. One woman is a dressmaker, two have knitting machines. There is a priest, a village president, a secretary to the community, an agricultural guard, and a miller who has a small clientele for the brown and, it is thought, rather inferior flour that comes from his paraffin-driven mill. However, all these occupations are engaged upon to provide only a supplementary income to that gained from the fields and the forests, for it is these which together provide the chief means of livelihood.

Shepherding, which used to be a general occupation in the past, began to be abandoned by the villagers in 1958, but even when there were, as it is said, over 2,000 head of sheep and goats on the hillsides of Ambéli, the fields were never left unworked even

---

more children and usually one or more elderly dependants. A household consisting only of an old couple will plant very much less.

			Expected crop per str.
Wheat:	10–25 *str.*	(20–5 *str.* are sown only by three families, the usual amount being 12–15 *str.*)	125 kilos
Oats:	2–5 *str.*	(Sown in the proportion of hay : seeds, 2 : 3)	100 kilos / 50 bales
Vetch:	1–3 *str.*	(Animal fodder)	
Broad beans:	2–5 *str.*		75 kilos
Barley:	3–5 *str.*		100 kilos
Lentils:	½–2 *str.*		60 kilos
Chickpeas:	3–4 *str.*		110 kilos
Maize:	2–5 *str.*	(Occasionally as high as 8 *str.*, but very few people have enough fields of the quality which permits this acreage being given over to maize)	90 kilos

Before the advent of fertilizer in the mid-1950s, and the emigration of 1960 onwards, every last half-*strémma* was cultivated, with an average of 50 *strémmata* being put down to wheat by every family. The present agricultural pattern is the result of a diminished population together with a greatly increased productivity per *strémma*. One villager told me that before the days of fertilizer he used to get 1,200 kilos of corn from 40 *str.*, whereas he now sows 12 *str.* and gets 1,500 kilos. The old average yield of 30 kilos per *strémma* has thus risen to 125 kilos. These figures, with minor variations, are confirmed by other villagers.

though the forests were deserted at times when the resin trade failed. Thus while the fields have always been used for subsistence, cash was gained from the cheese, wool and meat from the sheep and goats, and from the periodic sale of resin from the forests whenever trade was good. There have been times, also, in the past, when the forests were leased by all the villagers jointly to a local timber merchant, and the rent then divided among them proportionate to their holdings.

Because of the emigration from the village in post-war years, all but one family now own more agricultural land than they can cultivate, and most own more pines than they want to tap. Except for the one family which has never owned any land,[1] and the one relatively poor shepherding family, no family owns less than ten acres of arable land and between 500 and 700 pine trees, while some own as much as thirty acres of arable land and 3,000 pines. It would therefore be financially economic today for every villager to concentrate on tapping all the resin he can and only secondarily cultivating those of his fields that he has time for, although for reasons which will be examined later only two families in Ambéli do this. Subsistence farming of the fields is still, as it has traditionally been, the villagers' chief means of livelihood.

The working day, in the fields, lasts from about 7 a.m. to 7 p.m., and the family returns to the house at midday if it is possible, eating the midday meal in the fields if it is not. The organization of the acreage under plough makes possible a reasonable working day at the same time as it demands a schedule as tight as the uncertain spring and autumn weather can allow, and gives the villagers a period of comparative relaxation from the completion of sowing at the end of November, until the intensification of the spring work when the weather clears at the end of February or the beginning of March.

The agricultural year[2] starts in the second half of September with the clearing of the fields and the burning off of bracken and rough bushes to prepare for the first ploughing. This period is also spent by the men making the most of the remainder of the resin season, taking the accumulated resin down by mule to Kateríni,

---

[1] This family survived by grazing its sheep off the fallow land belonging to others, and the two remaining old people now exist on their pensions and on gifts from their sons.

[2] See Appendix III on the Ecological Year.

and collecting fertilizer for the sowing. Odd days at this time are taken up by those who possess olive trees lower down the hillside, or on the plain of Kateríni, collecting the first windfalls, although clearing the trees is not done till late November or December. Ploughing starts after the first heavy rains, about the third week of September, and continues until the last of the wheat is sown at the end of November or early in December. Most families sow only what they need for bread for the year, although a few also sow enough to be able to pay off their fertilizer debt in corn rather than in cash. In 1967 five acres was the largest area put down to wheat by any one family.

Autumn days that are not being used for other tasks are used by the men to collect firewood, and to do repairs about the house. Winter is a time largely for the men to sit in the cafés and the women in the houses, as long as the bad weather lasts. Families rise late, 6 or 7 o'clock, compared with 4 o'clock in the summer, and though there are jobs in the fields during January and February if the weather is fit, it is usual for the weather of these months to consist largely of rain and snow when no one goes out to work, and the most urgent task is the collecting of huge piles of evergreen branches every three or four days to feed the household animals which have to be kept inside during the cold weather. However, as soon as the bad weather clears away in early March, and as the sun gets hotter and the days longer, a gradual impetus is felt in the work of the village, bringing the women out of the houses to plant the garden plots near the houses with lettuces, radishes, and spring onions, to beat their rugs at the fountain, and to do any agricultural tasks that have been left undone from the dark days of February. From this month on, the tempo of work intensifies steadily, beginning with hoeing the broad beans and vineyards, and planting the chickpeas, until the last two weeks of June when all the subsidiary crops are cut and gathered in, and, if possible, threshed as well, before the whole village, as they say, 'goes into the harvest'. This is the wheat harvest, and the whole month of July is given over to the gathering, threshing, and winnowing of this crop.

For two weeks after the threshing of the wheat, the work is hard and varied, threshing the subsidiary crops that have been left over from June and harvesting the maize and chickpeas—but the sense of urgency is over, and throughout all this time the tempo gradually subsides into a proliferation of household jobs for the women, while the men go to make up lost time in the forest, and make frequent trips to Kateríni with resin they have been storing from the summer, and to collect the autumn fertilizer. The final burst of activity is a brief, colourful period at the end of September, when the grapes are harvested and when families who are on good terms with each other once again work together and eat in each other's houses for the one day that it takes to pick the vineyard and tread the grapes. By this time it is autumn, the first rain has already fallen and everyone waits for the real break in the weather that signals the beginning of the ploughing as the year turns and the whole cycle begins again.

There is thus a very close interdependence between the house and the land which is the result of a way of life based on farming and a system of ownership based on inheritance. However, there is a further dimension according to which the house is linked with its environment, and is the result both of a mentality which has traditionally persuaded rather than coerced the natural world, and of a lack of mechanization which has made it impossible for the villagers to deny or defy nature in any significant way. Because of this, the natural world constantly makes itself felt in all aspects of the villager's life, and as a result the identification of the house with the family is automatically given a parallel on a purely material level. For instance, there is the fact that a house which is not lived in and cared for, is not 'smoked' (καπνίζεται) as they say, will within a year begin to rot and fall apart. No damp courses in the walls, an interior decoration which consists of plaster and white-wash needing continually to be renewed, an earthen yard outside, all mean that, when the family has finally left the house, weeds begin to grow up in the yard, dead leaves to gather in the corners, lumps of plaster to grow yellow and bulge and fall with the damp, rats, mice, and cockroaches to infest the attics and skirting-boards. Within a year the house begins to look abandoned, and in less than five it will have become a ruin.

In the same way, no electricity and the necessity for a wood fire to provide warmth and cooking, together with the fact that such a fire needs the continual presence of somebody—usually the wife or the grandmother—if it is not to go out, means that the hearth is literally the centre of the house, the source of light, food, and warmth. This practical association of the hearth with the woman, the two sources of life made interdependent, is an aspect of the total symbolic significance of the woman and the house, and it is consistent with this aspect of womanhood that fetching water from the fountain—another task connected with the elemental nature of the survival of the house—is also the exclusive prerogative of women.

The house is also the physical focus for the life of the family in the sense that, since it is in the nature of the agricultural work in the village to be fragmented between various different tasks, one or all of the members of a family may return to the house several times in the day. Except, therefore, at peak periods of combined work, the house is never left empty for long periods, and in houses where there is an old grandmother she may be relied upon always to be there. The association of the house with the family has therefore a purely concrete aspect in which somebody is about the house nearly all the time.

Because in many of the above-mentioned aspects of village life— the use of wood and whitewash, earthen yards, and so on—the villagers have no practical alternative, it may perhaps be said that many of the factors described above throw more light on the determination of the life of the villagers by their environment than on the nature of their values as the causes for their action. The relation between the physical demands of the environment and the values which order how these demands are to be met, is of course two-way, and it would be difficult, if not impossible, to determine in the dense texture of village belief and practice how far the villager's beliefs originate in the natural world by which he lives, and how far his beliefs condition his response to that world. But there is one area of his life where it may be shown conclusively how his sense of the house, as identified with the land, the seasons, and the corporate work and life of the family, is a value strong enough to predispose him strongly to subsistence farming, and to override the economically preferable alternative of abandoning the fields and depending on a cash-based economy from the forests alone.

Worked out in terms of hard cash, and with resin at a subsidized price of 4 drachmas a kilo,[1] it would in fact pay every family to

---

[1] In 1965 the resin prices were stabilized at 4 drs. a kilo by government subsidy, and in 1966–8, when the fieldwork for this book was done, the villagers could rely on this price. In 1967 one drachma equalled approximately 3*d*. (= 1·25p).

make the pines their first priority, and, in the days that are left over, to cultivate their fields. They do not, however, do this. Briefly, the situation may be stated as follows: the resin season lasts from the end of March to the end of October. A hard worker is meant to be able to tap a maximum of 400 pines in one day, every one of which he visits once every eight days in the cooler months, and every six days from mid-June to mid-September when the resin is running fast. Such a man may get an average daily yield from the trees of 60 kilos, that is to say an income of 240 drs. Thus, allowing for days off for festivals and for necessary jobs around the house and in Kateríni, 1,500–2,000 trees are enough to keep one man fully occupied in the summer months and to provide him with a maximum of 10,000 kilos of resin, or an income of 40,000 drs. On the other hand, such a man, working on the fields and the forest together, would make an income in cash and kind of approximately 31,000 drs. only,[2] which, when 2,500 drs. have been deducted for fertilizer, amounts to 28,500 drs. Even allowing for the fact that the figure of 40,000 per annum quoted above is a maximum income, the discrepancy between the two sets of figures is still considerable when the narrow financial margin within which the villager lives is taken into account. And this discrepancy is increased when it is remembered that if enough trees were owned to enable the forests alone to be worked, the family would no longer need a team, or 'pair', of animals, and so would sell one animal and effect a yearly saving on its food of the equivalent of 5,500 drs. Those who have only one animal anyway are forced into a still more uneconomic use of time and labour on the land, since a man with one animal in a situation that calls for two has to co-operate with another family and work jointly on two sets of fields.

It is thus incontestable that a full exploitation of the forests with a secondary emphasis being placed on the fields would be more profitable to the average villager owning—as many of them do—1,000 pines and over, than the reverse scale of priorities. However, of all the householders in the village, only six cultivate all the pines they possess, and these, with two notable exceptions,[1] are the people who own the fewest; and of the six families owning between 2,000 and 3,000 trees, not one of these taps more than

---

[1] See p. 38.

[2] Three farmers' budgets were taken down in detail. This calculation relies on that of the intermediate budget.

half its trees, and in every case the cultivation of the fields is now, as in the past, given priority.

When asked about this, the villagers advance various explanations, of which the commonest are, 'Why should I buy my bread when I can grow it myself?', and, 'Why should I sit doing nothing all winter when my fields lie idle?' Others say, 'Look how much bread one family eats in a year, it's not worth our while to buy it. And the animals have to be fed too.' A typical comment is, 'A little from here, a little from there, that's how we manage to keep things going', and someone once said to me, of resin gathering, 'Don't talk about it. It's hot work in the forest, you tear your clothes, you come back filthy and sweaty, the snakes eat you . . .'

Resin gathering is indeed an exhausting and dirty task which involves the resin gatherer climbing the steep mountain slopes loaded with anything up to fifteen kilos of resin, and often climbing twenty feet up a pine-tree if it is old and has already been heavily tapped. This, if the tree is in a difficult or precipitous position, can be dangerous, and one man in Ambéli, many years ago, was killed by falling from such a tree. However, in spite of this, the villagers need cash ever more badly as the years go by and as their values come more and more to approximate to those of the more urbanized people in the plains. Grammar-school education, particularly, is gaining in importance, and involves very heavy expenditure on rents, food, clothes, and books. In the face of this necessity, it seems that to continue in the fields rather than in the forests, simply because work in the forests is especially exhausting, is not a logical answer, but just one of many answers that the villager might give when asked this particular question. And the truth is of course that the traditional villager has never sat down and worked out why he does one thing rather than another; he simply follows the course that seems to him to be 'good' and that is not obviously inconsistent with his necessary material progress.

It seems plain, then, that what causes the villager—still in his traditional environment and, because of his geographical and social isolation from much of the modern world, still among many of his traditional values—to continue to place the cultivation of the fields before that of the forest, is some powerful value which is quite independent of rational and materialist argument. Since it is with his family that he is primarily concerned, it is to the house and its symbolic significance that we should look for the answer to this

question. In this complex of values the villagers' traditional
attitude to cash is significant.

For the villager the spending of money to buy commodities to
bring into the house is not thought of in at all the same way as is
the direct storing of the house with farm produce. The villager is
used to his labour resulting in two different types of acquisition—
cash or kind—and he looks on work as something which should
bring one or other *into the house*. If, however, the cash that is
earned by the family labour is immediately expended, even though
the result of that expenditure is to stock the house with something
vital, a different process has taken place—one that is less satisfac-
tory to traditional village thinking and which could almost be
described as dissipation rather than conservation. The difference
therefore to the villager between bringing in his foodstuffs
straight from the fields to the house, and spending money to buy
those foodstuffs, may be summarized as in the first instance vital
commodities being brought into the house, and, in the second, a
vital commodity leaving it.

The difference is not a rational one, but rational argument of
a kind which deals only with material expedience is a way of
thought which is not used by the traditional villager to order all
his actions, but only some of them, and many of his actions depend
also on the way in which he perceives his relation to the natural and
spiritual worlds which are so vital a part of his cosmology.

Another example of this type of thought was often demonstrated
to me in the reluctance with which anyone would accept, for
instance, an egg from me.

'You've paid for it,' they would say, in horror.

'Well, you've given me lots of eggs, and you work for yours.
It's the same thing.'

'No,' they would reply. 'You've paid for yours with money.'
The comment of another woman, when asked which season she
liked best, illustrates the same turn of mind. She said that the
harvest was to her the best time of year, and when I expressed
my surprise at this, since this time is notorious for gruelling work
in great heat, she replied: 'Up to the harvest time you're filling
your house with grain—wheat, lentils, beans, chickpeas. . . . After
then it all disappears little by little.' It was the harvest (June and
July), not the gaining of cash (the season for which is August to
December) nor the spending of cash on things for the house, which

represented for her the security of the house and insurance against the winter. The simple exchange between man and nature according to which he tills the ground and gets his bread in return is a relationship which the traditional villager finds comprehensible, and totally different from the more dislocated process of working, exchanging the produce for money, and buying bread.

Relevant to this question is, of course, the villager's distrust of cash which a historically unstable political and economic situation has most bitterly impressed upon him. However, this is not the cause of his preference for subsistence farming, it is merely contingent upon it: his attitude to cash is conditioned, not by a fear that he will not, if he depends on it, be able to buy and sell enough —it is conditioned by a basic reluctance to buy and sell at all. And in this context the use to which cash was put in earlier times is illuminating, for money was not, to former generations, a commodity to be parted with, it was to be kept in chests, given in dowries, it was to be used as an adornment, it was to be *worn*. It was an indication of the 'strength' (δύναμη) of the house, and as such it was to be stored, not to say hoarded. The people did not live by money, but by the land.

The villagers are traditionally farmers, and according to traditional thinking to be a farmer is not just to have an occupation but a way of life: and the owner of the land—in Ambéli known as the owner of a *zevgári*, a *zevgoulótis*[1]—is by heredity and destiny placed to follow through this particular pattern, to be the link between the house and the land, between the land and its fertility, between the corn in the field and the bread given to the church for the liturgy (λειτουργιές). Commenting one day on the practice of townswomen who buy such bread instead of making the loaves themselves, and judging whether such a practice was suitable for the people of Ambéli, an old woman said, 'I don't know. I'm just a stupid, toothless old woman, but *I* say that the farmer himself should produce the corn from his own land to make the liturgical

---

[1] Ζευγουλότης. This is the word used locally for a farmer, or one who tills his *zevgári* (ζευγάρι, pl. ζευγάρια), in this sense used loosely for 'property'. Technically, one *zevgári* equals, in Ambéli, 300 *strémmata*, and it was this amount of land that each householder originally acquired when the village was bought from the *Agá* in 1853. *Zevgári* is the word normally used for a 'pair' of anything, and the use of the word in this context is derived, I was told, from the fact that a form of measurement in earlier days used to be the amount of land a team or a pair of oxen could plough in thirty days.

bread. That is what is good.' And it is interesting to note that the heads of the two families who have abandoned their fields for the sake of more intensive work in the forests are both men who are noticeable for their adaptability to and longing for the customs of the modern world.

The house, therefore, according to this way of thinking, is not simply a place from which its members go out to work in the morning and to which they return at night; it is a sanctuary from the hostility of both nature and society, it is a monument to earlier generations who built it and lived in it, and it is a cornucopia which is filled, not just with fruits but with fruits of the family land gained by family toil. And this last image is an image so vivid that its preservation far outweighs the advantages to be gained by sacrificing it to an increased cash income. The extent to which this image still has reality for the villager is the extent to which he literally fails to see the rational advantages in exchanging subsistence farming for cash-cropping the forests. When this image fades, as it is already beginning to do, in the face of the altered attitudes to house and land which are making themselves felt from outside, the villager will have nothing between him and a purely economic and expedient way of organizing his household.

The villager's attitude to hospitality illustrates particularly clearly the living reality of this image of the house, and in Ambéli the householders still take pride in the fact that they can at a moment's notice provide cheese, bread, eggs, wine, and so on from their own land, of finest quality and in almost unlimited quantities, for any guests who may arrive. In a sense it is the index of a house's security and an element in the honour of its owners to be able to provide for the unexpected, and to give hospitality where it falls due. Here, therefore, the concept of the house as a cornucopia is not simply an image of the well-stocked house, but of the house that is, like nature herself, full to overflowing, and able to share some of its abundance with others.

In the giving of hospitality, the part played by fear of misfortune attending the house that turned the stranger away was, in the old days, clear; and certainly in the thinking of the older generation in Ambéli the necessity to placate or to win over the equivocal presence that the stranger represented seems to have been strong. There is a folk tale in which a man who had just refused hospitality to an old beggar turned back to the meat stew that was bubbling on the fire, only to find that it had been turned, hideously, into human flesh. The beggar was, of course, Christ. And I was told by a certain family, 'In the old days you never knew who a guest would be. Then you, for instance, might have been the All Holy Mother of God.' And even though a more materialistic age has robbed the stranger of a possible divine origin, the gipsies and vagrants who pass through the village occasionally are, I was told, given something by every house—a hunk of bread, some eggs, a lump of cheese.

Nevertheless, whatever negative motives may be attributed to rural Greek hospitality, its effect is to cause not only a remission of fear and caution on the part of the house, but a positive release of generosity and affection not only to people who are friends and relatives, but also to those who are complete strangers, totally beyond the usual village economy. Thus the way the house relates to the stranger or the guest has the effect of keeping the circle open, of breaking the inward-looking exclusiveness of the group, and providing the means whereby the house can, without endangering the material basis of its integrity, relate positively to the society from which in the normal course of events it is separated by mistrust and hostility.

In the house, therefore, the fruits of the perfected cycle of nature are garnered against the turning year and the hard times when nature is hostile once again, and these fruits, following the pattern of nature herself, are not to be hoarded but given freely. The attitude towards the farmer's own produce which is demonstrated in the context of the house is a reflection of the villager's sense of the house as his own unique and perfect world—a microcosm—a symbol which draws together the present family and the past generations with the land and its produce into a comprehensible and independent unity. It is a preference expressed for a way of life as opposed to a standard of living, and one which is a continuing assertion of the validity of the family as an integral part of the natural rhythms, in perpetual communion with the natural world in which it lives, the past generations to which it owes its present existence, and the supernatural powers which watch over its destiny. In this communion the intervention of another element, cash, and the processes which cash involves, could only act to disrupt and unbalance—ultimately to challenge the very bases on which the integrity of the family is thought to rest. The antinomy which is seen throughout Greek rural life is very clear here—the dependence and even sycophancy of the villager's relations with authority, the avid search for relations (σχέσεις) with any who he thinks can help him, and the extreme independence and social isolation of the family group and the way in which it chooses to get its bread.

The villagers, then, have a way of life which is automatically in tune with the natural rhythms of the physical world and its recurrent cycle of birth, fruition, death, and re-birth. It is linked with the practical observance of a high code of honour in the behaviour of one member of the household to another, and with an intricate pattern of responsibility according to which the living care for the dead in the long sequence of memorial services. In it the children are born who carry the names of the grandparents and who, in older times at any rate, would perpetuate the traditional way of life and the history of the family into the future and thus ensure, in one aspect, a type of immortality for the ageing and the dead. The same patterns, therefore, in which the villagers participate and which they help to promote in the natural world, are also re-enacted in their own lives and within their own houses, as generation after generation reaches maturity, fecundity, and, with the grandchildren growing up around it, sinks gradually into old age and death. There is thus a natural correspondence between the house and the land which is implicitly recognized and perpetuated in the villager's way of life. It is partly this correspondence which gives to the house in rural Greece its great symbolic content, and provides the family which lives within its doors with something of nature's own permanence and her possibility of endless regeneration.

III
THE COMMUNITY

THE vitality of family life and the strength of the love and loyalty which are generated within the house are reversed in the social relationships lived out in the total community. Simply because the individual's identification with his house is so exclusive, his identification with his village is of an entirely different order, and is one which is, in practical terms, very much less effective. The village as a whole carries out its social activities not as a village but as a series of houses.

Nevertheless in spite of this there are times when this diversity is overcome, and when an awareness of common membership in a group larger than the family motivates in the individual an identification with the community as a whole. This sense of common identity rests to a very large extent on the sharing of common values and a common culture of extreme intricacy and detail. In the translation of this sense of identity into practical social action, much, inevitably, is lost, for as soon as ideal values and perceptions are projected into action in the social world they are immediately modified by the conflicting tensions and loyalties generated within it. However, even though their manifestation in community life is much weakened by having been passed through the filter of competition and self-esteem, these values may still be recognized for what they are. For the sake of clarity and at the risk of over-systematization, I analyse this sense of community in three aspects: in united social action responding to an emergency or a challenge from an opposing social group; in conscious identification with a common situation and culture; and as an understanding of the common religious identity of mankind—an understanding which is projected into the life of the community by a series of customs which cause the social year to go, as it was said to me, 'proportionately with the Faith' (ἀνάλογα μὲ τὴν θρησκεία).

As a brief introduction, however, to this localized sense of community which is found in the village, it must just be said that the Greek villagers do also in various ways identify themselves personally with the world in general. There is a sense in which they recognize all mankind to be one, all brothers, but separated from each other by gulfs of misunderstanding resulting from the work of the Devil and typified in the variety and incomprehensibility of the languages of different countries. In this motley of nations they recognize, though they do not understand, the right of each country to have its own customs, and the existence among these nations of 'savages' and 'wild men' who worship cows and have peculiar practices is often described in terms of high comedy. Their own religion they consider to be the only correct path to God, for they find on the whole what they hear of non-Christian practices incredible and ludicrous, and what they hear of other denominations of Christianity strange and shocking. Inevitably, therefore, except when they are consciously defining ethnic and cultural differences, their concept of mankind is either an implicit extension of the Christian Orthodox world to cover all humanity of whatever actual faith, or the idea of humanity in general as Christendom, from which non-Christians are unconsciously excluded.

Once the sense of the religious community narrows down to the Orthodox world—and this, since the Greek villager has little awareness of Orthodoxy as a possession also of other nationalities, means in fact the Greek-speaking world—it becomes an entity which is emotionally and intellectually more immediately comprehensible. This world is also the one with which the villager is more immediately concerned. *Kósmos* (*κόσμος*), the word used in Greek both for 'people' and for 'world', is therefore on the whole used for the people with whom the villager is able to identify, and may be extended to cover a wider concept of humanity when this identification is made less in the narrowly religious sense as in the awareness of common proneness to sin and liability to suffering.

This apprehension of humanity, however, is complicated by other strands of thought, because the tendency to link it with the Greek-speaking world carries with it political and social overtones of which no Greek is unaware. Generations of school-children brought up by generations of chauvinistic school-teachers as a deliberate state policy have an ineradicable knowledge of the harshness of Turkish rule during the 400 years' occupation, of the savagery and brutality of the oppressors, and of the nobility and honour of the oppressed. The sacred right of Greeks once again to occupy their lost land in Asia Minor is a chimera from which few village Greeks are free, and results in an unhappy mixture of vainglory for past victories and self-pity for present obscurity; and it is often, especially in the political crises, with these concepts of Nation (ἔθνος)[1] rather than with the idea of Orthodox Christendom that the villager will identify. The villager is, however, for far the greater part of his life, concerned purely with the locality of his village, and the surrounding area, and it is in terms of this local awareness that the following analysis is carried out.

In these days of low population and relative social security, community responses to death and danger are comparatively rarely evoked. Two examples of the community as a whole rising to the occasion of a sudden emergency were related to me as having happened in 1958 and 1967. On the former occasion a disappointed legatee threatened to kill his brother-in-law, the husband of the successful heiress, and went out into the fields looking for him with his gun. He was only prevented, it is said, by the community who 'fell between them' and separated them until the heat of his anger was spent and the danger over. In 1967 a woman of sixty-four, harvesting alone, collapsed through the heat and later died. She was found an hour or two after she had collapsed, and again 'all the people ran with clothes, with water, with methylated spirits . . .' to try to revive her. An instance of a similar sort I witnessed in 1968 when a mule came alone into the village with a deep gash in its flank and some of its intestines hanging out. Without thought of whose mule it was, all the people in the nearby café turned out with lamps, water, and advice, and tried, albeit unsuccessfully, to save the animal's life. Another occasion, brought about by the events of the civil war, is described later.[2]

On these occasions people say that quarrels are forgotten and everyone is bound up in self-forgetfulness as they combine to fight a common enemy. Such self-forgetfulness, however, lasts for only as long as the emergency lasts, and immediately following the unity caused by the concentration of the community on the unfortunate mule, the families fragmented again as the wife of the man who owned the mule screamed out at another woman, 'Now your heart rejoices . . .!', accusing her of having caused the mis-

---

[1] For a study of the development of the Greek national consciousness and the foundation of the modern Greek state, see J. K. Campbell and P. Sherrard, *Modern Greece*, London, 1968.

[2] See p. 241.

fortune by cursing them a few days before. And the tale of an individual reaction to a different event in 1961 reveals how hard it is for hatred to be lost even in the extremity of death. This was the remark of a certain woman to the news that another woman was dying in child-birth: 'May her stomach burst and may she come to the same fate as Manoli!' Manoli had been the speaker's brother-in-law. He had been cursed on his wedding-day by the same woman who was now lying ill, and had been murdered in 1960. It must be added, though, that this degree of animosity in such a situation is unusual, and the woman who told me of it—by no means a gentle person, and with cause for rancour herself since it was her husband who had been murdered—said, 'Look how unyielding she was. I couldn't be as hard as that'; and added 'God forbid that you should ever see such a thing, but when this happened, when Maria died, there were gipsies in the village, and they all gathered round the house wailing and shrieking. Everyone mourns such an event.'

The community, therefore, is at one in its awareness of a common situation in the face of life, death, and danger, but at the moment that this awareness is revealed in the social world it inevitably becomes conditioned, however slightly, by the social situation in which the different individuals find themselves.

These two attitudes are revealed particularly clearly in the attitude to death, where the whole community will be united in a common experience of mourning although the particularities of their grief will differ. Since death is an event which concerns the community as a whole, every villager, old and young, will attend the wake—if only briefly—to bring a candle and a little bunch of flowers for the dead. All will be genuinely sorrowful, and many will weep, particularly if the person concerned is considered to have been 'young' to die, that is to say under sixty-five or seventy. And while some will be weeping for the dead person before them, the grief of the others is no less genuine as they are stirred by the grief they see around them, by the thought of their own mothers, their own dead, and for the inescapable tragedy of mortality. In the particularization therefore of its grief the community is divided, but in mourning the fact of death it is one.

Where the challenge comes not from individual threat, accident, or act of God, but from an opposing social group, the response is similar, though such instances are also, in these days, comparatively rare. This is partly because there is no pattern of institutionalized enmity between the villages, and because no political or social situation exists in which the members of one community might be considered a permanent threat to the next. The only possible event which could arouse the animosity of the whole of Ambéli against all the inhabitants of another village, and thereby stir in the villagers of Ambéli a strong identification with their locality as opposed to that of their opponents, is the one concerned with a project to take the water from a spring in property belonging to Ambéli and pipe it to Kateríni. Although the villagers of Ambéli get little benefit from this water at the moment, the spring being almost at the limits of the property high up on the flank of the mountain to the south-west, they are adamant that the people of Kateríni should not get it, and that if anyone has a right to it, they have. I asked them what they would do if the officials came and took the water, and got the answer, 'We'll go by night and cut the pipes. Let them do what they want, we won't let the water go.' Nothing more has been heard of this scheme, and it is likely that it was never seriously contemplated; however, the villagers' reaction to it leaves no doubt that a type of cohesion in village life is directly dependent on the degree of menace from outside, and that the present cordial relations between all the villages in the neighbourhood has got a certain amount to do with the general lack of social cohesion within the villages themselves.

It must be added here, however, that this principle of solidarity in the face of an external threat is dependent on the type of threat involved, for to certain types of bureaucratic and administrative interference such as land consolidation proposals, the decision to ban goats from the area, and so on, the resistance is individual rather than communal. The issue here is concerned with whether the village as a whole is threatened, in which case its members will unite; or whether the different groups within the village will see in this threat a chance to further their own interests, in which case the normal divisions within the village will be intensified. It seems also that the degree of cohesion or fragmentation produced by an external threat is related also to the degree to which the villager understands the nature of that threat. In opposition to the impersonal threat of bureaucracy the villager has little to relate to other than his own self-interest and the reality of his family group;

and it is this therefore that provides him with the overriding criteria by which to act. In opposition, however, to a personal challenge from an individual, a village, a group, or from an event like death which touches the village mind deeply and conditions a significant part of traditional thinking, an intense personal response is generated which throws the community into a renewed understanding of its own common identity, and unites opposition against the insurgent element.

Events in which village loyalty is called up in response to an individual rather than a communal emergency from outside are also rare, for in the sphere of social relations with the outside world the main impulse of the villager is not towards division but unity. And although a strong sense of community still binds the inhabitants of Ambéli together with reference to the common nature of their beliefs, values, and way of life, the endeavour in the social sphere is always outwards, towards the ease, prosperity, prestige, and wider horizons of the towns, and away from the poverty of their village lives.

However, simply because a person's village is his village, in the sense of the 'land of his fathers' (πατρίδα), the village will often be defended in social terms even when both parties know that no valid social defence is really possible. This is illustrated by the following conversation between two women, one from Ambéli and the other from a neighbouring village, Kalýva, to which very many girls from Ambéli have married in recent years, and one which has the advantages of a population of more than double that of Ambéli, a situation in the valley, and a subsidiary road, although it has as yet no regular communications. The woman from this village, through which we were walking, began the conversation by saying to me how nice it must be for me, up in Ambéli, so quiet and with none of the hurly-burly of the towns.

'Yes,' took up the woman from Ambéli, 'and here you're all surrounded with hurly-burly, what with the trains and the trams. . . .'
'We've got a road, we see a motor-car from time to time. Up with you what happens if someone gets ill? They die.'
'The people here have eternal life, I suppose? No one dies in Kalýva.'
'Eh, you know our village is better than yours.'
'You've taken all our girls.'
'Even though they weren't virgins. Have you got any more for us?'
'One or two still.'

Apart from the wit demonstrated by this exchange, this conversation illustrates that the social cohesion within the village, and
the sense in which it is felt, is divided with itself. For while there
still exist certain situations which call individual loyalty from the
family to the village, the villager nevertheless is always deeply
conscious of the failure of his village in the competitive social
scene and in comparison with those urban values which he has
come to believe are necessary to a decent life.

This is one aspect of the continual ambivalence in the villager's
attitude to himself and his village which is produced by the rapidly
changing face of society, and is illustrated by the following two
comments, both of which were prompted by the same situation—
the engagement of a man from a nearby village to a girl from
Ambéli. The first comment was from a woman: 'I don't know why
it is, but any stranger coming up here for our girls seems to us to be
ugly.' And the second, from a man, 'If Polyxeni's fiancé had been
from here they wouldn't have looked twice at him, but we have a
mania about strangers here, and so they've taken him.' The
situation in this respect therefore reveals itself in a verbal and
emotional subscription to some vaguely defined qualitative superiority that they feel their village to hold, while the practical fact
of the matter is that confidence in the village as a social unit has
failed so completely that anyone, however ordinary, from outside
the village, is thought to be better than someone from Ambéli.

Bearing in mind, therefore, this over-all social disillusion with
the village, it can be said that in spite of this there do occur
situations in which the villager, identifying himself with something in his village other than its economic and social disparity as
compared with the outside world, will both verbally and practically
identify himself with the community and with other members of
that community in defence of its interest or its honour.

Both these aspects of community solidarity which have been discussed above reveal that the villagers' sense of unity, while originating in an absolute similarity of commitments and beliefs,
manifests itself on a social level as an identity which is expressed
chiefly in opposition and separation. There are exceptions to this
which are discussed later, but on the whole it is true to say that
because of the fragmented nature of society the forces which are
able to overcome this fragmentation are only those which are

mobilized in the face of an even greater danger than that posed by the various competing groups within the society. It is only then that self-interest and loyalty are forced to move out of their normal sphere—the house and family—into that of the village as a whole, and the individual to assume the role of protector not of the interests and honour of his house alone, but of the total community.

However, there is a sense in which the villager identifies himself with his village which, while it results in and is the result of a feeling of exclusiveness in relation to outsiders, does not depend on danger to be evoked, and is a more continuing and positive manifestation of solidarity within the village than the examples quoted above. This is a sense which is rapidly being undermined by the knowledge that many of the values it represents are being outmoded in the increasing urbanization in the modern world, yet there are several contexts in which it may still be found.

It is found, for instance, in a story which the villagers are fond of telling—of how an Athenian, amazed at the communication between shepherds by means of shouts and whistles, left the area in despair exclaiming that he would never be able to speak Greek. It is found in the pride with which they admit to a mutual understanding derived from the nature of their life and work, and expressed in the acknowledgement 'we understand one another here'. It is expressed too in the instinctive and completely mendacious defence of the reputation of the village with regard to the problem of whether its inhabitants would blacken the reputation of any of its girls who were being sought in marriage, 'no one would give anyone away here'. It is often voiced in praise of the beauty and fertility of the village, the 'we have everything' sentiment which expresses a pride of place counterbalancing the increasing tendency to discontent and self-denigration provoked by comparison with the modern world. Most significantly of all, it is revealed in the absolute and unquestioning acceptance by any one member of the community of the same values and customs of all, a fact which binds together the whole community in the solidarity of the single unit 'We'. This sense of community is, in Ambéli, reinforced rather than undermined by the knowledge that these values and customs do not prevail everywhere, and that even in the local market town the same standards are not demanded by the community as are demanded by the people of Ambéli; and this awareness of locality simply lends an edge to the statement often heard about, for instance, heating water and washing clothes on a Wednesday or a Friday, failing to change clothes after being with anyone as they die, sending unmarried girls out to work, and so on, '*We* take exception to that here' (ἐμεῖς τὸ ἐξετάζουμε ἐδῶ).

These customs are thought of as having been preserved and handed down by past generations, and as being similarly entrusted to the present one—a sentiment which is voiced in such terms as, 'That's how we found it' (ἔτσι τὰ βρήκαμε), or, more explicitly, 'That's how we learned it and that's how we leave it' (ἔτσι τὰ μάθαμε καὶ ἔτσι τὰ ἀφήνουμε), and although changing values are working to undermine this sense of community, this has not as yet by any means been totally compromised.

The balance on which rests this assumption of the innate rightness of We against They is precarious, and it is the alteration of this balance which is probably, when it occurs, one of the foremost agents of social change. Emigration alone, occurring as a phenomenon unrelated to a moral collapse in the community, does not shift this balance, for the body of values left in the community from which the *émigré* has departed remains unchallenged, and the *émigré* himself, removed from the traditional environment and placed in a different society, adapts himself without too much trauma to its different values. The *émigré*, that is to say, has become in certain senses one of Them. It is when the We of the community leans towards the They of the outside world that social change, as a phenomenon occurring within a community, really begins to make itself felt, and it does so by virtue of the fact that the self-sufficiency of the villager within the communal value system, and his automatic assumption of the superiority of this system over those of other places, have begun to collapse. In this event, the villagers remain united in so far as the whole community lives in the same place and is bound by the same values, even though these may be in disintegration; but the community has begun to lose confidence in itself in so far as its identification with its traditional and inherited value system and way of life has begun to be discredited, and that of the modern world to draw its loyalties. This is the situation in which the villagers of Ambéli now find themselves. But it is a stage which is more integrated than that which is found in the less remote villages, where a deep fragmentation of values is seen to have occurred within each village itself. In these villages there are immediately apparent various strata of respectability—a word coincident in this context with modernity—and where the old women, for instance, will dress one way and refer their way of dressing to a particular set of values, while the young women, with their refined way of speaking and their smart sleeveless dresses, will say to me, 'You don't want to pay any attention to backward old women.'

This situation does not obtain in Ambéli where, in spite of the degree of depopulation, the culture to be found in the village is still relatively homogeneous. The villagers' ambition, in the sense of their desire for an easier life for themselves, for the glamour of the towns, and for education for their children, is focused on the outside world. In that respect—their failure to translate their traditional values into an acceptable twentieth-century good—they may be heard referring to themselves as backward people, living like animals. Yet, although shaken, the central core of their self-respect has not yet been mortally wounded, and this is because the main body of their traditional values is, although increasingly questioned, still generally upheld within the society. The villagers' identification as social beings with that which has socialized them—the body of beliefs and customs which inform their life—remains still centred relatively solidly within their own society, and so there remains a coherence between the totality of the physical and social existence of the village, and its ritual and moral life.

All this is not to say that there are no secondary or other standards of behaviour to which people may appeal, or that none of these secondary standards is derived from contact with the modern world; still less to imply that no social change in the sense of a feeling of increasing isolation, and a disruption of the internal moral structure of the village, has been felt. But it is to emphasize the moral solidarity of such a community where a central self-confidence in the main body of its own traditional value system still survives, even while it runs concurrent with the obvious economic and social discrepancies between that society and the outside world. This moral solidarity has a vital effect on the social structure, for it is by means of the common body of values and beliefs that the speech and actions of all the individuals within the community are perpetually related to the totality of the community itself. In every statement, judgement, and action which is referred to or is derived from this body of traditional beliefs, the individual who is speaking or acting does so in his capacity not as a solitary individual but as a member of the total community. In illustration of this I quote an incident at which a young woman was preparing to lay out the *loukoúmia* (sweets known in England as Turkish delight) for a name-day, and put the whole box on the tray. It was an untidy box with ragged bits of paper hanging out, and I said I thought she ought to take out the bits of *loukoúmi* and put them on a dish. 'No,' she said, 'that's not as it should be.'

'I don't agree,' said I.

'It's not that you don't agree, it's that you don't know,' she replied, with finality.

This sense of the village as a common cultural and geographical entity relies in many ways on features which may be called secular—that is to say on elements which are not overtly connected with religious belief. However, beliefs regarding the metaphysical nature of the world and of human thought and action within that world provide a permanent sub-structure to the totality of village life, and are overwhelmingly responsible for the degree of coherence and solidarity still to be found in it.

These beliefs fall roughly into two categories, one derived from Christian Orthodoxy, and the other from the religious beliefs of pagan or 'folk' philosophy which persist still into the present day and underlie much of the villagers' religious thought. These latter beliefs are very complex, and because of their ambiguous position in relation to much of Christian doctrine are combated by the Church and often semi-consciously repressed by the villager. They find frequent expression, however, particularly in concepts of 'luck', or, more correctly here, 'fate' (τύχη), and in attitudes to death.

Some mention of the various customs which originate from these pagan elements in village thinking will be made later in this chapter. However, a detailed exposition of this whole system of thought needs a special study of its own, and would be out of place here. All that can be said at the moment is that it is based on an understanding of the world according to which man, far from being the child of God, mediated for and protected by the sacred presences of the Orthodox hierarchy, is the object of impersonal and irrational forces, in the face of which all his own efforts for his immediate prosperity and ultimate salvation are useless. It is a philosophy in which an ineluctible fate is woven around men by chthonic powers, a fate which, good or bad, is 'written and cannot be unwritten' (τὸ γραφτὸ ἄγραφτο δὲν γίνεται). Within the limitations of this fate man has a certain autonomy, and can strive to propitiate and placate those forces which he feels to be bearing upon him. Nevertheless the main course of his passage through life has already been decreed and must come to pass; and at the end of this passage there lie the grave, the earth's 'black mantle' (μαύρη τσέργα), and final dissolution, which puts an end to all eating, drinking, dancing, and happiness—to all, in fact, that is of any value to man.

In spite, however, of the prevalence of this type of thinking and all that it involves, it is the Christian philosophy which forms for the villager the more coherent and explicit system, and it is in terms of this philosophy that his ritual and ceremonial life is largely organized. For the purpose of the present analysis, therefore, it is this system which is the more relevant, and this which is analysed in the following pages.

In their understanding of Orthodox doctrine the villagers have naturally been influenced by their traditional folk mentality, and by the particular cultural clothing in which some of the presences of the supernatural world make their appearance. But while this adds a particular colour and quality to the way in which the canonical doctrine is understood, it in no way diminishes the genuine Orthodoxy of village belief. This belief is one according to which the world, created and sustained by God, is continually being fought for by the Devil who sends out his emissaries—the demons in all their various guises, the evil eye, the evil hour, the nereids, and so on—to torment and corrupt mankind. Man is thus seen as being in a central position between God and the Devil in a world where these two powers strive endlessly for mastery. Thus the world is in a sense a cosmic battleground, and man the microcosm where this battle finds localized and specific expression. An ultimate value is thus given to men's actions and to the outcome of each individual situation in which he finds himself, since in these situations he reveals not only a sequence of human and temporal events—in themselves relatively insignificant—but the fluctuations of the cosmic drama concerning the ultimate forces of good and evil.

However, while man is thus in the most absolute sense responsible neither for good nor for evil, he is not absolved from respon-

sibility for two reasons; first, because in each situation he has the
freedom to listen either to Christ or to the Devil, and therefore
knowingly to ally himself directly with the good or the evil whose
power he then enables to express itself through him; secondly,
because, although in terms of each single confrontation the outcome of the battle is uncertain, in terms of the ultimate redemption
of the world the victory of God is inevitable, since Christ, the
second Adam, has already brought about the defeat of evil. Man,
therefore, lives in a universe in which the dualistic principle has
been irrevocably conquered, and therefore is doubly guilty if he
rejects or sets himself against the principles embodied by Christ.

In spite of the villagers' uncompromising awareness of the duty
of man and the sacrifice of Christ, they realize all too clearly that
in fact man does not, as he should, turn a deaf ear to the Devil.
He quarrels, he fights, he curses, he is suspicious, jealous, and full
of hatred—things which the villagers see not as the deliberate
will to evil but simply as a built-in inevitability, a fatal predilection
to sin. Man is thus seen as a victim of his own weakness, of the
wiles of the Devil, and of the sinfulness of a world which, seen
in pragmatic rather than ideal terms, he cannot successfully com-
bat. He suffers not so much because he is evil himself, as because
he lives in a world in whose structure a degree of evil is tragically
involved. 'The Devil has many feet' (ὁ Δαίμονας ἔχει πολλὰ
ποδάρια), the villagers say, meaning that if the Devil cannot bring
about the downfall of a man in one way he will do it in another.
This is a saying which is founded on bitter experience.

In his dealings with the social world, where society in general is
seen as being set against the family and in competition with it,
the villager does indeed find the temptation to evil virtually
irresistible. He is socially committed to lying, concealing, competing, undermining, in sheer defence of his house. However, in the
case of his relation with the world of nature he is better equipped
to resist the working of the Devil, for here the identification of his
family with his land makes possible the projection into the land of
the ideal values found within the house. In this context the original
destiny of man is particularly clearly seen, and is expressed in the
story of Adam and Eve which all villagers know. Man as the head
of material creation has the natural world as his inheritance, and
his God-given relationship is one of dominion over it. This
original relationship was upset by the Fall, and as a result man is

continually bedevilled in his efforts to win a living from it, and the toil and sweat of the man at the plough the villager sees as a direct result of the sin of Adam. It is not so much, therefore, that nature is in itself hostile to man, as that it is infested with inimical presences which struggle, through the natural phenomena, to defeat him.

These presences man cannot, on his own, conquer, but only with the help of God, to whom he normally appeals in Christ, and through the figures of the Mother of God and the saints; and it is therefore only by man's co-operation with these powers that he can bring some of the original order and harmony back into the natural world. The fruits of these efforts are seen in cultivated fields, bulging hay-sheds, healthy animals, and houses which are stocked with bins of corn, sacks of chickpeas, beans, lentils, and maize, strings of onions and garlic, tins of oil, jars of honey, barrels of wine and cheese, bunches of wild marjoram, bay, and mountain-tea.

The natural world, then—the unsocialized regions which lie outside the village—holds ambivalent significance for the villager. It produces his livelihood and yet at the same time it is dangerous, inhabited by the demons, and is in purely practical terms a place where the lot of man is toil and sweat and exhaustion—torments (βάσανα), as the villagers put it. The house, on the other hand, is a place where the demons are already defeated, and where the victory of Christ over the Devil—already in the eschatological sense a reality and seen recurrently in the festival of Easter—is in the human and social world also achieved. Here is the area where man may physically and spiritually relax, lapped in peace and surrounded by order. Here the icons in the corner, with the lumps of incense, the dried sprigs of basil or withered flowers, the bottle of holy water, all testify to the presence of God in the house and to the differentiation of the house from other types of dwelling. As one villager said to me, 'What is a house without icons? A shelter for animals.' In such a situation, the abundance of natural produce in the house is not merely an assurance that the family is not going to starve—it is witness to the triumphant battle that man has fought with the help of God in re-establishing and reaffirming man's original relationship with the earth.

It is because of this that the meal in the Greek village house takes on its particular significance, for because of the relationship

3. The Honey Harvest

between the family and the land, and because of the way in which the house is thought of, even the simplest meal produced from family land by the work of the family becomes an act of communion. This communion is naturally between the members of the family who gather at the table and any guests who may be present. But it also extends far beyond these limits to include both the family in its more enduring aspect, and the principal figures of the sacred world. In the presence of the family itself and the food which comes from family land, there is implied a sense of continuity from the 'grandfathers' (παπποῦδες) from whom the living family draws much of its identity; the power of God is implied in the very existence of the meal and the house at all; Christ the Saviour is invoked in the sign of the Cross which each person makes at the beginning and end of every meal; and very often the Mother of God is ritually invited in the words, 'All Holy Mother of God, come and eat with us' (Παναγία, ἔλα νὰ φᾶμε). The village meal therefore is a communion which involves not only the living family but also the 'grandfathers' who have preceded it, the natural world which nourishes it, and the sacred world which created and supports it.

The symbolic significance of the meal is made even clearer by the fact that the formal meal—that is to say any but such meals as the bread, cheese, and olives eaten in the fields or on a journey—is almost always eaten in the house, and by the exceptional character of the chief occasion on which this custom is broken. One exception is the meal which takes place at the time of the shearing of the sheep and goats, when because of the custom of any recipient of labour to feed those who work for him, and because of the distance of the fold from the village, a meal of meat and spaghetti, bread, wine and possibly yoghurt, is eaten on the site where the work takes place. There is one other occasion, however, in which the formal meal is eaten outside, and this is the threshing of the wheat. Here it would be possible, because the threshing-floors are all around the village, for the workers to go back to their host's house and eat there, returning after the meal to the threshing-floor; and this is in fact done at the grape harvest or at the hoeing of the broad beans—other occasions on which a number of hands are needed. But at the threshing of the wheat all the workers remain outside at midday while the meal is brought out from the house with ceremony, the housewife leaving the house first with her helpers after her, and the meal is eaten on the edge of the threshing-floor. Ouzo or raki is available throughout the day, and great plates of *loukoumádhes* (λουκουμάδες)—balls of yeasty dough which are fried and eaten with honey, and are made in the village only at the time of a festival—are also taken out to the threshing-floor. On this day also a special decorated loaf of bread (βιτταλιά) is eaten—bread richer than the normal type and baked with a little oil. The meal on this day is thus conspicuously a ceremonial meal, and the choice of the threshing-floor in preference to the house is plainly deliberate; not the result in any way of convenience or necessity but springing instead from the symbolic value attributed to the house and the fields.

Of all the villager's crops wheat is the most vital, and the phrase 'to eat bread' is still a typical way in the village of saying 'to eat'; but the winning of bread from the rocky fields is, as the villagers say, 'an agonizing struggle' (ἀγωνία). For the greater part of the year nature, if not actually hostile to man, is at least relatively intractable. Day after day the farmer wears himself out in clearing, burning, ploughing, double-ploughing, sowing, hoeing, weeding; all through the year there are risks from hail, floods, drought, locusts, diseases, any one of which could, particularly in the past, reduce him to debt and hunger. The house, on the other hand, at all times is, or aspires to be, an image of the perfect society—the sanctuary where man, God, and nature unite in harmony and peace.

All through the year, therefore, nature is thought of as being in opposition to the house, a place of struggle, hardship, risks, and sometimes danger, from which the villager returns home exhausted to be refreshed for another day. However, once a year this continual counterpoint is overcome, and the original relationship with the earth which was granted to man at his creation is again fulfilled. Man emerges as the creature whom creation serves; and at the high point of the year when this occurs—when the wheat is gathered in—the natural world also becomes a sanctuary for man and is thus symbolically unified with the house. Because of the necessity for the presence of God if this process is to come about, it is not by accident that it is the harvest of the wheat rather than of any other grain which is chosen for this symbolism, for bread is to the villager both the staff of life and the Body of God. The normal opposition between nature and society is thus transcended by means of a single divine principle, and the meal on the threshing-floor is the formal celebration of this event.

To the image of the house as a cornucopia is, therefore, added the image of the house as a microcosm in its fullest sense—as the complete society in which divine and human elements are merged, and in which the perfected cycle of nature is revealed in the stores of grain and farm produce. The family within the house looks continually to the figures of the Holy Family—Christ in the dual aspect of Saviour and Son, and the Mother of God—as the authors, guides, and guardians of its life, and thus inevitably models itself according to this divine archetype,[1] and the love and trust which bind the members of the family together are reflections of the values of love and peace which are those of the sacred world. The house, the family, and the principal figures of the family, are thus united in a complex symbol which images the world restored to its original integrity—the ideal configuration of man and nature in communion with God and redeemed from the possession of the Devil.

It is plain from this that the villager's religious understanding is put into practice in terms which relate very dynamically to his house and family; and it is in fact largely the strength and exclusiveness of this understanding that prevent the villager from extending his commitment beyond the confines of his family into the wider society. However, there do occur times when the villager's religious sense creates in him a positive identification with his village as a whole. The annual village festival is one occasion on which the social and religious worlds fuse to create a noticeable feeling of community solidarity and pride, and Easter, which will be discussed later, brings about a sense of common identity of quite a different order. But in addition to these two occasions, the villagers' participation in the liturgy—enacted in Ambéli every alternate Sunday because of a scarcity of priests—brings about a situation in which the ritual action of the community is, instead of being confined to private houses and individual people, communalized in a single activity in which a common identity between the villagers is recurrently expressed.

[1] 'The family and the flock are both forms divinely confirmed, the earthly family being a refraction of the Holy archetype Family, while the sheep is a sacred animal blessed by God. These things have always been so, they always will be so.' J. K. Campbell, *Honour, Family, and Patronage*, Oxford, 1964, pp. 34–5.

Attendance at the liturgy is nominally a matter in which the village as a whole is concerned, although this is not thought of in terms of every individual having a duty to the community to go to church, but in terms of the need of every house to send one representative. For a variety of reasons even this minimal attendance is not always thought possible, but at the service of the Resurrection (*'Ανάστασις*) on the night of Easter Saturday, every house is always represented, and the priest has been known to hold up the service until full representation has been achieved. The congregation, therefore, in gathering, demonstrates not the brotherhood of the community in the hands of God so much as the need of each house to reaffirm its individual relationship with the divine powers; and it unites not as one single unit with one single conscious aim, but as a collection of disparate units each with its own self-centred, or rather, house-centred, aim.

In the village setting the liturgy is a social event of some importance. Young girls and women will dress in their best, the men will come in suits, shoes will all be cleaned, and gumboots or shabby clothes are never worn, no matter how warm they are or how cold the day. In the event of an engagement—which is always celebrated first in the girl's village—one of the first public acts of the engaged couple is to attend the liturgy together on Sunday, where everyone can see what the prospective bridegroom looks like, what clothes and jewellery he has given his betrothed, and so on. Attendance at the liturgy therefore holds within it all the everyday conflicts and jealousies of the village, and carries unspoken competition between the young unmarried girls to appear better dressed than any of their rivals, while the best efforts of the older women are directed towards, at the least, not giving the 'world' any chance of laughing at them for not being well turned out. Existing rivalries and animosities are not overcome by attendance in church—on the contrary they may even be tacitly demonstrated within it—and people who are not on speaking terms with each other in daily life will leave the church at the end of the liturgy as if unaware of each other's existence.

Nevertheless, in spite of these disruptive elements, the church is still one of the focal points for the community's consciousness of itself as a community, and, according to the paradigm of religious events which it presents, the holidays and festivals of the village are predominantly organized. And in spite of the fact that the congregation attends the liturgy as part of the process of ensuring the prosperity of their various mutually opposing houses, there is a sense in which the community recognizes an interdependence simply by virtue of the fact that it shares a single body of beliefs. On one level the social separation is projected by the congregation into the spiritual sphere, yet on another this separation is transcended by the universal desire of the villagers for a relationship with the sacred world represented in the liturgy.

The attitudes of the villagers revealed in their conduct of the remembrance services for the dead also throws light on this point. These services are held throughout the year, except during the period between Easter Sunday and Pentecost, and there are certain special days known as Soul Saturdays (ψυχοσάββατα) at which a special service is held both on the Saturday evening and again on the Sunday morning. At these services the traditional remembrance food (κόλλυβα) is blessed, and after the service it is distributed to all the congregation. This remembrance food is a mixture of boiled corn mixed up with sugar, raisins, pomegranate seeds, and sugared almonds, and in its distribution no one, friend or enemy, is omitted, and only in the rarest circumstances would anyone refuse it or fail to say, as they take it, 'May God forgive' (Θεὸς σχωρέσει). The explicit idea behind this distribution of food is that it is literally a service to the dead, and that just as the community is eating on earth, so the soul who is the object of the commemoration is feasting in heaven; and stories are related of how the soul who has been forgotten by his relatives sits alone and desolate, while all the other souls around him are merry-making. However, in this event not only are the communities of the living and the dead symbolically linked, but the different elements of the living community itself are momentarily reconciled. The dead have moved, not out of relationship with the living but out of that particular social relationship in which jealousy and competition are relevant; and in its acknowledgement of the reality of a different sphere of relationship with a different community in which personal hatreds do not exist, the community on earth also briefly acknowledges its unity.

It is apparent that the sense of community brought about by a similar commitment to identical religious beliefs causes, in this society, a solidarity which may be said to lie more within the sphere of religious experience than of social effort. There is, however, one

period in the ecclesiastical year when this relationship with a
world outside that of the tormented world of humanity is felt so
deeply that the experience breaks out of the purely metaphysical
sphere, and manifests itself in the social structure as a positive
demonstration of social solidarity. This is the Easter period, the
culmination of which is reached at the liturgy of the Resurrection
on the night of Easter Saturday.

Eleven weeks before Easter Sunday the community begins to
prepare for the events of Holy Week with the three weeks which
gradually work up towards the Lenten fast. On the last Sunday
of these three weeks is the feast of the Carnival or Great Apokreas,
and on Clean Monday, the first Monday of Lent, the true fast
begins. This fast, strictly, should involve abstinence from meat,
fish, eggs, milk, cheese, and any other animal product, and,
according to the strict monastic rule, from oil and wine. The
villagers, during their normal fast, abstain from all these things
except for the last two. On the Sunday and Monday at the beginning of Lent in the area of Ambéli, the event is celebrated by the
children and young men of the village dressing up in transvestite
costumes, and going from house to house singing bawdy songs and
collecting eggs or money; and on these two days the men and
married women of the community are also permitted speech and
songs of great obscenity. Traditionally the Lenten fast was kept in
all its severity, but now although many of the old people and some
of the younger women keep the fast for the whole of Lent, the
majority compromises by fasting only for the first and last weeks
of Lent. During this period, however, everyone takes especial care
to observe the Wednesday and Friday fasts which are customary
throughout the year. The Holy Week fast is strictly observed by
everybody, and on Holy Friday the custom is to abstain all day
from oil, and from eating and drinking anything at all until after
the midday service in church which ends at about 3 p.m. After
that time people may eat, but without ceremony, because they
say, 'Christ died today, so how can one sit down to a meal?' The
customary fare on this day is bread, olives, and some boiled wild
greens (βρνές), or bracken shoots, both of which should be eaten
with vinegar as a re-enactment of Christ's taking of vinegar when
He was on the Cross.

Communal activity really begins with the Holy Week services
which take place in the evening and which the majority of the vil-

lage attends. The reading of the twelve Gospels in the long service
of Thursday night is awaited with particular reverence by the
villagers, and on the following morning, Holy Friday, women and
girls will go into the countryside and collect flowers and wild bay
to bring for the tomb of Christ (᾽Επιτάφιος). Friend and enemy
work here side by side decorating the arched wooden bier, and
after it is finished it is placed in the church, and the girls gather
round and sing the traditional Holy Friday lament, 'Today the
sky is black, today is a black day.' Just as it is the custom never to
leave a dead body alone, so the symbolic representation of the
death of Christ must be similarly honoured and guarded, and from
the time of the completion of the bier until the evening service
when Christ is taken down from the Cross a continuous vigil is
kept.

Finally, on the Saturday evening at about 11 o'clock, the three-
hour service of the Resurrection is held, the climax of which is the
moment of the Resurrection itself when the church is darkened
completely, one candle is lit by the priest, and as the flame is
passed quickly to all the people from candle to candle, everyone
cries out 'Christ is risen!' (Χριστὸς ἀνέστη). After the service
everyone goes home to break the fast with a spiced meat soup, red
eggs, and yoghurt, and the next day is given over to celebration.
People will eat as much as they can, red eggs will be given to anyone who enters the house, and in the afternoon the final service of
the Easter period is held, the *Agápe*, at which a state of harmony
among the earthly community is celebrated—a harmony which
used to be (but is now in Ambéli no longer) confirmed by the
exchanging of kisses as the people leave the church.

Easter is the greatest festival of the Orthodox year, and, because
of the intensity of feeling which it evokes, it reveals particularly
clearly certain characteristics of Orthodox village thinking which
are present but less easily discernible in religious practice during
the rest of the year.

One of these characteristics is the villagers' belief in the living
reality of the events of the Gospel—a belief which is particularly
evident as the villagers guard the tomb of Christ with an absolute
conviction of His presence there. Another characteristic is their
sense of participation in the mystical life of the ecclesiastical year,
as a result of which they endeavour constantly to ensure and
perpetuate a living relationship between social life and its divine

counterpart. These efforts may be seen in various areas of the villager's ritual life, but never more clearly than in his emotional, social, and spiritual participation in the events which lead up to the liturgy of the Resurrection. Belief in this correspondence between human and divine actions is not unique to this Easter period; what is unique is the degree to which this correspondence is actually made manifest in communalized behaviour. At this time in particular—a festival which holds all the tragedy and all the enlightenment of the Christian faith—the objectivity of the people's belief becomes overwhelming and materializes, so to speak, into their physical and social world. This event in the religious cycle, above all others, calls into play the villagers' enduring sense of the true correspondence between divine and human actions, and generates not only an individual but a social reaction. The normal tension between the family and the village is thereby transcended, and a social community linked by the reality of metaphysical belief is formed.[1]

In conclusion to this topic it must just be said that although this tension between family and village loyalties is very pronounced in rural Greek society, this does not mean that the villagers' spiritual life remains normally on a conceptual or theoretical level. The religious life of the villagers is one which is deeply experienced, but it is experienced in its own terms rather than in, for instance, those of the morality of North European cultures; and thus while this religious life may appear to an onlooker from an alien culture to be superficial or even hypocritical, it is in fact not so. The villager does not feel that he is outraging his religious commitment by telling lies, for instance, or by laughing at his neighbour, or even, in older times, by killing an enemy in a feud; but he feels it vital to observe the important fasts, to carry out punctiliously his ritual obligations, and he dedicates his whole life to the well-being of his family in both social and metaphysical terms. Since the house is the material representation of the villager's religious values, the terms in which he dedicates himself to the house are thus an expression of his religious understanding. Whereas, in the cultures of Northern Europe, morality tends to be looked on in

---

[1] See Campbell's description of the celebration of Easter among the Sarakatsani (op. cit., p. 351). 'As my friend Aristoteles left the church, he smiled and said, "A weight has left me" (μοὔφυγε ἕνα βάρος). In saying this he was not referring to personal sin.'

terms of concepts of justice, equality, and tolerance, held by each member of the community for all, in rural Greek culture the morality of the villager lies in the faithful perpetuation of his house and family, and in the simultaneous perpetuation of his relationship with the sacred world on which the family is founded and from which it is derived.

While it is largely in terms of Orthodox belief that the religious sense of community in the village is expressed, there exists also a body of customs which is an important aspect of the ritual year but which, while deeply related to Orthodox thinking, is not directly a result of its dogma.

The villager, by the very nature of his work and by his unavoidable participation in the ecological year, is linked to the natural cycle of the seasons. This natural rhythm, however, is interpenetrated for him by another, supernatural, rhythm—an additional dimension of experience which he achieves by correct observance of customs relating to the performance or avoidance of certain acts proper to the particular time or season concerned, by means of which he and his work are dynamically related to the whole ebb and flow of the ritual year. These observances are concerned not only to ensure the personal protection of the divine powers of the Christian hierarchy, but also to activate on the villager's behalf the favourable influences of all the other unnamed and impersonal powers with which his universe is informed.

Some of these practices relate to both men and women, and concern taboos on working in the fields or forests or on visiting the vineyards on certain saints' days, for fear of misfortune following. The majority of them are the concern of the women only, even though their effect is thought to spread throughout all the activities of the whole family. The following rhyme referring to the Orthodox practice of fasting on Wednesdays and Fridays throughout the year illustrates this clearly:

Friday your husband	*Τὴν Παρασκευὴ τὸν ἄντρα σου*
Wednesday your children,	*Τετάρτη τὰ παιδιά σου,*
And if you have neither husband nor children	*Καὶ ἂν δὲν ἔχεις ἄντρα καὶ παιδιὰ*
Protect yourself.	*Φύλα τὴν ἀρχοντιά σου.*

The ritual and spiritual basis from which man goes out to work and whose energies protect him when he is away from home, thus emanate from the house and from the woman within the house.

Taboos regarding women's work are based on two different concepts—that of the sacredness of certain days (Wednesdays, Fridays, Sundays, and certain saints' days) and that of the sacrilege, on these days, of certain kinds of work. Spinning, in this context, is universally admitted to be particularly serious, and weaving also. The particular danger about these types of work is, so people say, the bits of wool or fluff that drop off on to the ground, for these, as popular mythology goes, find their way into the bread that Christ and His Mother are eating in heaven, so that their bread is full of wool and impossible to eat. Slightly less dangerous on such occasions, but only fractionally so, are implements such as scissors, needles, and pins, since the function of these objects is to skewer or impale, and these functions are associated with the death of Christ, nailed to the Cross and finally pierced with a spear. On such evenings, therefore, work in the house is meant to stop at 6 o'clock when the bell for Vespers sounds, or, at the very latest, 8 o'clock, after which the women sit talking without working with their hands until they go to bed. The responsibility for such avoidance is particularly heavy on married women with children, and unmarried girls are excused if, on the less important occasions, they continue with their sewing or knitting all evening.

On the same occasions, also, baking (which involves lighting a fire) and heating water to wash clothes with, is prohibited, the reason for this being given as protection of the crops, for lighting fires on these days is inauspicious and may cause the crops to shrivel up in the summer.

These prohibitions, grafted on to the Orthodox notion of the sacredness of these days, have acquired the sanction of religious practice and are so regarded by the community. It is difficult therefore to distinguish clearly between the varying degrees of belief and practice which shade off those of Orthodox Christian doctrine from those of a more popular religion which surrounds it. These one might describe as practices which, although connected with the patron saint of the particular day on which that practice is carried out, nevertheless carry strong overtones of sympathetic magic, and are more concerned with manipulating natural influences than with honouring the sacred world.

There are many such days, of which I shall mention only a few.

On the day of Saint Trifona, on 1 February, it is thought to be dangerous to pick up needles, scissors, or kindred objects, the explicit analogy here being not that of the piercing of Christ, but the piercing action of an insect which bores into the corn and destroys it. This same day is also important for guarding against hail by refraining from heating water for washing clothes, and also from washing rugs by beating them in cold water at the spring. Scissors, needles, and pins also figure in observances on the first Thursday after Easter, and on 1 May, on these occasions their avoidance being part of an apotropaic ritual against snakes. At Pentecost, and half-way through the Pentecost period, it is considered unlucky to weave, bake, wash clothes, or do any household tasks, for fear of the mice coming and destroying all future products of such work throughout the year. On the feast of Saint Theodori on the first Saturday of the Lenten fast there are a number of customs which young men and girls observe in order to dream that night of their future spouse. On New Year's Day, just before the midnight liturgy, one member of each house goes, in silence, to the spring to draw fresh water and take a round, egg-shaped, stone back to the house with them; this they put under a cushion for someone to sit on for half an hour on return from the church, after which it remains for three days at the back of the hearth and is then put in the hen-house to make the hens 'like stone' (σὰν πέτρα), strong and healthy. Emptying out all water vessels and filling them with fresh water is done by every family at a funeral; and on all important ritual occasions such as deaths, baptisms, marriages, exhumations, and so on, the auspicious nature of odd numbers (with the exception of thirteen) is invariably invoked.

Although there are numerous other customs of this sort, these are not listed here, because the present intention is not to give an exhaustive description of such customs but merely to indicate their nature and prevalence, and to show how tightly and by what various means the villager is bound to the ecclesiastical year.

In the matter of spells and divination the villager enters into a different realm and one which is actively discouraged by the Church. In conjunction, for instance, with the 1 May ritual against snakes is used an apotropaic spell, and invocations to Saint Theodori accompany the divination practices of the first Saturday of Lent. There are spells against various kinds of sickness—

unaccountable swellings of any sort, pain in the breast, snake bites, a painful eye, a disease (ἀστέρα) which is contracted by children under one year old through having had some garment of theirs left out at night under the stars, and there is a practice by which the nature of an illness is divined and its cure ascertained (ψύχισμα). Most commonly used of all are spells against the evil eye.

Use of spells is condemned as a sin by the church confessors, who stipulate instead the use of holy water (ἁγιασμός), of which every household has a bottle—or the ritual known as 'reading' (διάβασμα) by the priest. But the community doggedly stick to their spells (in conjunction, frequently, with holy water) for they find their use quick, easy and effective, and say, 'Why should we pay a priest when we can cure the trouble ourselves?'

These customs merge in with those concerned with cures through homoeopathy and natural healing—for warts, for the polyp which is known as an 'octopus' and which is often found inside pregnant goats and more rarely in women, for hernias, and so on, where the use of a herb is combined with a spell to effect a cure. However, the knowledge of such spells and herbs, once extensive, is now gradually dying out along with the art of the village midwives and practical healers (those who can set bones, pull teeth, and reduce sprains and dislocations) in whom guilt regarding their spells is being induced by the Church, or who are being driven underground as regards their practice by the medical profession.

Also condemned by the Church is the practice, continually indulged in as an amusement in winter, of telling fortunes from the shapes patterned in coffee-grounds at the bottom of a cup, and, less often, for fewer know the art, from beans dropped on the floor, or by means of cards. All these practices the villagers regard with a certain ambivalence, tending, in the case of cards and beans, to cross themselves against misfortune before beginning, and ponder, 'Is this a sin? Isn't it? . . .', even though the enjoyment they get out of it causes them more or less to ignore the strictures of the confessors, and to be only temporarily disturbed by omens such as dreams warning them against such acts.

Of all these three types of divination, that by means of coffee-cups is considered the least serious, while beans are thought to be more dangerous, and cards more or less diabolical, because, as was told to me, 'When the Jews wanted to find out how they would catch Christ they went to a sorcerer, and she threw a Knave of Clubs—a dark man—and this was Judas whom they found and bribed with thirty pieces of silver to betray Christ so that they could kill him.'

At the very end of the scale of these observances, where they tip the balance over into the acknowledged sphere of anti-Christ, is found the practice of sorcery. This is universally acknowledged to be evil, the product of demonic powers and a practice in which only the 'stupid' ($\mu o \nu \varrho \lambda o i$) meddle. It is thought that there used to be professional sorcerers, resident particularly in Chalkis, who possessed a full range of diabolic powers and could perform acts ranging from rendering a man impotent, causing a quarrel between husband and wife, or casting a love spell on a particular man or woman, to interference with the cosmic powers to the extent of bringing the moon down to the earth in the shape of a cow. It is generally agreed now, however, that sorcerers of this order are hard to find, and that the majority of the sorcerers of Chalkis are charlatans who know nothing and merely cheat the people out of their money. Sorcery, however, in common with the practice of all the spells mentioned in this section, does not appear to require any particular initiation or talent for evil, but is a matter strictly connected with the correct performance of certain actions and the correct recital of certain words. The possession, therefore, of a certain text by a family, can give that family the power to become sorcerers and a tale is told of two men of the village, one of whom obtained a text which enabled him to summon devils, and the other a book by which he learned the art of performing such feats as finding lost articles by causing their image to be seen by a child in a plate of water. No good, however, came of such deeds, for the first man, so the story goes, succeeded in summoning the devils but was unable to dismiss them, and his wife and two of his children have been mad ever since; while the family of the second man had to flee for ever from the village in 1957, for fear of vengeance when their son suddenly murdered a fellow villager as the climax to a quarrel that had lasted two years.[1]

In spite of the fact that it is universally recognized that sorcerers appeal to the powers of evil, it is thought also that the guilt, not to say the danger, involved in seeking a sorcerer's services, is also linked to the type of service required. To destroy another human

[1] See pp. 4 and 178.

being or to damage them in any way, is considered very serious, while to seek such things as a love potion, to ask advice about the auspiciousness of a certain venture, to try to put an end to cruelty from a husband, or to find something that is lost, does not in village thinking come under quite the same condemnation, and if one is to believe village rumour, visits to sorcerers for such purposes are by no means unknown.

These visits are kept under a heavy cloak of secrecy, and although villagers may justify themselves on the score of expediency, and even justify a desire to destroy another person on the grounds of the validity of their cause for complaint, there is in village thinking a fundamental value according to which sorcery and all appeal to it are condemned as evil. There is only one exception to this, and this is appeal to a sorcerer to unloose a spell cast by an enemy. Such a visit is considered regrettable but necessary, since it is thought that sorcery alone is capable of dealing with sorcery. Even this remedy, however, is not invariably effective, since there are ways of binding a spell which render it totally impervious to all further efforts against it.

In conclusion to this topic it is relevant to point out two aspects of sorcery which concern the role it plays in society. First, sorcery is thought to achieve practical results in the social sphere—it causes the materialization of the seeker's wishes—while the link between the religious life of the villager and his relationships with his neighbours is more subtle and less direct. Secondly, the appeal to a sorcerer is nearly always an individual and not a social affair; the appeal is made by the individual and not by the group, not even by the family group, and frequently the fact that the individual has visited a sorcerer is kept a secret even from the family.

In the context, therefore, in which sorcery is appealed to, one sees a situation in which extreme social emergency creates a reaction of extreme individualism—a movement which draws the individual away from his correct relation with society as a member of the whole and which places him on his own, separate at times even from his family. The social movement in the individual is paralleled by a corresponding metaphysical movement in which he departs from his correct relationship with the divine hierarchy and enters into the sphere of the demonic powers. This particular heresy (for so it is regarded by the villagers and expressed by their use in this context of the word 'stupid')[1] is tempting to the villager, for according to its logic the power of God becomes related to inaction, and that of the Devil to action. Thus the normal values become reversed, for since action is what is so ardently desired action comes to be equated with the good. This is denied by the villager's fundamental conception of the world, according to which the powers of good as well as those of evil are thought to be continually active, and the whole of the universe, the whole of man, to consist in a cosmic battleground in which the forces of good and evil, of Christ and the Devil, are engaged in continual conflict. However, the competitive and troubled nature of relations within the community can cause a situation in which the villager, if he is 'stupid', may be so bedevilled by hatred, jealousy, misery, and rage, that he sees as infinitely more desirable than further apparently non-productive appeals to the Mother of God, the practical aid of those whose business it is to produce tangible results in the social world. In this state he loses sight of the essential nature of good as an active force, and turns instead to demonic energy as the only release from an insupportable situation.

Sorcery, therefore, when it seeks to affect the natural course of social relations, is seen as an offence against society by the individual, and the individual is presented as 'stupid', a deviant, who has lost his understanding of the nature of good and evil and of the relation of the divine powers with the activities of man, and who seeks illicitly to affect society by the violent intrusion of forces from which the community as a whole continually endeavours to protect itself.

---

[1] μουρλὸς means 'stupid', 'foolish', or even, in some contexts, 'mad'.

PART II

IV

THE SELF AND OTHERS

ANY understanding of a society needs an explanation not only of structural elements of that society, but also of the emotional realities which that structure involves, for it is only in this way that a reader who has experience only of quite a different system, can understand in human terms the logic and morality of behaviour quite foreign to his own. Some of the puzzles of this community are how the slander (λόγια, lit. words) of others have such genuine destructive power; how it is that honour resides not in the individual conscience but is conferred on the individual as a collective assessment of the community; how people can lie so often and yet not lose touch with their personal integrity; why the marriages which are arranged through the family group are nearly always much happier than those which are contracted on the basis of 'love'; how it comes about that friendships are made so frequently and broken so disastrously. In this chapter therefore I attempt to throw some light on the nature of personal insight and the experience of others which underlie these phenomena.

In Ambéli, in spite of the changes brought about by the various contacts with the outside world, the broad structure of community relations seems to be still very much as it has always been. Elements have appeared within this traditional structure which are working increasingly towards a radical change, and elements extraneous to this structure are also beginning to make themselves felt; but in principle it is still the case that relationships in the community are organized in accordance with a commonly held value system and a tightly knit system of roles. Since there are in the village few official positions, and since common subscription to the same values prohibits the making of too many deviants, at the same time as inhibiting the rise of new standards according to which new roles might be created, these roles are limited in number and very clear-cut.

It is in keeping with the importance of the family and the house in village life that the principal roles of the community are defined in relation to it—husband, wife, father, mother, son, daughter, aunt, and so on. Roles of host and guest, important also in their capacity of mediating between the hostile outside world and the sanctuary of the family group, also take place largely in the context of the house. Other roles—those defined in relation to official positions, such as priest, president of the village community, secretary, and agricultural policeman; those defined by such peripheral and extraordinary situations as that of an outcast, a stranger, or an enemy; or those defined by non-related and interfamilial relationships such as neighbour and fellow villager—are all subordinate to these primal family roles. Hence the overriding duty of any person, in a case where he has to act two (or more) roles simultaneously, is always to his family. The duty of the neighbour gives way, in such cases, to the duty of the son; the obligations of the official to that of the father. And these obligations are often such as to make it a moral duty to quarrel with, cheat, or deceive the outsider in support of the house.

The implications of this fact of social relations in terms of the villager's insight and understanding are considerable. The pious mother of a family, for instance, involves herself in quarrels, abuse, and unrelenting hatreds in defence of her house; a child is conditioned to deceit from a tender age, because deceit is necessary to safeguard the family from the curiosity and malice of the community. A village priest, although he is a priest, does not, nor is he able to, act according to a moral order different from that which constrains his fellow villagers—for he is no less involved than the others in the basic duty to defend his family, and he, with the others, has to carry out this duty in a competitive social situation.

It is plain from this that the structure of social relations in the village encourages the development in the individual of qualities which, though they are a necessary part of family integrity, act against a certain type of self-awareness. This is by no means to say that the individual has no personal integrity, nor that he is totally lacking in self-awareness; it is to redefine the concepts of integrity and self-awareness in terms which relate to village culture rather than to more introspective types of thinking, and are thus oriented more to the group than to the individual. Thus, to the extent that the villager's personal integrity is identified with that of his family, he is correspondingly involved in a type of self-awareness more extrovert than introvert. He acts more as the protagonist of his family group than as a person with his own individual moral existence. In the following analysis, therefore, I intend no moral evaluation whatever of the relative merits of the different types of experience; it is merely my aim to analyse a certain area of the villager's understanding and show how it is conditioned by the social situation in which he finds himself.

The effect of the role system in conditioning behaviour is clearly seen in the phenomenon of 'self-assertion' (ἐγωισμός). The fact that the dominant roles of society are defined with reference to the family creates a situation in which every villager is, in his meetings with other members of the community, seen as the protagonist of his family and as its potential defender against the attacks of other non-related groups. Thus it comes about that public behaviour—particularly among men, who are the chief representatives of their families—comes to be associated with a type of self-assertive behaviour known as *egoismós* (from ἐγώ = I). As was said to me, 'In the house, *egoismós* disappears. But outside the house everyone tries to make himself out a bit larger than he really is'. Thus self-assertion is not an essential and integral part of a person which is reflected consistently in all that person's attitudes and relationships; it is a type of *persona*, worn in public and discarded in private, which has as its conscious aim the achievement of a relative prestige for the wearer, and the vindication of himself or his family from the accusations and criticisms of the community. It is a type of behaviour which is best understood as 'me-ness', a display of personality essentially bombastic and competitive, and for this reason the transliterated Greek term will be used in this section, although the rendering 'self-assertion' will be used in general throughout this book.

Because of the essentially competitive nature of *egoismós*, it reveals itself as one of the prime motivators and consolidators of quarrels, and it is recognized as such by the villagers. Two people, for instance, deadlock over a particular situation, and neither will draw back. Both parties say, 'I'm not at fault, you are'—a simple expedient which, by denying the fact of fallibility, obviates the need for apology. The quarrel is then consolidated by one means or another, and in order to establish their claim to infallibility in the eyes of the world, both parties will withdraw into their own seclusion and 'not speak' to the other.

A man's instinct for self-assertion is often called into action by the fear that someone else is making a fool of him. In a situation such as the trespass on his land by goats belonging to another person, a quarrel could very often be avoided if the offender admitted reasonably to his guilt. If, however, the trespasser (in a reciprocal display of self-assertion) attempts to gloss over the fact of his trespass, it is this, much more than the trespass itself, which offends against the *egoismós* of the other, forcing him then to take up the matter openly and press for payment. 'Does he think that he can make a fool of me?' is the type of comment often made in these circumstances. To 'make a fool of' someone is an effective way of enhancing one's own ego and of damaging that of another, a fact which creates a situation in which everyone is continually on the look-out against a possible cheat or leg-pull, and in which the slightest unintentional insult may be interpreted as gratuitous offence and give rise to a quarrel.

Egoismós is essentially a quality which reveals itself in relation to people outside the house, but it also is seen deeply entrenched in insoluble situations when a person has committed himself too deeply to a particular stand to withdraw without losing face, and yet in which all the community are united in thinking him wrong. In such a case, by keeping to his own version of events and by refusing to speak to the other party, the man concerned continues to attempt to preserve his ego even while the community laughs at him for it. *Egoismós* therefore is capable, unlike honour,[1] of continuing to have an existence in spite of the mockery of the community.

In the cause of self-assertion a man may also take the offensive, and it is as an expression of *egoismós* that the community as a whole indulges in socially regulated forms of stealing, such as tapping a pine-tree belonging to someone else, or cutting firewood from a neighbouring property. It is from the same impulse, too, that a man will shift with his foot the boundary stone which marks off his field from a neighbouring one, and plough an extra six inches down all its length; and it is out of a reciprocal *egoismós* that the neighbour, although he probably has more land than he can cultivate, will waste a lot of money taking the first man to court, saying, if pressed, 'What if I have more land than I need? Does that mean I must give it away?'

Important here is the concept mentioned earlier of the involve-

[1] See p. 182.

ment of the householder in his house and land, according to which an offence against any part of these constitutes an offence against himself. This is not to be seen as an offence at one remove, in the sense that the theft of his property involves him in a reduction of income, although it may well do that; it must be seen as an offence, literally and directly, against the integrity, the wholeness, of his own existence; for this existence he bears not in isolation, but as a member of a group, as the recipient of his father's land and wealth, as the heir to a body of customs about which he says, 'This is how we found them and this is how we leave them', and as the gateway to a future generation from whom he and his forebears will gain renewed validity. He occupies, that is to say, a particular network of relationships with people and things, and it is that, rather than any individual characteristics he may or may not possess, which is the charter for his social existence and the basis from which he derives his identity.

It follows, therefore, that when a man gives vent to his *egoismós* by appropriating someone else's property, or defends it by repelling the attack of another, something much deeper than sheer egotism is at stake; it is not an empty vanity which is being satisfied, but a social personality and its very desire for existence which are being vindicated. It is because of the villager's particular involvement with the complex of people and things with which he is surrounded from birth up, that quarrels over material objects, land in particular, are inevitable. This is a point which is illustrated particularly sharply in the present day when nearly everyone in Ambéli has more land than they know what to do with, but when, nevertheless, the whole of the resin season is bedevilled by quarrels over the pines among the men who, as it is said, 'kill each other in the forests'.

Because *egoismós* is such an important part of public behaviour, and because it is so intimately related to the defence of the family, it is plain that there is a sense in which the sheer preservation of *egoismós* is a value in itself and supersedes the value of sheer justice or truth. One of the results of this on the mentality of the villager is that, since he has been prevented by his culture from identifying, consistently, what is (in a purely literal sense) true, with what is good, and indeed is forced in certain contexts to separate the two, his capacity for telling lies is highly developed while his personal integrity and his sense of honour are not necessarily compromised thereby.

In normal life, therefore, lying is not something which disturbs the villager's conscience, for his integrity is not crucially identified with the value of telling the 'truth', in the immediate practical sense, at all times. This is not to say that there are not occasions on which the villager is troubled by the fact that the social situation imposes on him the necessity to lie, and it is when he is considering his social life in the light of the divine law that he sees most of it, including its lies, as 'sin'. But the fact nevertheless remains that although the incongruity between the divine law and the social reality does not go unobserved or unlamented by the villager, he at the same time feels in no way compelled to defeat it by his own efforts, or to load himself with guilt because of his complicity in it. The two standards of social action, the ideal and the actual, exist side by side in unresolved paradox because the system of roles in this society is simple and straightforward enough to allow this. Because the villager's loyalty is categorically due to his family, and because it is through the family that the ideal values are realized, his criteria for action are, in the last resort, quite clear. Thus, therefore, the villager can accommodate without difficulty a deep understanding of the reality of the commandment to love his neighbour with the fact that very often he hates him; he can simultaneously accept the principle of the supreme importance of his own family, and the ideal of equal regard for all.

Since the villager is not forced by his society to resolve the paradoxes inherent in this situation, it follows that the capacity of village thinking to resolve such paradoxes has remained relatively undeveloped. The villager remains at peace with his faults, and along with his role he accepts without too deep questioning and torment the social situation into which he has been born. This is not a situation which leads to reform or social revolution, but to a continuing self-perpetuation in its own terms, and the stability of such societies is due to this, and to the fact that there is no room within this traditional pattern for the individual to develop other criteria for belief and action which seriously challenge it. Social change, therefore, where it occurs, occurs as the destroyer of this tradition, not only on the level of specific phenomena, cars versus mules, or literacy versus the oral tradition, but, at a deeper level, as a new culture which demands, if it is to be successfully lived, the one thing the villagers cannot give it: that is to say the capacity for individual choice, and, if necessary, for individual rejection. It is for this reason that the villagers all over Greece are succumbing so quickly to the new values which are being brought in from outside, for in this cultural matter they can only make cultural decisions, not personal ones, and culture in this case is the voice of the majority.

One of the key points of social change, therefore, occurring in traditional societies, may be seen as lying in this factor of self-awareness, and in the need for this to change, as a culture in which most social action is consistent with a single internal moral order, develops into one in which a proliferation of roles forces on the members of society the necessity to discriminate between differing moral values.

To examine social change in Ambéli in these terms is outside the scope of this book, but it is evident that the organization of roles in the village carries with it certain demonstrable effects on the nature of the villager's self-awareness and on his relationships with others, and some of these are assessed in the following pages.

Because roles in this society are limited and clearly defined, there is no doubt in the minds of the community as to what is proper and what is improper action, and, as a result, behaviour within these roles is strongly sanctioned. Thus a strict conformity of behaviour relating centrally to the family is achieved. As a result of this close association of the individual with the group, there is little latitude for the development in the individual of any sense of himself as a being other than one who gains his validity through the correct and responsible fulfilment of certain well-defined courses of action. Where this is so there can necessarily develop in the individual no consistent criteria by which to act if for any reason he chooses to reject his proper role. Such rejection, therefore, if it takes place, takes place not as a result of a mature and reflective judgement on what is or is not in accordance with the deepest needs of personal fulfilment, but merely according to a self-willed and irresponsible self-assertion. This is a very different state of affairs from that found in societies where the individual is faced from early youth with a number of different possibilities of role which he can assume, and in whom therefore the capacity for evaluating the merits of these different roles is, to some extent at any rate, given the chance to develop. It is in these societies that 'individuality' (in the sense of personal fulfilment) has come to be associated with a type of independence, almost with nonconformity, whereas in Ambéli such fulfilment is gained, and is seen to be gained, only through conformity to the common norms.

Mild demonstrations of such individualism are known as *houï* (χοΰϊ)—a characteristic which has been described by Campbell as '. . . an aspect of personality to which one may attribute those idiosyncratic actions and attitudes which are in some way unusual or even deviant'.[1] Among the Sarakatsani, he says, it is John Charisis who tears his shirts to shreds when he dances at weddings; in Ambéli the principal possessor of *houï* is the unpredictable, clever Anastasia Planas, the convolutions of whose *houï*, in the sense of her capacity for amusing herself with devious jokes at other people's expense, no one can fathom. *Houï* is disapproved of as an irrational and potentially disruptive element which society is better without, even while it is tolerated as a feature which is not actually outside the structure of accepted behaviour.

More extreme expressions, however, of individualism occur only in the socially outcast, either as the cause or the result of their ostracism, and consistent nonconformist behaviour is noticeable only in such people—in the local simpleton, in the girl who is 'stupid' and behaves in a loose and irresponsible way; in the woman who was hopelessly crippled in youth; and in the man who has always drunk excessively and has never married, and may now neglect the fast, ask to be given glasses of ouzo, and make a fool of himself in various different ways, because he has 'lost his turn' (δὲν ἔχει σειρά) in the community life, that is to say he has created no family of his own, he has no issue.

In all these cases, individualism occurs not as the expression of identity, but as the loss of it. Such people may or may not be condemned by society according to how far their present behaviour is seen to be the result of a character defect, and how far it is the result (as in the case of illness) of sheer ill chance. But leaving such issues aside, such people all come under the single category of those who have forfeited, or been denied, full membership of the community, and who as a result have developed relationships with the rest of the village of a different and inferior order from those which obtain between all other members of it. These people are, in fact, considered unworthy of the struggling competitive

[1] J. K. Campbell, *Honour, Family, and Patronage*, p. 45.

relationship between equals which characterizes the village at large, and are treated in various modes of pity, condescension, sympathetic amusement, mockery, or disdain. Such people are, as it is said, 'apart from the community' (ἔξ'ἀπ'τὸ κοινό).

It is with this complete acceptance of customary social values, then, and with the corresponding lack of self-examination that such acceptance involves, that the villager engages on all his relationships.

Because it is the community rather than the individual that is the custodian of social values, the villager's honour is, broadly speaking, something which is granted him by public opinion and which may not be possessed in defiance of it. A man who is denied a reputation for honour by the community has, except in a very specialized sense which will be discussed later, no honour. Avoidance of social condemnation therefore equals retention of honour, rather than avoidance of doing wrong. Thus it comes about that there is a very significant sense in which it is considered more important to be seen to be honourable than it is actually to be so, and the villager passes much of his time in trying to extract from public opinion by whatever means he can (including lying and deceit) such a reputation. The result of such a situation is that, although theoretically it is the reality of honour that is considered to be fundamental to personality, it is in practice the appearance of honour which is in this society the vital arbitrator of behaviour.

It is very important here to make it clear that these words 'appearance' and 'reality' must be understood absolutely literally to signify the factual occurrence or non-occurrence of a specific event, and to hold no overtones of moral evaluation whatever. For so strong is the identification of the individual with the group and with the over-all judgement of society, that the appearance and reality of honour, according to the villager's categories, have in many situations a significance quite different from that which these concepts hold in societies with a different type of conscience. In Ambéli, as the following examples show, the sharp definition between the appearance and the reality can get blurred to the point at which they both overlap, and where it is the maintenance of a good appearance which, regardless of the factual events behind it, is seen to maintain the honour of the house. At this point the appearance has in a sense become the reality. This point is of vital importance to the discussion of lies and concealment which will be the subject of a later chapter.

The two examples which illustrate best this overlap of the appearance of honour with the reality, and the equation of honour with the concealment of wrong done, are given in two folk tales. One of these stories concerns the idea of fate—the irrevocable destiny given to a child by three old women, the three Fates, during the first three days after its birth. In this story a girl was born who was fated to grow up and to marry well, but eventually to prove unfaithful to her husband. However, in later years one of the Fates grew well disposed towards her and contrived it that, although what was fated for her had to come to pass, she would nevertheless not 'lose her honour'. By devious means this came about. The girl married and found herself later in a situation in which she committed adultery with another man, but, being protected by her Fate, the affair went undiscovered by the community. Thus her fate was 'mended', she retained her honour, and her life was not ruined. The crucial words in this story are those of the Fate to the husband: 'It will come about that she will be unfaithful to you. This is what must happen. But you will arrange things so that although this thing will come to pass, she will nevertheless keep her honour'; and the son of the story-teller explained this as follows: 'She didn't lose her honour because the community didn't find out. Only her husband knew, and he decided to let it pass, and so she kept her honour.' This interpretation was echoed by other villagers.

The second story from a different woman tells of a mother who attained great sanctity because she concealed the infidelity of her daughter-in-law from her absent son, so that when he returned to the house he was not forced to divorce her and to break up the family. So good was this woman's action in concealing her daughter-in-law's lapse and in saving the household from catastrophe that when she died three lamps hung miraculously from the sky at her head. The explanation of the story-teller was as follows: 'God wants people to cover things up, He wants there to be no fuss. If the community had got to hear of it, the son would have got angry and turned his bride out, and the whole house would have been scattered. As it was she covered the sin up, and the son forgave his bride, and no one got to hear of anything, and the house was saved. That was the miracle that the mother did, and why lamps came out of heaven when she died. God wants concealment.'

It is as a direct result of this state of affairs that the villager is on the whole concerned only with sanctions imposed on him by others as a result of his doing wrong, and only very marginally, if at all, with the damage he may have inflicted on himself by the act itself. He therefore remains relatively limited in his knowledge of that area of himself which is affected by internal conditions rather than by outer actions. To be in a state of hatred, jealousy, or promiscuity, for instance, the villager sees not as conditions which *in themselves* can damage the person who is in their grip, but only as conditions which are potentially damaging in so far as their public effects are concerned. Several conversations on the subject have revealed a complete incomprehension of a type of thought which sees in the very presence of hatred, for instance, in a person, a process which can damage the one who hates; and the result of this in terms of the villagers' lives is that their passions tend to need violent outlet because their lack of insight in this respect denies them any other means of coping with them.

Life in Ambéli with its quarrels and gossip furnishes abundant evidence of this situation, and a discussion of these topics follows later. Here I give only one example—of a woman whose chances of marriage had been ruined and whose life made unbearable by the slander of a certain man. This woman spent her evenings weeping in her house and dreaming of revenge, and as I talked to her I realized that there was nothing in her philosophy which would serve to take the edge off her passion, nothing that she would even momentarily assent to as being a reasonable way to try to cope with her situation, except the solace of positive action. All courses of action being closed to her except that of sorcery, she remained throughout the winter and until the man had married and left the village in the spring, obsessed with the idea of trying to organize his partial destruction by such means, saying, probably truly, that unless she was able to damage him in some way she would carry a weight inside her heart until the day she died.

All this is not to imply that, even in societies where this type of self-awareness is more encouraged, other people may not be similarly possessed by similar passions. But what is being discussed here is the effects of culture on the individual, rather than individual responses in themselves, and, whatever is true of other societies, it may be said that the villagers in this one are culturally committed to placating their passions rather than surmounting them, though they may subdue them if self-interest is strong enough.

The nature of the villager's conscience is similarly related to the nature of his self-awareness, for when sanctions on behaviour are predominantly a matter for the community rather than for the individual, the individual fails to develop criteria for self-reproach other than those which are the community's and which are given him by the community. In this way a man may feel ashamed of some action even if no one discovers it, but what he is ashamed of is not the consequences of his action with relation to his own inner balance, for he is not aware of this or of the ways in which it can be upset; he blushes at the slur on his integrity which would follow if the community were to find out about it; he fears for the possible damage to his reputation.

Since the villager's self-awareness is in terms of dedicated fulfilment of his roles rather than in terms of introspective self-knowledge and contemplation, it follows that his awareness of others is similarly influenced—for where you do not know yourself you cannot know others. In any situation, therefore, in which his role does not give him a clear indication for action and in which, therefore, such insight would be useful—for instance when he is required to use his own judgement as to the character of another, unaided by specific knowledge of that person's actions—he is often literally at a loss. This sense of incapacity when faced with the imponderables of another person's being, as opposed to the more accessible facts of their actions or of their particular social relevance to the individual, finds its characteristic expression in two oft-quoted phrases: 'How do I know what you're really up to?' (τί ξέρω ἐγὼ τί κάνεις ἐσύ;) and 'Do you ever really know anyone else?' (ποῦ ξέρεις τὸν ἄλλονε;). I have heard the former phrase used often between married couples, and the latter is used particularly often in contexts where the character of someone outside the family is being discussed.

Although, therefore, the villagers speculate about the characters of others and are often shrewd enough in their assessment, they have not, and they know they have not, developed very deeply the capacity to assess the inner characteristics of others from minor outer indications. It is because of this that in the harrowing business of trying to assess the character of a prospective son- or daughter-in-law from a few meetings, the villagers are almost totally in the hands of their informants—true or false—and because of this that the gossips, knowing that they are on fertile ground, are most prolific round an engagement.

The type of friendships found in village life is also related to this lack of insight, and to the latent suspicion which is a part of every friendship in the village and gives to that friendship its unstable psychological foundation, rendering it permanently liable to rupture. In structural terms the flexibility of friendships is the result of the exclusive nature of the family and the fact that non-related liaisons inevitably involve only marginal loyalties. This explanation does not, however, throw much light on how the villager sustains in personal terms such a volatile situation; and what is noticeable about the villagers as they make and break friendships is that, since in those friendships they are relating less to some characteristic in that person which they find sympathetic than to the emotional or practical convenience which that person represents for them, the ending of friendship when convenience ends is a perfectly logical conclusion.

Friendships therefore occur as a compromise between the necessity for the family to look after itself by concentrating on its own material advantage, and the need of its members to create around themselves little nuclei of supporters and confidants. Two different types of need are balanced against each other, and while this equilibrium lasts—and it may do so for years—it lasts well. But because the central element in such relationships is not the deep personal significance of the one for the other but a more or less fortuitous union of self-interests, it follows that when self-interest fails the friendship must also fail, for in this case the roots of friendship have been destroyed. It is because of the innate and inescapable identification of each member of the community with the good of his own family group that there lies a latent antagonism at the heart of every friendship; and it is this antagonism which, when the particular combination of circumstances occurs, arises in a flood of accusations and mutual disillusionment and bursts the friendship apart.

All relationships therefore between the family group and people who are outside it hold a measure of distrust; and even within the

family the love that is felt between the various members of it is
generated less through sheer relationship, insight, and knowledge,
than through means and objects—the relationship that joins them
is less a direct one of mutual understanding so much as an indirect
one which is formed as they look outwards in their common concern for those objects which are in their care. This element of
objectivity which, since it springs from a general characteristic of
village thinking, is a characteristic of all village relationships, finds
its most extreme manifestation in the villager's relationship with
his animals.

The villager's feeling for his animals may be described as
originating in a utilitarian though not unkindly attitude according
to which an animal is loved if it is useful and is rejected if it is not.
It is an attitude which is demonstrated, for instance, when a mother
prevents a small child from pestering a goat by saying, typically,
'Be kind to our goat, she gives us milk'; when a child, asked if it
likes its cat, answers, variously, 'Yes, she's good, she catches mice',
or, 'No, she's a useless cat, she doesn't catch mice', and when a
woman one day, commenting on my love for my cats, said as she
gathered up an armful of kids that she would sell at Easter, 'These
are the animals that *I* love.' Nevertheless a distinction must be
made here between mere appreciation of the work the animal does,
and the love of an animal because it is useful, for it is the latter
which obtains here.

The village household cannot afford to carry non-working
members, except for the very old, or the ill, and even these do what
they can. Animal members of the combine, if they cannot for any
reason work, must sooner or later be jettisoned, even though this is
done with sorrow. But an animal which qualifies by reason of its
usefulness for inclusion into the household is then granted full
membership, on a basis of mutual rather than unilateral service.
This relationship is quite explicit in the mind of the villager who,
as he tends to his animals before seeing to himself, will often say,
'They work for us, we must work for them.' The relationship is
incurred on the basis of sheer utility, but when it is so to speak
ratified by inclusion of the animal into the household it immediately transcends that utility and becomes not one of exploitation
but of reciprocal obligation. The criteria one then observes in the
attitude of the villager to his animal are those which make it a
point of honour, as well as of expediency, to care for the animal

reasonably well, and which cause him to honour this obligation at the expense, sometimes, of financial gain. One notable example of this is given in the attitude taken by the villagers over the annual threshing.

This is still done by teams of animals roped together in numbers of up to ten, which take about ten hours of fast walking or trotting around the threshing-floor to break up the stalks and separate the grain. This on a hot July day exhausts the animals, and their owners sympathize. Where the corn to be threshed is the household's own, or where a system of reciprocal aid is agreed upon in which a man and his animals will go to the threshing-floor of another, on condition that the reverse applies, the animals are used and forced to work until the job is completed. But when I asked if anyone ever hired out his horse or mule in the threshing season in order to make money, the answer was, 'No, everyone says, "Why lend my animal to be killed all day?" It's different if it's your own threshing.' In other words, it is within the contract for the animals to be 'killed' in threshing the corn of their own household, or in maintaining a system of relations which enables that corn to be threshed, or in providing corn for a household that otherwise has none, but it is an abuse of the duty the owner bears to the animal if he hired it out to do excruciating work for money.

One last example is the event in the village when a mule was accidentally killed.[1] I was talking about it with another woman who had previously impressed me with her utilitarian attitude towards animals, and when she said that the daughter of the house concerned had been in tears all the following day, I took up what I imagined to be her line of thought and said, 'It was a good mule, of course, how much was it worth?', to which she replied hotly, 'It's not just a question of the value; that mule had been in the house for years. They had ploughed together, worked together, and now it's gone.'

Animals are not loved for themselves as members of the animal kingdom with their own beauty and peculiarity, but nor are they thought of in crude terms which involve only total exploitation of their productivity; they are cared for because they are members of the household which contribute, each according to its capacity, to the viability and the prosperity of the family group, and which share, inevitably, in its fortunes.

[1] See p. 43.

At this point cruelty to animals must be analysed briefly, because it is often misunderstood by Western visitors to Greece, and it may be thought that evidence of such cruelty conflicts with the basic assertion that membership of a household involves not only humans but animals also in a relationship of reciprocal obligation.

Since the degree of affection given to the animal is related to its membership of and usefulness to the group, there are occasions in which the animal must be sacrificed for the good of the group. These occasions comprise one category of cruelty to animals, and include such events as the threshing, when a man or boy runs behind the animals all the time with a whip to force them round and round the threshing-floor; irrigation, where the water has to be drawn from a well by a succession of little buckets worked by a blindfold animal who walks round and round the well-head; or when a sick animal which is past work is eventually taken to a remote spot and left to die.

A second category of cruelty to animals arises primarily through ignorance. The fact that the original relationship between man and animal is based on a need for the type of usefulness the animal represents, rather than on an understanding of and a liking for the animal's particular nature, results in a fundamental lack of direct relationship between the two. They form a unit whose elements are linked to each other by virtue of the total community of which they are a part, and which meet each other not in a process of mutual understanding, but in the process of working for the common good. Cases of cruelty, therefore, such as the over-punishment given to a dog which has done wrong, of failing to remove an animal's heavy saddle while it waits for hours at a time, of cuffing a cat away from the fire or knocking it off a stool—all common occurrences—have their basis not in gratuitous cruelty but in a lack of knowledge of the finer points of how to relate to an animal, how to treat, and how to train it. Added to this is also the attitude indicated previously that animals occupy the lowest position in the community, which carries with it the implicit, and sometimes explicit, feeling that they must be kept in their proper place. However, even cats, the least valued members of the household, are accepted with a sort of tolerant impatience as being under the protection of the household and therefore entitled to food, shelter, and a reasonable degree of kindness, and it is understood that more must not be expected of them than is in their nature to give. This attitude is often revealed by such a comment as, 'They must eat too, the little creatures', as the dry bread, the cats' diet, is thrown on the floor at the evening meal. And if a cat is ever kicked or stoned gratuitously, uncommon in Ambéli although more frequent in the nearby towns, it will almost inevitably be a cat belonging to another house.

There is a third category of cruelty, which more nearly approaches viciousness than the former ones, but it too is related to the fact of common membership of the household which is at the basis of the animal/man relationship. In cases where a family is in great hardship, the animals will be likely to suffer too, on the principle, 'Why should they eat while we starve?' Since an animal's position is, in the order of things, lower than a man's, it is not uncommon to find in very impoverished parts of the country a man taking it as quite normal that his animals' lot is, relatively speaking, even worse than his own. Here, where the economic balance is loaded heavily against the family, there occurs a diminution in the quota of kindness the householder can afford, both economically and psychologically, to give his animal, and a justification of what in many cases amounts to callousness or cruelty by a more absolute reference to the man/animal hierarchy. This type of maltreatment or carelessness of animals springs from the same system of values as the care and, frequently, affection, described above; the essential difference lies in the imbalance between the needs of the family and its economic resources, which, on the essential principle of the primacy of the family, necessarily involves any animal within its household in a relationship which is oriented more towards a sharing of its suffering than a receipt of its benefits.

All the foregoing is not to say that there are few occasions of deliberate cruelty to animals in Greece—still less that there are none; but it is to say that this type of cruelty, where it exists, exists as a deviation from the norm which in general persists as an understanding by the villager of responsibility and a kind of comradeship gained through common toil for a common end. The concept of the house, therefore, as a sanctuary in which all who are admitted find a reciprocal relationship centred round the highest and most positive standards of the community, gains added force when it is realized that the energy generated by the house is sufficient to socialize the relations between all its inhabitants, down to the least important animals which make up its complement.

The quality which is so noticeable in the villager's relationships with his animals is not absent, though it is very differently expressed, even where his capacity for relating to others is most developed—in the case of his marriage; and here too his concentration on the more external aspects of the relationship is a central feature. The resulting objectivity, however, shows itself not, as in the case of the villager and his animals as a relationship based purely on their use and value but, for men as for women, as one based on the need for self-fulfilment.

Initially, it is plain, when two people get engaged they see each other not as persons but as symbols. They embark upon marriage, not as a result of a deep affinity of character, nor because they see in each other any unique personal significance, but in order to form a social and symbolic unit—to set up house together and to procreate children. And the point of marriage is to create a unity in which each one may realize his or her own social personality according to its ideal role. Within this unity each one leads interdependent yet self-contained lives, each looking to the other for no more than the faithful fulfilment of that role—the whole-hearted carrying out of the social contract. Affection grows with the passing of time and the sharing of children, grief, and joy, and this affection can grow into a dynamic relationship. But still the essential nature of the relationship is that it is extroverted, engaged upon by both members for their own ends, connected with their own achievement of a certain role and position, and maintained chiefly not through deepening awareness and knowledge of self and other, but by a focus always outwards to the material, social, economic, and religious world within which this relationship is set, and by means of which it is maintained.

The initiation of this relationship is at the first formal meeting between the couple, and was illustrated for me by a married woman in the following words: 'He is attracted to her, he buys her clothes . . . they get married.' And she elaborated, in a personal sense, 'First of all', looking at the cat on my lap, 'you pity him.' It is plain from these words, even if it were not from the pattern of the events themselves, that apart from the initial attraction, love grows not as

4. Harvesting the Oats

a direct relationship in terms of mutual understanding but rather as a result of a series of acts. Clothes are bought and received, and the first tentative liaison is strengthened. Then the engagement ceremony is held, the union consolidated, the community informed, and the close kin included explicitly in the relationship. And the crucial act which joins the couple is an act not of love but of decision—the pronouncing of the marriage vows on the wedding-day. It is these vows rather than any interior sense of commitment which form the basis to the whole of the couple's future life together, and these vows and their centrality to the whole marriage relationship are symbolized by the 'crowning' (στεφάνωσις or στέψις) which is an essential part of the Orthodox marriage service, and which in the popular mentality is inseparable from the fact of marriage. The word meaning 'to crown' (στεφανώνω) as well as the word for 'to marry' (παντρεύω) are both used indiscriminately for the marriage ceremony, and in the eyes of the villagers the Protestant marriage, with no crowns, cannot be said to be a marriage at all. It could in fact be said that the crowning, symbolizing the mystical union of the couple in the eyes of God as well as of the community, is an act which does not serve merely to make the marriage relationship binding, it is the effective creator of the relationship in the first place.

Thus the man and the woman are joined originally not by any love they bear each other, because love is consequent on marriage and not the cause of it; they are joined by the act of decision inaugurated at the time of the engagement and consolidated on marriage. The significance of this decision with regard to the vitality of the later relationship is well illustrated by the comment of a girl who was at one time hesitating about whether or not to accept a man whose looks she did not altogether like. I asked how she would become fond of him later if she did not like him then. 'Now I couldn't care less about him,' she said. 'Later it will be different. I shall have made my decision.'

Marriage is in village society a social necessity for both men and women, and those who do not marry fail to do so only because of extreme necessity. In Ambéli the six unmarried villagers have remained in this state due variously to crippling illness, schizophrenia, and in one case to chronic drunkenness. Lacking disabilities such as these, no girl in the village will remain unwooed by some man,[1] although according to her evaluation by the community the quality of the bridegroom will vary. The one girl in Ambéli who was notorious for her immodesty and reputed unchastity was sought several times during my stay in the village, but her suitors were all men who had been rejected by better girls, one being slightly paralysed through a heart disease, another being very poor and uncouth and having in his household an old mother and a blind brother, while another was simple-minded. All in the village thought that she should have accepted one of these men—'Ioanna is a fool, so she must take a fool' was its united opinion; a comment which voices the people's general belief that in the sphere of marriage some kind of economy is seen to operate according to which girls get the men they deserve. No girl, therefore, is praised if she consistently refuses suitors, however unacceptable they may be, for in the final analysis the fact that only such people seek her is illustration of her deserts; and in the judgement of the community, since it is the proper state of women to marry and set up a family, the sort of pride which causes them continually to reject men on the grounds that they are not good enough, is seen not as a proper sense of discrimination but as a perverse and destructive instinct.

Engagements are always—except in cases of a 'stolen marriage' (κλέφτικος γάμος)—embarked upon as part of an authorized contract between two families, in which the principals have often had no more contact with each other than to see each other once and exchange a few formal sentences at a meeting organized by the match-maker. It is thus primarily a social rather than a personal act, one that is seen as linking two groups together in an affinal relationship and in socially regulated acts of obligation and co-operation, and as founding a new and separate social unit, rather than as linking two individuals for the purposes of their own happiness.

There are two types of 'stolen marriage'. One is reputed to have

[1] There are a number of unmarried women over 40 in Kateríni with no obvious disabilities, whose spinsterhood is due to the fact that on account of the possession of a certain degree of refinement and a moderately large dowry (over 100,000 drs.) they expect a husband from the professional class, or from the civil service. Such men, however, are few, and the majority of the offers for girls in Kateríni come from farmers, artisans, or shopkeepers. Some of these girls therefore prefer to reject such men in the hope eventually of acquiring a man who measures up to their expectations.

occurred from time to time in the early part of the century, although there have been no instances of this in Ambéli since 1940, and comes about when a man abducts a girl against her will and violates her, thus destroying her reputation and forcing her parents to give her to him in marriage. Such an act could lead to blood feud between the two houses concerned, but it appears that, in order to avoid such mutual destruction, it was the more common practice for the parents of the girl to make the best of a bad job and consent to the marriage. The second type of 'stolen marriage' has occurred twice since 1960, and is the result of an illicit liaison between a man and a girl initiated without the parents' knowledge or consent. Such a marriage, when it comes about, may be voluntary on the side of both parties, but it frequently occurs that the man, growing fearful of a girl who has so patently demonstrated her lack of chastity to him, draws back, and is persuaded into marriage only by threats from the wife's kinsmen. Both the recent cases in Ambéli were of this sort. In one case the girl's family put pressure on the man and, without threat of violence, talked him into marrying her. The other case was more serious involving the union of second cousins which is according to village custom the last degree of kinship between which marriage is prohibited. The girl became pregnant, and the man fled to Athens. He was called back, however, by the news of a threat by the girl's brother to kill his entire household if he failed to come back and marry her. He returned and they were married, shamefully, in their house, with no church service, no guests, and no celebration.

It is not surprising that such marriages are thought of by the community as the least successful, for they are embarked on not by mutual agreement between two groups but by individual defiance of village opinion and family preference, and although they are frequently consolidated by the combined action of the girl's family group, this is a unilateral unity achieved only on the negative principle of preventing a bad situation from becoming worse, rather than in a positive act of communion and support. The girl has lost her honour before marriage, and the man his chance of negotiating for a good dowry; and since, as was demonstrated earlier, neither party has the ability at this stage to have any real idea of what the other is like, such a marriage is inevitably inaugurated not by a deep affinity of character but merely by sexual attraction. This attraction, it appears, is incapable of resisting successfully the combined pressures of economic discrepancy, family disapproval, and the suspicion generated by the man's inability to have confidence in his wife's fidelity to him since he himself was the chief witness to her unchaste behaviour with him before they married. Village opinion therefore is that such marriages for 'love' will almost certainly be regretted by both parties, and that the arranged marriage is not only the only dignified way for a couple to unite, but also the only way which promises any happiness for the pair. This view is certainly supported by the first case cited above, in which the couple are seen by all to lead a very tempestuous life, the wife being forbidden by her husband to see her mother or to take her children to see her, and being frequently beaten on account of her husband's jealous suspicions.

The customary engagement follows a different pattern. The suit may, in the present day, come either from the man or the girl, who chooses as match-maker or go-between[1] a man or a woman who is preferably a relative of theirs, and, if possible, also a kinsman, friend, or acquaintance of the family to whom the suit is being made. Marriages may also be arranged on the initiative of the match-maker, who goes independently to each of the two families which he would like to unite by marriage.

This match-maker approaches the particular family concerned, sounds out the prospects, and, if all is promising, arranges a meeting between the two families and mediates in all ensuing negotiations. It is the match-maker's business somehow to reconcile the high expectations of two mutually opposed families with the inevitably disappointing reality which either offers to the other, and for this reason it is said that a match-maker must be an accomplished liar.

The meeting between the two families always takes place at the girl's house, with the groom's party, consisting usually of the groom himself, his father, and the match-maker, being entertained to a meal. This meal may be at midday, but it is more frequently the evening meal so as to enable the visiting party to come and go under cover of darkness, and maybe escape the curiosity of the neighbours. At this meeting the couple assess each other, and the girl, particularly at the serving of the water, liqueur, and preserve

[1] The usual word for a match-maker in Greek is προξενητής. In Ambéli however, such a person is known by the term used also for affines, συμπέθερος.

which is, in these circumstances, her traditional duty, knows that her deportment is being minutely scrutinized. After the initial pleasantries the match-maker will initiate the serious discussion, the most important features of which are, for the man, the size of the dowry, and for the girl, the financial position and social status of the groom, his economic prospects, the type of work she will be expected to do in her new home, and the number of relatives by marriage she will have living in the same house. Important also to the bride is the fact that the groom should own property in his own name, for under existing Greek law a woman who is widowed, before she has a child, by a man who owns no property in his own right, has no claim to any of her parents-in-law's estate; but of her husband's estate she will inherit half if he dies before she has a child, and all if she has one or more.

It is unusual for there to be explicit agreement at this meeting, for the girl is normally too shy to express her liking for the groom openly in front of the company, and it is usually hoped by one or both sides to gain further concessions from the other by more negotiations, and the meeting usually adjourns with promises to send messages to each other within a few days.

Each side will of course make exhaustive inquiries about the character of the proposed partner, but it is recognized that these inquiries will not necessarily elicit all the truth, partly because the informants will usually be biased either in favour of the person or against him, and will weight their information accordingly; and partly because it is thought that even the community does not know the real nature of a man or woman, which only emerges within the house. Even the minimal requirements of virtue in a spouse—that the man should not be wasteful, drunken, cruel, or lazy, and that the woman should not be immodest and extravagant —are not thought to be capable of discernment by the interested party in any meeting, brief or prolonged. As one woman said to me, 'A bad man turns out good, and you take a man for a good person and he turns out bad.' A person reveals himself through action alone, within the house, and apart from the reports of the community his character can be inferred or deduced in no other way than that of direct observation.

It is partly because of this that the concept of Fate (*Τύχη*) has such currency in the village with reference to marriage, for it is a way in which people abdicate from responsibility for an act

whose ultimate outcome they cannot even guess with any degree
of conviction. So it is universally accepted in Ambéli that although
people do what they can, organize and plan and foresee as far as
they are able, marriages in fact take place as the Fate of each
person decides, as the outcome of an inexorable pattern laid down
for that person from the hour of their birth. The explicit attitude
of both parties after an engagement, therefore, is one of hopeful
fatalism. They have done everything they can, they have tried to
foresee and forestall all the difficulties. Now . . . time will tell. It is
because of this fundamental uncertainty about the characters of
others that visitors to an engagement party will be asked earnestly
what they think of the bride (or bridegroom) and a favourable
answer will visibly please the questioner, although it will not re-
assure him. I was asked by one prospective mother-in-law what I
thought of the bridegroom, and said I thought him very nice.
'Good, bad, that's what we've decided now. Marriage is a matter
of luck', was her typical reply. On the other side, in this instance,
the bridegroom was equally ignorant of the character of his
prospective bride, for some of the community had, as it always
does, slandered her, rumouring that she had had an affair in the
previous year with a man who was at the moment of the engagement overseas. Others in the community assured him that the
girl was 'good'. I met the two of them together visiting a house on a
name-day, and the conversation turned to his engagement. 'People
say she's not good,' he said at one point. 'How do *I* know?' It was
plain that this was the literal truth, and until the day of her
marriage this particular girl was anxious lest her fiancé should
come to believe the rumours and desert her.

After coming to a conclusion about the advantages of a match,
the respective families will tell the match-maker of their decision,
upon which, if it is favourable, there will usually ensue further
negotiations with regard to questions such as the size of the dowry,
the possibility of the addition of half an acre or so, the amount of
furniture the groom will buy—at which each party tries to extract
the best possible terms for themselves. These negotiations may
entail another meeting between the man and the girl, but they
may also be carried out between the two families without recourse
to any further confrontation between the two principals.

The decision to ratify an engagement may not be reached for a
period of weeks or even months, and the first definite indication to

the community that such a decision has been reached is the departure of the girl with one or two female relations to 'go shopping' with her future fiancé. This is an event at which the bridegroom with various relatives and advisers meets the bride and her company in Kateríni or some other market town and buys for her clothes and jewellery which are expected to total approximately between 7,000 and 8,000 drachmas, or about £100; and it is considered by the bride's family to be a kind of extension of the battle for advantage that characterizes the whole match-making period. The couple have not been joined yet, still considering themselves as representatives of opposing interests, so the bride's relatives tend always towards extravagance, while the groom laments the amount of money that is being spent but dares not for the sake of his prestige look mean. Once I was present when a generous-hearted girl, having refused a watch from her fiancé on the grounds that she already had one, was rebuked by her relatives when she got back home and was told, 'You were a fool, you'll never get another chance.'

A few days later the engagement party will be held in the bride's house at which the bride gives gifts to the groom and to her future in-laws, has the ring put on her finger, and there is eating and drinking and dancing until the groom's party have to leave. The engaged couple may go out on their own after this party and sit for a little while in the café, but this is not invariable custom and it is on the following Sunday, when the groom comes again to the village, that the two incorporate their act into the life of the community by going to church together. On this occasion the bride, resplendent in all the finery he has bought her, will submit both herself and her fiancé to the judgement of the village in a conscious public action which is both an appeal to the community for their approval of the marriage, and an affirmation of the fact of her engagement and the successful ending to the preceding period of hesitation and anxiety.

The making public of the engagement in this way, the din of the record-player from the girl's house 'so that everyone may know that they are rejoicing', and the proud acknowledgement of the people concerned of the congratulations of the community are in striking contrast to the tortuous secrecy which cloaks every action during the match-making period, and are an indication of the binding nature of the engagement as it is understood by the villagers. Although it is not unknown for engagements to be broken off, it is rare, and it is looked upon with disfavour by the community if a man 'deceives' a girl in this way and ruins her reputation and her future.[1] Because of the malice of certain sections of the community a girl is in fear of having her engagement broken off until the day of her wedding, but the main force of gossip, activated by the impetus of a developing situation and fed by the rumours and counter-rumours and inquiries which congregate around any engagement negotiations, lessens very considerably on the achievement by the parties concerned of the engaged state, although it may start up again if there is a particularly long interval between the engagement and the celebration of the marriage.

Coincident also with this change from secrecy to publicity is the change in the relations between the two families from a latent antagonism and mutual exploitation to an admitted harmony and mutual interest. The two families after the engagement share a common concern for the well-being of their children (or grandchildren, first nephews or nieces as the case may be); they have acquired a large number of affinal relatives and unite in a common hope of future descendants; the bride and groom have the common cause of their future life together, and the present extension of their circle of relationships to include the entire kindred of their future spouse. In the kinship terminology little difference is made, except in the case of the immediate relations within the family, between blood and affinal relations; the aunt of the bride becomes the aunt of the bridegroom, similarly with uncles and cousins: and even the mother of the bride—technically 'mother-in-law' (πεθερά) to the new groom, may be addressed as 'mother' (μάννα or μητέρα) during and after the engagement ceremony.

The fact that this situation takes place in a competitive environment renders it of paramount importance that the final conclusion should be, and should be seen to be, successful. Where success is the criterion, the tendency is, inevitably, that people should be used in an instrumental way. This in itself accounts for the apparently overnight change from competition to co-operation which occurs between the two parties which are negotiating for a marriage, once the engagement has been celebrated. However, the nature of village relationships and the type of self-awareness

[1] Such a girl would be able to marry only 'as a widow', that is to say as a used woman, to a man who was poor, or old, or had some disability.

which has been analysed above, and the fact that marriage is genuinely thought of as a social act rather than as an individual preference, does cause there to be released, from the moment of the engagement, real sentiments of goodwill in both parties. The social occasion is accompanied by an emotional reality. The engagement party which first celebrates the new relationship with communal merry-making and the exchange of gifts is thus a genuine *rite de passage*, and symbolizes, while it creates, cements, and makes viable, the new estate.

V

MEN AND WOMEN—THEIR HUMAN
AND DIVINE NATURES

IN this type of society where the villager's individuality is
essentially implicated in a limited number of clearly defined
roles, every person has, from the moment he is born, a pattern
of socially approved actions and sentiments laid down for him
which accord with the particular group into which he is born, with
its particular relation to the community of which it is a part, and
in particular with his or her sex.

Traditionally this inclusion was from birth up, and small
children as young as five years old were required to help on the
farm in such duties as herding the animals for long hours winter
and summer, and were strictly trained in total loyalty and complete
commitment to the system of friendships and hostilities in which
their family was involved. Since 1950, however, this system of
roles for children has become weaker, because the children have
been associating together more regularly in the primary school,
and the teachers have consistently tried to prevent the continuance
there of family hostilities. Today this trend has been increased by
the departure of children for the grammar school immediately
they have finished their primary education, as they continue to
learn different attitudes and modes of behaviour from the outside
world and gradually disengage from the tightly introspective
network of village relationships; but in the young girls who are
still part of the traditional village organization it is noticeable how
completely they are included into the family system of roles after
they leave school, in contra-distinction to the more diffused
loyalties and generalized friendships of those children who are
still attending it.

The types of roles played by any one person at any one moment
depend very largely on his age, status, and the type of situation
in which he finds himself. A married man may in his own house be,
at the same time, husband, father, son, and brother, and his roles
proliferate with respect to his kindred outside the house and in the
context of the community in general to whom he is the representa-

tive of a particular grouping. But however much the roles may vary for any one person, they may all be finally reduced to two basic categories—those of sex. Because of this primary differentiation in the basic role patterns between men and women, this chapter begins with an analysis of the Greek symbolic classification of masculine and feminine nature.

According to this classification, men and women form a complementary opposition according to which men have a natural association with the sacred world, and women with that of the demons.

The prime faculty which man possesses, which both indicates his closer derivation from God and enables him to act more in accordance with God-like attributes, is that of the intellect. Man is 'logical' (λογικός)—a word which should not be understood merely in the sense in which it now has currency as the capacity for the precise use of the *ratio* or purely rational faculty. Here it implies an unimpassioned vision of the true values of society and the ability to enact them in everyday behaviour—values which involve particularly the idea of the protection of the family and a proper sense of obligation to others. This quality is opposed to the illogicality of women who, made vulnerable to passion by the vice of sensuality, are swept away from an understanding of the long-term good of their family for the sake of temporary gratifications and trivial victories. However, the frequent association of the word 'logical' with concepts of man's innate superiority, and the continual relation of that superiority to his creation at the hands of God, indicate quite clearly that to this way of thinking the capacity for logical thought is not only a social virtue but also a gift of divine grace, and confers, if this is not putting it too highly, a kind of relative divinity. Logicality is valued, not solely because it is a useful attribute which enables man to achieve a type of material success which non-logical creatures are not able to achieve, for this is the expression not the cause of its superiority. It is valued primarily because it is a capacity which enables the possessor to use his mind in a way which corresponds in some aspect to the mind of the creator—to discern and to follow his true destiny as it lies in society and in the natural world. It is a quality, therefore, which is more properly translated in this context as 'intelligence'.

In relation to women, men are invariably defined as 'superior' (ἀνώτεροι), and the connection made by the villagers between this superiority and the basic charter given to them at their creation is based on their knowledge of the story of the Fall, and by their association of men and women with Adam and Eve. The story as told by different people tends to vary in the mode of telling, but the words with which God curses Adam and Eve are always the same: 'You, Adam, shall till the ground with toil and with sweat, and you, Eve, shall bear children with pain and with torment' (ἐσύ, Ἀδάμ, θὰ καλλιεργεῖς τὴν γῆ μὲ κόπο καὶ μὲ ἱδρωτα, κι' ἐσύ, Εὔα, θὰ κάνεις παιδιὰ μὲ πόνο καὶ μὲ βάσανα). And often the speaker ends with his own comment, 'Are things any different now?' These attitudes to men and women are expressed in such phrases as, 'Men are somehow superior, that's why they are men' (οἱ ἄντρες εἶναι κάπως ἀνώτεροι, γι' αὐτὸ εἶναι ἄντρες); and 'Men are other, ordained by God' (οἱ ἄντρες εἶναι ἄλλο, ἀπ' τὸν Θεό). Women, on the other hand, are referred to as 'worthless women' (παλιογυναῖκες) and as 'Eves' (Εὔες)—an expression which carries with it implications of the weakness and predisposition for making trouble which are thought to be inseparable from feminine nature. 'Men are intelligent', they say, 'but women are gossips' (οἱ ἄντρες εἶναι λογικοί, ἀλλὰ οἱ γυναῖκες εἶναι κουτσομπόλισσες).

Thus man is seen symbolically as standing on the right-hand side of the woman, while she on his left is 'from the Devil' (ἀπὸ τὸ Δαίμονα), his weak link, the aspect of his creation and his nature through which he becomes vulnerable to evil and may be drawn away from his true purpose.

Other male and female attributes also fall according to this basic symbolic classification, and are seen as deriving in principle from the inherent superiority of the man, and in particular from the degree of intelligence possessed by either sex. Men are thought to be responsible, cool-headed, and brave; they alone bear the economic burdens of the house, stand between their families and starvation, fight in wars, and protect their women's honour. Women are thought to be seductive, credulous, and fearful, endangering the house by their sexual weakness and their basic irresponsibility in the matter of gossip.

A further differentiation between the sexes is made according to an overtly physiological classification, according to which the sexual nature of woman is judged as intrinsically impure. The fact of menstruation is seen as evidence of this impurity and, in accordance with this, various ritual activities in the house, such as making the sausages before Christmas, or preparing the bread for the liturgy or remembrance food, are strictly prohibited for a menstruating woman, as is the lighting of candles in church and the veneration of icons. Stricter opinion holds that a woman in such a condition should not even set her foot inside the church, or light the sanctuary lamp in her own house.

Although there are occasions on which lack of care in this respect is reported to have led to misfortune to the house or family, the language in which this taboo is most commonly explained stresses less an actively diabolical principle, than a state which is an impediment to the flow of grace or to the proper contact between the human and divine worlds. It is a negative condition in which, it is universally stated, an action such as lighting a candle or kissing an icon 'does not take' (δὲν πιάνει), that is to say does not do any good, and which, by implication, must be avoided as a useless and sacrilegious act. The word πιάνω, 'to take', is used colloquially, as it is in English, to signify the successful outcome of a plant graft, and the use of the word in this context shows clearly a conception of action and reaction between man and the divine powers. Thus, to the traditional view, it is necessary not only for God to be favourably disposed to man, but also for man to take the correct steps in continually re-establishing and perpetuating a relationship within which the power of God can operate. While women, therefore, are periodically in a state in which the nature of their sexuality prohibits them from taking positive steps to contact the divine world by any type of ritual action, men are permanently in a state which by nature allows free passage between their own divine aspirations and the God to whom they aspire. This is yet another facet of man's inherent superiority which is expressed in the word 'pure' (καθαρός, also 'clean')—and an interesting connection between this state and the stability and responsibility of men was made in the statement, 'Men are the more responsible—they are pure'.

While the whole conception of the superiority of man over woman is related basically to the superior spiritual capacities of man's nature, and as such is explicitly a part of the people's symbolic classification, the differentiation also extends to a more physical field which concerns the relative strength and weakness of the two sexes. The fact that men are physically strong has an important repercussion on the nature of the personal relationships

between them and their women, for where the force of the traditional charter for male superiority breaks down, or is challenged,
the man can always rely on the use of force as his final and in-
vincible argument. Even in the case of a bridegroom who is
brought into the bride's house and cultivates her property, where
one might expect the wife's greater economic power to bring about
a reversal or diminution of this situation, the man can and does put
an end to prolonged arguments or grumbling with a blow or two;
and although there is only one house in Ambéli in which the wife
is beaten frequently by her husband, there is hardly a woman who
cannot relate tales of how she has been struck by her husband for
argument, opposition, or some indiscretion.

Thus far, therefore, we have a series of oppositions which de-
lineate the differentiation made by the villagers in their conception
of male and female nature:

Man	Woman
Adam	Eve
Superior	Inferior
Right	Left
Closer to God	Closer to the Devil
Intelligent	Unintelligent, 'stupid'
Strong-minded	Credulous
Cool-headed, brave	Fearful
Reliable	Unreliable
Strong	Weak (seen also in the aspect of sensuality)
Responsible	Irresponsible

To this list must be added honour (τιμή), and shame or modesty
(ντροπή). Both honour and shame are qualities which are thought to
be possessed naturally (although they may be lost) by both sexes,
since to have a sense of shame is to be aware of the significance of
honourable and dishonourable actions, and to prefer the former.
In a more specific sense, ντροπή implies a sense of sexual shame
or sexual modesty which is thought of as being a quality which
women, specifically, possess by nature, and which is the one faculty
capable of redeeming them from domination by their other more
destructive attributes. It is a word for which there is no very
adequate translation in English, for although it can in many contexts be translated accurately as 'modesty', it must in principle be
rendered, more clumsily, as 'shame', since it involves not merely a

sense of discretion and propriety but, when it is applied to men, the sensitivity to be ashamed of failure within their role, and, in the case of women, a deep inner awareness of the dangerous potentialities of feminine sexuality and a natural ability to control them.

This, then, is the unchanging classification of masculine and feminine nature on which the society's value system and its understanding of ideal masculine and feminine behaviour are built up. No matter how important the feminine role, nor how dedicated the fulfilment of it, this essential classification of men as superior and women as inferior remains constant. This is so, even though the villagers are alive to the fact that men have faults, and often greater faults than their women, that they get drunk, fight, and curse, they fail to go to church, they are easily inflamed to physical violence and so on; for these masculine defects are seen not as defects of nature, as are those of women, but merely as defects of character to which humanity in general is susceptible.

Although, therefore, men may in individual situations be judged to be worthless, stupid, or lacking in honour, they are still collectively defined as superior. For since there exists as an intrinsic part of human nature a form of inborn and direct communication with the divine which is possessed principally by man and, to a lesser degree, by woman, and since this is primarily a question not of what a man or a woman does but of what he or she is, it follows that no form of deviant behaviour can rob mankind in general, or the male species in particular, of its inherent superiority. Men can be forced into socially disapproved actions by reason of the pressure of circumstances on their particular nature; or they can wilfully betray this nature; but they cannot, except in rare and specific circumstances, actually abdicate from it.[1] While woman,

---

[1] These circumstances are as follows: where a man is a passive homosexual, a πούστης, he is in the villagers' eyes no longer a man, and thus loses many of the attributes of the masculine symbolic classification. See also Peristiany: '. . . a procurer is a *man* who has *abdicated* his manhood. He is *adiantropos*, he has no shame, no self-respect, he is *atimos*, he lacks honour, he is *tou klotsou kai tou mpatsou*—he is, that is, a man who may both metaphorically and actually be kicked and slapped with impunity. A person of this kind is said to lack *philotimo* and to be *aphilotimos*. The same may be said about a woman. Immodesty marks woman's abdication of her femininity, the betrayal of her nature and therefore of her divinely prescribed role, of her family of origin or marriage which, of necessity, entrusted her with its honour, that is with its most precious possession.' 'Honour and Shame in a Cypriot Highland Village', *Honour and Shame. The Values of Mediterranean Society*, ed. J. G. Peristiany, Athens, 1965.

therefore, whatever her potentiality, is the agent through which evil may become active and challenging, man is not capable of being in himself the vehicle of evil, although he may through weakness become the victim of it. It is consistent with this view to state, as the villagers do, that even if a man were a gossip, a card player, a wastrel, and a drunkard, he would still be superior, and he would maintain his superiority in spite of all, even though it would become his wife's duty to remonstrate with him and attempt to restrain him if his behaviour became excessive.

By nature, therefore, and as a consequence of the Fall, men and women are unequal, men being superior to women and having power over them. In the relative situation between them, man never loses his position as head of material creation and leader of the house. However, having established the absolute nature of this classification of men and women, it is important to emphasize that the difference between them is one of degree rather than of kind. Women are not thought to be totally lacking in intelligence, merely relatively lacking in it when compared to men; and men and women together, along with the whole of the human race, are thought of as intelligent when they are considered with reference to the animals and to the rest of creation, in which context they are defined collectively as 'the superior intelligent creature' (ἀνώτερο λογικὸ ζῶο). Since men and women, therefore, share the imperfections of human nature, it is not a question of man being innately divine and woman innately demonic, but of a situation in which man, whatever his social actions and human failings, is always 'somehow superior' (κάπως ἀνώτερος), and woman, however virtuous, always 'on his left-hand side' (στὴν ἀριστερὴ πλάτ').

It is important also to make it clear that this particular differentiation of men from women relates only to the quality of their sex; as human beings they are all the children of God, and therefore all ultimately of equal significance in the total scheme of things. There is potential divinity in women as well as in men. The way in which these two ideas are accommodated simultaneously in village thinking is well illustrated by the attitude of parents towards their children, where although boys are ardently wished for and are in a sense preferred to their sisters when they are born, all the children are, at least ideally, equally loved and valued. This has been many times expressed to me by both men and women as they

5. Grinding Corn

hold up one hand and say, 'Look, my fingers are not all the same, yet they are all equally necessary to me.'

It is this potential divinity—this, so to speak, ultimate spiritual equality—which provides woman with the means of fulfilling her highest role, that of wife and mother; and it is this which allows for the creation in society of the ideal marriage relationship, that of symbiosis, or, as the villagers put it, one in which both husband and wife are equally necessary.

The link between woman as Eve in her natural classification, and as the wife and mother of her ideal role, lies in the one positive quality which she possesses by nature, that of shame. A woman who has no sense of shame has, literally, nothing, since lacking this crucial virtue she lacks also any inner defence against the compulsion of the rest of her nature, and so will inevitably succumb to it. If a woman is to be redeemed from all these negative qualities to which she is by nature vulnerable, it must be through this one virtue which she also possesses by nature, and which she must develop and strengthen by her own efforts and those of the man under whose protection she is. It is for this reason that such a high value is placed on shame for women in this society; and for this reason that one of the crucial elements in the definition of honour for a man is his ability to protect his wife and children from shame.

The notion of honour ($\tau\iota\mu\dot{\eta}$), is, like that of shame, one which is not easily rendered in English, for it is a concept which involves not only the specific idea of honour, but also the notion of social worth. It involves, that is to say, the evaluation of the community.[1] It is, as thus defined, applicable to women as well as to men.

Although the concept of honour is basic to the society's system of values, the word $\tau\iota\mu\dot{\eta}$ itself is not very often used by the villagers. This is largely because honour is not a commodity which may be gained or lost easily in the seesaw of social competition, but is something with which men and women are born, which they lose only in an extreme situation, and which, once lost, tends to be lost for ever. The contexts in which honour may be lost are, therefore, comparatively few, and it is truer to say that honour is something which must be preserved rather than that it must be competed for,

---

[1] '$T\iota\mu\dot{\eta}$ expresses the idea of worth, whether this is an economic value in a market, or social worth evaluated in a complex of competing groups and individuals.' J. K. Campbell, *Honour, Family and Patronage*, p. 268.

even though in the process of preservation there is inevitably an element of competition. It is therefore over matters concerning prestige and self-regard as observable in the minutiae of everyday behaviour—matters which are related to honour while not comprising the whole of it—rather than over honour itself, that competition is carried on. Competition, it may be said, is over reputation rather than over honour as such.[1]

In this society, therefore, where honour is closely related to reputation and where reputation lies unequivocally in the hands of the community, honour must be seen as residing largely in public opinion. However, it is evident even in this situation that there must coexist, with this public type of honour, a personal awareness of honour which is in a sense anterior to this public recognition. There would be nothing to compete about if no one were already convinced of the justice of his claim. This personal honour is experienced by every individual in the heart of his own family where the ideal values of society are pre-eminently realized, and it is this that provides the virtually unshakeable foundations on which the individual's activities within the community are based. Except, therefore, in the case of extreme catastrophe, each family remains through all vicissitudes convinced of its own essential virtue, and of the community's unfounded envy which prevents it from recognizing that virtue.

This statement regarding the villager's personal and independent sense of honour must not, however, be taken as modifying that regarding the essentially public nature of honour, but rather as complementing it, and the paradox may be put as follows: the villager has a sense of his own honour which continues in all but the most extreme circumstances, but this is not strong enough on its own to support him in his public life. Its recognition therefore by the community is indispensable to his social and moral exist-

---

[1] See J. K. Campell, *Honour, Family and Patronage.* p. 272: 'It is the natural birthright of most Sarakatsani to be manly and of their sisters to have shame. Therefore, in the sense that τιμή is used by the Sarakatsani, it is difficult to talk of competition to win more honour than another man or another family. Honour is something which most families are presumed to have, but which they may very easily lose if they do not guard it with all their resources of courage and self-discipline. There is, rather, a constant struggle to maintain an ideal state of equality in honour between most individuals and families. And since the downfall of one family validates and in some sense improves the status of other families, men attempt by every means of allusive gossip and criticism of conduct to deny each other their pretensions to honour.'

ence, and it is over this recognition that so many community struggles are carried on.

Since, as was shown earlier, the crucial element in loss of reputation is not in the actual fact of wrong-doing and its effect on the wrong-doer's character, so much as in the discovery by the community of the wrong done, and its effect on the wrong-doer's reputation, public opinion becomes, in effect, the villager's conscience. Someone who has no honour, no sense of shame, will not know or care what people think, and so will do whatever he or she pleases without reference to the social ideals enshrined in popular opinion. Such a person is known as 'lost' (χαμένος), 'stupid' (μουρλός), or, in extreme cases, 'without honour' (άτιμος). The degree of shame, therefore, that a person possesses is an index to the degree of his personal integrity.

The function of shame in enforcing honourable behaviour is illustrated by the almost invariable explanation given for a person's refraining from doing something he wants to do—'he is ashamed' (ντρέπεται). Widows do not go visiting on name-days, 'they are ashamed to go'; a woman denies having quarrelled with her mother-in-law, 'she is ashamed'; Ioanni Milios has stopped going to such-and-such a café, 'he is ashamed to, he quarrelled last week with the owner'. What they are ashamed of, in each case, is not simply the disapproval of the community, but the way in which this disapproval is voiced—in 'laughter' (γέλοια), that is to say in mockery, or scorn—for community mockery is the reverse of community respect, and therefore the enemy *par excellence* of reputation.

If a man or a woman is to be thought of as honourable, that is to say if they are to be admitted as having a good reputation in the community, they must have certain basic characteristics which were described by one villager to me as 'being reliable and honest, being a believer, and keeping the law'. However, social life in Ambéli being what it is, the ideal standard of honesty in all situations, of being reliable to all people at all times, tends to be interpreted more negatively as a type of discretion and a knowledge of proprieties which limits the inevitable cheating, lying, quarrelling, and bearing false witness, to its proper proportions, and which prompts the positive qualities of honesty and reliability only where they are unquestionably due. It is in fact a sense of obligation, of restraint and social responsibility, rather than a standard of ideal behaviour, which forms in practice the basis of reputation.

While these basic qualities of restraint and social responsibility are thought to be necessary for both sexes if they are to possess a good reputation, honour is not normally thought of as lying in this generalized set of obligations to society so much as in a series of differentiated modes of conduct depending on role, and thus, ultimately, on sex.

Unlike the more traditional societies of the Maniots or the Sarakatsani, the values informing honour in Ambéli are, for a man, thought of less as concerning exclusively characteristics such as courage, quick temper, and sexual potency, and more as those which in general terms make a responsible and authoritative husband and father, and a good provider for the household. Both with the Sarakatsani and the people of Ambéli, the values of manliness have the same orientation—to guard the virtue of the women and the honour of the house in both economic and moral terms. But whereas for the Sarakatsani these qualities include pre-eminently the physical strength and courage to endure hardship while guarding the flocks or repelling insults and dishonour from the family, for the people of Ambéli the qualities necessary for the defence of the house are centred increasingly round the values of patience, hard work, non-interference with others, and the avoidance of excessive quarrelling.

The reason for this change is found in the changing world round the village and in the changing ambitions within it. The villagers have always been interested in 'progress' (προκοπή), and they have always given their best efforts to see to it that their children fare as well as they possibly can in the material world in which they live. While in the past this progress was seen in terms of activities which perpetuated the living village tradition—in building up a good flock, in making a successful marriage into a prosperous family, in acquiring more land, or simply in the basic terms of becoming a householder and having a family—the terms in which progress is now realized involve education, emigration, and final abandonment of the old way of life. Traditionally, progress in Ambéli was located unequivocally in the villager's immediate social world; now it involves eventual removal to the world outside the village. Prestige—an inseparable concomitant of progress—

used to be demonstrated in Ambéli, as among the Sarakatsani, largely in relation to the surrounding community in terms of personal confrontation and a continual reaffirmation of verbal, physical, or economic superiority; now it is with the people of Ambéli revealed primarily in the application, sincerity, and efficiency with which a man dedicates himself to the task of promoting the fortunes of his family into the life and values of the modern world.

The older expressions of the search for reputation are, however, not entirely lost, and side by side with this standard of behaviour according to which prestige is gained as an independent function of honest hard work and the ability to save money, there exists also the more traditional code of values according to which it may be acquired or lost in verbal or physical confrontations with fellow villagers. This finds expression in the heroic image of the young man (παλλικάρι), one of whose qualities being that he is able to take up the cudgels, verbal or physical, in defence of his family's interests. While, therefore, quarrelling over 'trifles' is according to the former standard considered a waste of time and something for the community to 'laugh at', according to the latter it is a quality indispensable in the demonstration and vindication of family honour.

Thus two standards exist, one which accords with the image of the householder as a diligent and sober provider, whose reputation depends increasingly on his intrinsic merit as regards his opportunities and what he does with them, and only secondarily on direct confrontation with others; the other which accords with the image of the volatile defender of family interests against the depredations of others, and is primarily concerned with demonstrating his comparative merit over that of his neighbours.

It is difficult to estimate the comparative strength of either ideal in regulating behaviour in the village, but it may be said that, strong as the urge to competition and self-assertion may be, the theoretical strength of the ideal of the householder who makes progress by attending single-mindedly to his own affairs ensures that there is a powerful sanction against excessive litigation, and now limits almost totally the tendency for masculine honour to manifest itself in physical violence and feuding.

Unlike the double standard of prestige discussed above, there is in the present-day society in Ambéli only one standard of feminine modesty—that which concerns sexual shame. This is still thought of as an absolute prerequisite for the honourable woman, and involves a conception of purity which places an unalterable value on the virginity of the unmarried girl and the chastity of the married woman. Such chastity is demonstrated importantly in direct confrontations with men, but it is also demonstrated by attributes such as modesty in speech, dress, and behaviour, as well as by the decorum with which the unmarried girl acts within the authority of her family and with which the married woman runs her household and looks after her husband and children.

The public element in the organization of village life has an important bearing on the way in which the quality of sexual shame is lived out, for since honour is given to the individual by the community, and since feminine honour depends on the possession of shame, it is vital for the possessor of shame that this fact should be demonstrated to the community. It is in fact as important to be seen to be chaste as it is to be chaste.

In practical and personal terms the logic behind this, in addition to that relating to the public nature of honour and of conscience in such a society, is one which depends on the theory that it is safe always to assume the worst of women. This is because a woman, however genuine her sense of shame, is thought always to be in danger of losing her honour since men are insistent and she is by nature frail and easily deceived. And since it is assumed in this way that she will inevitably fall if she puts herself into temptation, it becomes her business as an honourable woman not to put herself into temptation at all. If, therefore, she is seen in a compromising situation, she will inevitably be assumed to have been compromised, whether or not this is actually so; and she is at fault not so much because she has necessarily been promiscuous as because, first, she has shown herself willing to risk her honour in this way, and secondly, because in doing so she has laid herself open to speculation and gossip. The woman's role, therefore, is to be seen to be honourable, for it is this evidence and this alone that indicates the presence in her of the quality of shame. No woman is ever believed to be beyond temptation, but a woman who is scrupulous in her deportment in front of the community proves that she is capable of keeping herself out of it.

In terms of personal experience—that is to say experience which involves the individual alone, rather than the individual and her

relationship with society—the situation is thought of rather differently, and with a sort of essential tolerance. Sex is considered
to be something that every normal person wants, and that it is
natural for them to have, and it is thought therefore that any girl
who is on her own, away from the sanctions of her society, far
from the protection of her father and her brothers, will automatically have sexual relations not with one man only, but with many,
both because she is weak and also because, since the only criteria for
such relations are those of physical attraction, she may legitimately
go where she is physically attracted. In the sense therefore in
which she may be considered as a being with an individual, rather
than a social, sense of values, it is plain that in this individual sense
she has violated nothing by such behaviour, for according to the
'natural' law she has only done what is normal. It is only on the
intervention of the social law—linked as it is with the community's
metaphysical understanding of human behaviour and human
potentialities—that she has both in actuality damaged herself,
and is made conscious of this damage by the effect on herself of
society's condemnation.

The damage to society by promiscuity in its women is seen by
that society as the gravest possible menace, since it threatens the
existence of the central social group—the family. Unchastity
reveals a lack of sexual shame, and lack of this one positive quality
deprives a woman of the possibility of overcoming her other
natural, and baser, characteristics. The unchaste woman is therefore incapable of being the support of the house which it is her
role, not to say her destiny, to be. This is illustrated by the sanctions for unchastity, which are in exact proportion both to the
gravity and to the type of the action, and reveal in practical and
social terms the moral and symbolic failure that has taken place:
they imperil the chances of marriage for an unmarried girl, and
they rupture the life of the married woman. It is interesting,
however, to note that the sanction for the unchastity of an unmarried girl is slightly less severe than it is for a married woman found
in adultery. This is a discrepancy which reflects the conception of
chastity as a responsibility the woman bears to society rather than
to herself alone—for since it is possible for a girl who is unchaste
to acquire a husband, if she is clever enough, and thereby 'mend'
(μπαλώνει) her position, this lack of shame is seen as a less grave
offence than lack of shame in a married woman on whose virtue

depends an already established family, and in whose fall the whole family is inevitably involved.

This attitude towards unchastity in unmarried girls is amply demonstrated by the community reaction to stories of girls in the neighbourhood of Ambéli who, after a period of more or less dishonourable activities, achieved husbands by trickery of one sort or another. One girl, it is said, having had a great many lovers, decided one day that it was time she got married. So she invited a certain man to come to the room where she was weaving, promising that no one would be there. When he came, she made a joke about making nooses, and managed to tie both his ankles to the legs of the loom, upon which she called to her sister who had been hiding behind the door, who promptly ran off and got the police. At the same time she got a best man, and a priest, and the next time the man's mother set eyes upon her son he was married.

Such a situation epitomizes both the hostility which is normal between unrelated families, and the antagonism between the sexes, and in this case competition is extreme and success is the chief criterion of behaviour. In the eyes of the community the fact that a girl has got herself into such a situation brands her as lacking in honour, but the fact that she can achieve as a husband someone who wanted only to be her lover diminishes criticism and evokes, from all non-interested parties at any rate, a certain amount of praise. A girl who is successful in such a manoeuvre would say, I was told, 'He came in order to make a fool of me, but I made a fool of him instead.'

There are various points to be drawn from such a story. First it is recognized that such a marriage is shameful for the girl, in that it provides the community with a good deal to laugh at, and reveals the girl's lack of honour for all to see. However, at the same time it is a brief period of shame which the achievement of marriage and the establishment of a household more or less conclude; whereas the shame of having lost one's reputation, albeit in a less public fashion, and of remaining unmarried and sought after only by suitors whom no other girl will accept, is a longer-lasting and more bitter experience. To attempt to compel a marriage of this sort is, however, dangerous, in that it may not be crowned with success and in that case the girl will have lost everything. It is for this reason and for fear of the shame involved that it is said only one in a hundred girls will attempt a marriage of this kind, and so men on the whole continue in the knowledge that they are unlikely to be trapped suddenly into an unwanted liaison.

Secondly, it is made clear that the loss of honour attendant on a woman who allows herself to be seduced lies both in the fact of her unchastity, and, more importantly, in the fact that she is, by reason of her unchastity, diminishing her chances of marrying. If by her wits she can achieve what by her unchastity she was in danger of losing, her unchastity is virtually forgotten, and she is received as any other married woman into full status in the community. What is important then is that she should remain chaste, and not jeopardize by further promiscuity what she was able to salvage from her former stupidity. It is the case, however, that even where marriage 'mends' a woman's honour, the original loss of it remains in the minds of the community as ammunition in quarrels and recriminations, even if in the normal day-to-day ordering of life she does not carry a continual stigma. There is therefore a distinction to be made between the loss of honour in the case of a girl who is promiscuous, and the loss of honour in one who is seduced by the man she eventually marries. For although theoretically virginity which is lost before marriage—or in present days before engagement—implies a total lack of shame and loss of honour, in fact the community finds this more easy to 'forget' than the continual scandal that accompanies a promiscuous girl's behaviour.

The final point is linked with the foregoing, and involves the equation in village thought of lack of honour with the state of being 'stupid', and in the value placed by the community on cleverness (ἐξυπνάδα), a word which means literally the state of being 'wide-awake', and which may therefore in the present context be thought of as being permanently on guard. One woman relating some long-past family history of certain women who cuckolded their husbands, made this equation quite clear: 'They were worthless, they weren't good; they were stupid, they weren't clever.' Similarly, in answer to the question referring to the loose behaviour of a village girl, 'Why does Ioanna behave like this?' the answer invariably was, 'Because she is stupid' (γιατί εἶναι χαζή); and with reference to the same girl one woman once said derisively, 'Ioanna is stupid. If a man approached me, I would either not have him at all or would get him to marry me, but she lets all the world make a fool of her.'

It is in fact stupidity rather than lack of honour which is the unforgivable sin in this society, for stupidity is seen as the root cause of shameless behaviour. Someone who lacks honour in the literal sense of lacking sexual modesty may yet make up for this lack by her cleverness, and redeem the situation adequately enough in the eyes of society for her to be virtually forgiven; whereas someone who is stupid not only lacks modesty and a proper sense of how to behave, but lacks also the ability necessary to redress the situation in any measure at all. Such a person is contemptuously or pityingly referred to in a variety of terms, all variants on the meaning 'stupid' or 'lacking' (χαϊβανάκι, μουρλή, χαζή). While it is possible, in fact, for a girl to be lacking in honour but to be clever enough to establish her social position in defiance of the evil intentions of the man who intended to make a fool of her, a girl who is genuinely stupid will inevitably lack honour as well. Thus it is not a question of it being thought better to be lacking in honour than to be stupid, for there is nothing worse than loss of honour. But since the root cause and perpetuator of the condition of dishonour is seen to be stupidity, it is this quality that is singled out by the community for derision and disapproval.

It appears from this that cleverness for a woman may in some senses be related to intelligence for a man, and may be valued for the same reasons. Women are not naturally clever as a man is naturally intelligent, but it is this quality, which women possess in common with men by virtue of their humanity, which may nevertheless be developed by them to the point at which it becomes one of the means by which they defend their natural shame. A woman's cleverness will prevent her from making a fool of herself in the first place, that is to say it will cause her to preserve her chastity; but, in the event of her loss of chastity, it will either enable her to keep this secret, in which case the wrong is, in a sense, righted; or it will enable her to achieve a husband in spite of the fact that the dice are by this time loaded against her. In all cases the virtue of cleverness is that it protects the individual against sexual dishonour, and therefore protects society against the greatest threat to its continued existence. It enables a woman to continue into marriage and to preserve that marriage in its integrity, and thereby to continue the development of herself into her ideal fulfilment, in the same way as the man's intelligence is the quality which allows him to consolidate his virtues, control his weaknesses, and to inherit his superior position at the head of material creation. It must not be forgotten, however, that the function of cleverness is always to preserve honour—it is never seen as an end in itself; and it is for this reason that while cleverness may in an unmarried girl legitimately exercise itself in opposition to any man who seeks to destroy her virtue, and is able, in effect, to redeem and consolidate that virtue, this is never so in the case of a married woman. The married woman with a family has no reason to succumb to another man and every reason to resist, since she is not, like the unmarried girl, open to being deceived with promises of marriage, nor is she free, as is the unmarried girl, of responsibility to husband and children. Concealment and trickery therefore in the case of the unchaste behaviour of a married woman may be seen as the best that can be done in bad circumstances, but it can never have the connotation of cleverness discussed above, nor be seen with the degree of approval and wry admiration that the cunning of a sharp-witted girl tends to attract.

Since the family is the basic unit of society which contains all the primary rights and obligations of the individual, the basic definition of roles is always with reference to it. The prototypes for all roles therefore appear in the basic masculine and feminine types which are expressed in the figures of husband and father, wife and mother.

The isolation of marriage as, symbolically and socially, the most important relationship in village life, may be explained essentially by the fact that since the family group is the basic unit of society, and since marriage is the institution on which this group primarily depends, the marriage relationship must plainly be the one which is central to the villagers' value system. But the particular stress that is placed on marriage in village thought is also the result of the symbolic classification of male and female nature, and of the attitudes to sex which this classification involves.

A villager, when he or she meets a member of the opposite sex, has to make one of two possible choices—either to respond to the sexuality which that person embodies, or to respond to the role which he or she bears at that particular time. Response to the role is the normal and accepted mode of behaviour, and the canons of behaviour with regard to cousins, guests, and so on, ensure that such a confrontation of the sexes is socialized and its dangerous implications rendered harmless. Even so, these implications are

thought always to be present, and the degree of chaperoning
which is considered necessary for the vast majority of meetings
between unrelated men and women in village society is an indication of the suspicion with which the community view the strength
of both men and women to maintain, unaided, their sanctioned
relationships, when the pull of sexuality is also present.

It has already been argued that in a culture which involves a very
strict conformity to roles and a considerable dependence on the
opinions of other people, the growth of insight and individual self-
knowledge, as well as of a certain type of perception of others, is
inhibited. In addition to this, the type of culturally determined
attitudes to other people which are found in this society are such
as to limit inevitably the degree to which one person may explore
the depth of another's personality. These two factors bring it
about that the Greek villager has, with regard to his relationships
with women, an attitude which is so dominated by the concept of
women as weak and sensual that any possibility of a personal
relationship with them which is not physical, or which is not
strictly controlled by ideal roles, is completely excluded. If for
some reason he lays aside the obligations of his proper role, he
finds that his response to women can find expression only in
physical terms. It is for this reason that personal relations between
all men and women, except those closely related through blood,
are thought to be inevitably characterized by overtones of physical
sexuality (*πονηριά*, lit. cunning, as it is called); a girl is thought not
to be able to have confidence in the honour even of her brother-in-
law, and there is a rhyme which illustrates the degree of mutual
trust which may be expected between men and women related by
marriage:

> *Συμπεθέρα, συμπεθέρα,*
> *Στάσου νὰ σὲ βάλω χέρα*

which, roughly translated, means,

> Wait a bit, 'in-law',
> Stop and let me grab hold of you.

The fact, then, that any direct response to the masculinity or
femininity of another person must inevitably be channelled into
physical expression makes it plain that, with the one important
exception of marriage, any type of individual personal relationship
between men and women who are non-related, or only distantly

related, is totally incompatible with role; for while feminine role is based on the absolute values of chastity and fidelity, the type of personal response discussed above leads automatically to the very reverse. The exception, however, is vital, for it is the one instance wherein the contradiction contained in the above situation does not occur, and where sexuality is not only harmonized with role but is indispensable to the fulfilment of it. Marriage is therefore revealed as an institution unique in Greek village life, for in it occur the only roles through which the sexual nature of men and women may be directly expressed and, by means of this expression, become harmonized and unified with the social and symbolic ideal. It is for this reason that the central roles of society are those held in the marriage relationship, and marriage conceived as the only means by which a man or a woman may realize fully their innate type and achieve the objective ideal represented by the words man and woman.[1]

It might be imagined by those unacquainted with rural Greek society that there would be a type of uniformity, almost of boredom, in a life organized by a few precisely defined roles and a code of conduct that has an absolute value, by an inherited philosophy, an unchallenged religion, and, until recently, by a customary dress dictated for all according to similar standards of sex, age, and situation. However, all these elements in society are not systematized by a controlling outer force but consistent with an inner metaphysical pattern,[2] and it is because of this that boredom is the last thing to be found in the lives of the villagers, and what is to be found is a great range of individual expression according to the way in which each person adapts himself or herself to the traditional wisdom which the culture embodies. There is, to recapitulate a former point, room within the terms of society and the understanding it incorporates, for a genuine self-realization.

The roles of this society thus act in two different ways. Where they do not relate to marriage they provide the means whereby men and women may confront each other in a way that expresses

---

[1] The more refined term 'spouse' (σύζυγος) is never heard in Ambéli, and the words for husband and wife are those used for man and woman, i.e. ἄντρα and γυναῖκα.

[2] For the distinction between a consistent and a systematic order I am indebted to A. Coomaraswamy, *Figures of Speech and Figures of Thought*, London, 1946, p. 218.

their essential natures while avoiding a direct sexual meeting; and they do this by transforming this personal confrontation into terms relating not to the localized and personal significance of the one for the other, but to their ideal significance to the total social order. In this way sexuality is not denied, it is transmuted directly from the basic symbolic classification referring to male and female nature into a series of corresponding ideal classifications relating to the particular individual's position in society. Where they relate to marriage they transcend the natural opposition between man and woman at the same time as providing a relationship based on the expression, rather than the repression, of physical sexuality. Thus, while the natural law acts, if unchecked, towards the destruction of the individual and the disintegration of society, the social law, based on the understanding both of nature and of the ideal human types, and articulated through the system of roles, becomes the agent of the divine purpose for men and women by which nature is overcome and the ideal human situation achieved.

VI

MEN AND WOMEN—MARRIAGE

THE essential superiority of all things in the masculine classification over those in the feminine, which was discussed in the last chapter, is reflected clearly in the way society is organized and is seen principally in the different focus of the masculine and feminine roles. Thus while the feminine roles are organized round a single element, that is to say the presence or the lack of a man, the masculine roles are organized not around the presence or absence of a woman as such, but around the total situation which can be created only by the presence of a wife. Thus, socially as well as symbolically, a man is the vital validating factor of a woman's life, whereas for a man a woman is merely the necessary condition to the creation of a particular situation.

For a man, the married state is important—it may be said that it is as important for a man as for a woman—but it is not important in the same way. A man who remains unmarried for no good reason long after his fellow villagers have married runs the risk of being an outcast, but what is thought to be wrong about such a man is less that he has not got a woman as that he has not founded a family or begotten children, he has failed to revitalize the house; he is a social anomaly, possibly a homosexual. If a man is thought to be capable of marriage and intending to marry at some time in the future, he is accepted by the community as a full member of society of equal standing with the married men. A woman, however, as long as she remains unmarried, whatever the reason, must observe the inferior status in which the lack of a man automatically places her. And it is consistent with this situation that while an unmarried man may be the target for various derogatory jokes and unflattering remarks about his state, these are never framed in the terms, 'He hasn't got a woman'; whereas of both unmarried girls and widows in contexts in which their behaviour is being criticized or restrained, it is said quite specifically, 'She hasn't got a man.'

It is around this conception of the indispensability to a woman of a man's protection that the crucial behaviour patterns of women of all ages are organized. An unmarried woman, it is said, cannot 'take liberties',[1] in any sense. She must not joke or laugh too much in public, she must not speak to men with any degree of freedom, she should not look around her too much but should occupy herself discreetly with her household duties and her work on the farm. An engaged girl, however, behaves differently. She dresses up on Sundays in her new clothes, receives the congratulations of the community, and bears herself in public with an added confidence and spirit; and a married woman is free to laugh, speak, and argue with other men, to travel alone if need be, and is given—always within the limitations of her role as wife and mother—the freedom of the community.

Most indicative, however, of cultural attitudes on this point is the role laid down for a widow of the community, and the comments of the villagers relating thereto. She is compelled to wear black, is prohibited from singing, wearing jewellery, dancing, and visiting houses, except for those of close relatives, and, particularly if she is young, is the continual and never-failing target for gossip, malicious jokes, and scandal. She may not talk freely with men: 'People say,' I was told, 'What business has she got to go talking with men? She who has no husband', and, 'She must keep the mourning, keep her eyes on the ground, and see to her house. Nothing else. She is a widow.' It is significant, however, that this state of affairs is not one of any set duration, though in certain respects it does fade in intensity with the menopause; after this, widows are less vulnerable to mockery and do, as do grandmothers, command a certain respect—although they are still bound in principle by the same prohibitions, and a grandmother of sixty-three, a widow, told me that she did not visit the houses on the name-days because people would 'laugh' (γελᾶνε) if she did. It is in fact only death, or, significantly, remarriage, which can release these prohibitions in any important respect. On remarriage, the woman puts away all sign of her former mourning and reverts totally to the full status of a married woman with all the liberties that this involves. It is plain from this that the indefinite continuance of mourning is kept less as evidence of grief for the loss of a companion than as, in general, a way in which society copes with death and, in particular, as evidence of submission to a code of

---

[1] This is a translation of two virtually untranslatable expressions: 'νὰ παίρνει ἀέρα', and 'νὰ κάνει καὶ νὰ δείχνει καὶ νὰ 'παφτώνει'

6. A Widow

values which excludes from full community life and from all institutionalized demonstrations of joy a woman who, having left her father's house and lost her husband, is without the essential factor she needs to validate her life. The observance of the mourning may also be seen as a protective code of behaviour, for it is the utmost that a woman who lacks a husband can do in her own right to protect herself against the hostility and the desire of others, and against her own nature which is thought to be always liable to betray her.

There is another aspect to the restrictive nature of role in the case of a widow, and this concerns the question of sensuality. As has been pointed out, all unmarried women come under the category of people without full status in the community, since they lack a husband. They are, however, relieved of the more extreme and repressive aspects of role which are seen in that of the widow, for they have the protection of a father or, if he is dead, of a brother or other male relative; and because they have, as the villagers say, 'never known a man'. The widow, however, is under the double disadvantage in that she has not only lost the protection of her husband and left that of her family, but she has also been sexually awakened and is now in the unenviable position of being the target for questionable jokes about unquenched fires, burning ovens, and so on. It is in this aspect that the widow offers most threat to the community, for since she is seen by all in a predominantly sexual aspect, and at the same time is known to lack the protection of a husband, she is in the position of greatest vulnerability to the vice of sensuality; and it is this vice which above all others is the enemy of shame, the destroyer of honour, and the wrecker of the family.

This difference in attitudes towards men and women is reflected also in attitudes to children, and even in present times, when many of the traditional views are fading, girls are still considered to be a 'weakness' (ἀδυναμία) and a 'liability' (ἀδύνατο μέρος), and two village women told me of their husbands' angry reproaches when they gave birth to girls in 1963 and 1964. This view of girls as a liability should not be construed, as it sometimes is, as deriving from the knowledge that girls are a drain on the family because of the dowry, for boys have always been equally or more expensive to marry since, ideally, they need a house and property in order to obtain a wife, and, in present days, require as much expenditure as girls need, or more, in education and training. The 'weakness' of girls is that they need protection, that through them the family can be dishonoured and that they are therefore a constant source of worry to their family, whereas boys can 'do what they like' (κάνουν ὅ,τι θέλουν) and are 'independent' (ἀνεξάρτητοι).

A woman, therefore, needs to be protected from her own nature and from her vulnerability to evil, and this is one of the main causes of her dependence on a man. A man is, in comparison, free from any inborn weakness in his own nature and does not need a woman to guard him from essential evil. Man, however, since he is dependent for the fulfilment of his social destiny on having a house and on being a husband and father, and is subject, as a human being, to the physical and metaphysical perils of humanity, cannot be said to be free from the need for a woman; and the ability of woman to transcend in marriage the weaknesses in her nature and to become, as a wife and mother, the guardian of her house, husband, and children, enables her to meet this dependence. The symbolic classification thus remains constant, but by a metamorphosis within this classification the man, having redeemed his wife from the weakness of her original position in the scheme of creation, then enables her to become the centre of the house and the guardian of all within it. The following discussion of roles within marriage illustrates the way in which this comes about.

The independence of man mentioned above is interpreted chiefly as sexual freedom. Whereas a woman of any age or status may lose her reputation if she is in any way careless in behaviour or deportment, a young man may do as he likes and will pride himself on the number of girls he has had, and it is considered unthinkable that a married man will survive a prolonged absence from his wife without seeking out some other woman, and an act of the grossest folly if he rejects any woman who presents herself. Yet although there is at this level a basic dichotomy between the codes of behaviour for men and women, there is another level at which sensuality is seen to be a potential wrecker for men as well as for women.

The crux on which man's behaviour in this matter rests is that of his intelligence. Men are intelligent by nature, but sensual only by virtue of their susceptibility to women; women, on the other hand, are weak and sensual in their very natures. Since it is the nature of women to be sensual and to attract men, but the nature of men to be intelligent, it follows that the responsibility for man's sensual desire lies with the woman who has generated that desire, rather than with the man who is merely responding to her. It follows then that a man is thought to be able to retain a detachment even while he indulges in sensuality, while for a woman such a thing is thought to be impossible since, lacking this degree of intelligence, she is incapable of controlling sensuality once it has been released. A man therefore may indulge fairly widely in pre- and extra-marital sexual activities while keeping his nature untouched by the evils of sensuality, provided always that his intelligence is in the ascendant; provided, that is to say, that he merely 'passes his time' (περνάει τὸν καιρό του) with women, making fools of them while in reality he keeps his mind and his loyalty where it should be—on his family. As long as he does this he is considered to be amply justified in his actions and such behaviour is merely thought to accentuate his virility. It is only if his desire possesses him to such an extent that he begins to neglect his proper duties and to waste on women time and even money that should rightly be spent on the family, that sensuality has usurped from intelligence the dominion of his nature. At this point, instead of his making a fool of the woman she is making a fool of him, the proper *status quo* is lost, and the man gains, instead of a reputation for virility, one of being a womanizer (γυναικᾶς). Honour is therefore not lost for a man by reason of any sexual adventures he may have, but by reason of the degree to which he allows himself to be possessed by desire at the expense of his awareness of his true responsibilities.

Because of this central point of a man's loyalty, however, it comes about that within the confines of the village itself or in its immediate area there do exist checks to the sexual freedom possessed by men, since in this environment a man's sexual adventures are not independent of his other involvements with his house and family. An unmarried man having an affair with a village girl runs the risk of being trapped into marriage with her, especially if her family discovers the liaison. A married man conducting an affair in the neighbourhood of the village tends also to be disapproved of, not because of the fact of infidelity but because such affairs inevitably lead to gossip and possibly quarrels which harm the family, and because in the normal ordering of village life any time spent on a woman tends to detract from the time that should be spent on the family. Also, when a man has his wife present it is considered superfluous to go with another woman. But it is considered perfectly normal for any man away from his wife to go to prostitutes or to have mistresses, and no village wife of an *émigré* husband harbours any delusion that her husband will remain faithful to her for longer than it takes him to find another woman.

Thus it is consistent with the way in which a man's sexuality is understood, that the principal role for the married man is to be protector, and, by derivation from this, provider; and the fact that this function of role is a stronger one even than that of biological fatherhood is borne out by the universal opinion in the village that a father who fails to provide for his family has forfeited his position as a father. Spiritually, the man must not only be strong enough in himself to resist the seductions of women and the evil of the world, but also to protect his wife and any women who may be in his care from the latent evil that is in their own natures. Materially he must implement this responsibility by providing a strong authority in the house, by careful management of the farm and all economic affairs, by practical hard work, and by constant dedication to the well-being of his family. In all things he must be the ultimate authority.

This concept of the unalterable superiority of the husband is well illustrated by the situation of the *esógambroi* (ἐσώγαμπροι), the men who marry into their wives' houses and cultivate their property. It must be said at the outset that it is not considered in Ambéli particularly desirable to marry as an *esógambros*, for it is accepted that a man who marries in this way is moving into a situation in which it is possible later for his wife to say to him, 'The property is mine, you brought nothing with you.' However, since the villagers all agree that there is no essential shame in marrying as an *esógambros*, it is plain that the shame of being one is only a possibility—a shame into which a man falls through not being able to manage his situation well, rather than one which is an inevitable condition of his status.

Ideally the *esógambros* should be deferent to his wife's parents, but superior in all matters relating to his masculine position in the house regarding his wife and children. This is so even though his wife is the legal owner of property and her signature is necessary if land is to be sold, or if loans are required or given.

The problem of selling land rarely arises, unless the family is leaving the village for good, in which case the couple are likely to agree. But several conversations on the possibility of a disagreement over the sale of land all went more or less as follows:

'If a woman has an *esógambros* and they disagree about whether or not to sell her property, what happens?'
'There would be no disagreement. They would do what was best for the family'.
'Yes, but if there was a disagreement?'
'There would be arguments, and blows. Finally the woman could say, "Go along, get out of here, I don't want you." '
'What ought she to do?'
'The woman, if she is good, will do what her husband says.'

It is plain from this conversation first that this kind of deadlock is rare in the village, but that in the event of such a deadlock the proper course of action is for the wife to give in; and secondly that the woman who pushes her legal power to its logical conclusion —and such a woman is by implication 'not good'—does so on the assumption that she no longer cares about her marriage.

Over the running of the farm, again the man's decision should prevail. For one reason, his decision is intrinsically more valid than that of his wife—as one woman said to me, 'The man must be superior. I don't know how it is with you, but women don't think so straight, a man is more intelligent.' In addition to this, it is his strength that causes the land to be productive, and this therefore gives him not only the right but the power to decide what is to be done with it. This situation is illustrated by the following conversation I had with a woman who has an *esógambros* who is both wasteful and lazy, and therefore in village eyes the most deserving of direction from his wife. She began the conversation:

'How I would like to be a man—I shall be a man in the next life! If I were a man I would plough for chickpeas in the autumn, and now I would be putting down fertilizer . . .'
'Can't you get Niko to do that?'
'Since he doesn't want to . . .'

It is plain then that even in a case where the woman has an *esógambros* in her house and cultivating her property, where all the legal and economic power rests with her, this power is in fact purely nominal and its exercise is in direct contravention to her status as a wife. Although such a situation is uncertain in that it provides a certain amount of latitude for a weak man or for a domineering woman to abandon their proper roles, it is one in which the proper course for a man is to gain and to keep control, and for a woman totally to accept this. Only a man who is 'stupid' or a woman who is both 'stupid' and a 'bitch' would accept or require a different situation.

It must not be imagined from this that the woman gets no good out of owning her own property, or out of the provisions of the Greek legal code. One of these provisions ensures her inheritance of at least a part of her husband's property if he dies before she has a child; another grants her the power of legacy over any land or property she may possess. This right is exercised, and is much prized by the villagers who wish always to keep their own land for their own descendants, or, if there are none, within their own family of origin. But it must be noted that the use by the wife or the wife's family of this privilege of ownership is brought about only when the woman concerned, or her spouse, is dead. The ownership of property is used by the woman to safeguard the interests of her family in the event of her death, or to keep her from starvation in the event of the earlier death of her husband; it is not, in village eyes, designed to give her unilateral power of decision over its administration within the marriage relationship. Material power and authority, therefore, regardless of any economic provisions in the Greek legal code, belong to the man; and any attempt by the woman to usurp this privilege, even in the case of her own property, is seen as a basic invalidation of the marriage contract and to rest, not on her proper role but on the destruction of it.

There is only one case in which such power may be legitimately used by the woman, and that is when the husband has *already* failed in his role as protector and provider. A man who is a drunkard, violent, incorrigibly idle, or in some other way proves himself incompetent to manage his family, forces his wife to assume responsibilities that are by right his. In such a situation the woman may, if she owns the property, exercise her legal right over it; and in the villages of this area it has been known, although it is extremely rare, for a woman to turn her husband out of the house, to leave and go to her parents, or even, if she has a rich relative, to get a divorce. Such courses of action, no matter what the provocation, are not praised by the villagers, who look on marriage as a lasting union; but it is tolerated by them if it is clear that only defence of the family and deepest necessity prompt the woman's action. In such a situation onlookers will say—'It isn't good, but since she has a worthless husband what can she do?'

While, however, it is crucial to the proper organization of the household that the man should retain in practical matters his symbolic and natural superiority, this does not mean that, where it is relevant, the wife does not, as they say, 'organize' either the house or the property (*κάνει κουμάντο*). There are four houses (out of thirty-three) in Ambéli in which it is said that the wife does this, but in three of these cases this independence in fact consists of the wife buying what she considers necessary for the house and then letting her husband know, rather than first waiting to ask him. This is never carried out in defiance of the husband's wishes but is rather done in anticipation of them, and such initiative is said to be greeted by him, when he learns of it, with the comment, 'You did well'. In the case of the fourth family it is said that the wife organizes the property, since she knows more about the management of goats, from which they make their living, and has a better head for figures and a harder sense of driving a bargain than her husband. In none of these cases therefore is the exercise of judgement by the woman thought of as a usurpation of role, since in these cases her judgement is being exercised for the common good of the family and with the full consent and approval of her husband.

One final point remains to be made about the male role, which is that it is concerned principally with occupations external to the house, with the fields, the forest, and the outside world of buying and selling, and, in leisure time, with the café. 'The man', it is often said 'is a guest in the house' (*ὁ ἄντρας εἶναι μουσαφίρης μέσα στὸ σπίτι*)—a sentiment which is well illustrated by a conversation I had with a housewife one day who was commenting on her husband's absence:

'He said he would be back, but he's not back yet.'
'Will you scold him when he gets back?'
'Of course not. You can't scold men. Anyway, what has a man to do in the house?'

The male role therefore gives the man considerable freedom, since so long as he faithfully fulfils his duty to protect his family and to provide for their well-being, he is free to do as he likes. And although this freedom is, in Ambéli, limited by the isolation of the village and by the demands of the agricultural life which take the man's continual and unrelenting labour for most of the year, it is still an essential part of masculine behaviour that a man is to a large extent independent in his behaviour and master of his own destiny.

For women the situation is otherwise. Unlike men, who, having no essential evil in their natures, have no need to suppress their natural tendencies but need only direct them towards the good of the family, women have always to battle with their innate weaknesses. While a man's role, therefore, depends on the successful fulfilment of various external duties, the woman's role is concerned always with the internal basis of her nature, and she is therefore never, in any context, free from the necessity to control and subdue it.

The necessity for sexual purity has been discussed already, and it remains only to illustrate the strength of this value in the village mind by mentioning the story of the women of Souli, who, in December 1803, rather than surrender to the Turks who were about to capture their village, took their children in their arms and, dancing one of the ring dances of the district, fell one by one over a cliff edge near the dancing-floor, and were all killed. Repeating this story to me, one of the village women commented, 'That was honour and glory'; and, in the same context, repeated to me a folk saying which appears to be common to much of Greece, 'It is better to lose your eye than your reputation' (καλύτερα νὰ χάσῃς τὸ μάτ', παρὰ τὸ ὄνομα).

There are two factors in village society which bring it about that a woman's reputation, essentially located in her sense of shame, extends into fields of activity which are not concerned with sexual relations. One is the practical fact that absence from the home or irregularities in customary activities which cannot be minutely and indisputably accounted for in society, will almost inevitably be taken as evidence of surreptitious liaisons. The other is the fact that since, according to the conception of feminine nature, a woman's shame is the seat of her virtue, lack of virtue in aspects of life completely unrelated to sexuality may, if occasion arises, be referred back to a woman's basic moral nature. Thus evidence of infidelity is direct proof of a woman's worthlessness in all other fields, and, conversely, careless behaviour about the house and neglect of household duties are referred back to the basis of a woman's honour and cause aspersions to be cast on her chastity. It is because of this that to be thought to be 'good' (*καλή*) in the sense in which this word is used to denote 'chaste', a woman must not only be literally chaste, but must be loyal, hard-working, obedient to her husband, and diligent in household duties such as cooking, washing, and cleaning. A woman's place, in fact, is in the home, and any prolonged absence from it except for matters directly related to the welfare of the family is disliked by the husband and adversely noted by the community. 'Do you know', one woman said to me, 'how a man rejoices and how he loves his wife when he finds her always in the house?'

Two other considerations reinforce the necessity for the woman to be in the house. First it is plain that, since the house is the feminine sphere of activity, it needs her continual presence there if it is to survive—if the goats and hens are to be fed, the rooms cleaned, the clothes and carpets washed, the cheeses made, the bread baked, the water fetched, the food cooked, and the children cared for. Not for nothing is it said that it is the woman who 'holds the house together' (*συγκρατεῖ τὸ σπίτι*). Secondly, however, there is the fact that the woman is thought to hold the house together not only by her physical activity in making the place a sanctuary from the outside world in which food, warmth, and peace are to be found, but also by the ritual activities by which in a metaphysical sense she guards and protects her family. It is therefore on the woman that the responsibility devolves of protecting husband and children by observing the religious fasts; it is she who may not curse, who is the chief representative of the house in church, and who perpetuates the history of the family by her observance of memorial services, her making of the remembrance food on the appropriate days, and her counting the strands in the home-made candles made from thread and wax with which, one by one, the dead in both her own and her husband's kindred are commemorated. It is the woman who, as they say, 'remembers' (*θυμᾶται*); and therefore it is she who, in keeping alive the memory of the dead, thus symbolically reveals the continuity of the kindred.

The woman, however, is not only the guardian of the past but also the bearer of the future, since there is a sense in which relationship is reckoned significantly as originating 'from the same womb' (ἀπ' τὴν ἴδια κοιλιά) rather than as deriving equally from both father and mother. This is not stated consciously as a general fact of relationship, for the bearing of his father's name is a vital matter for a son; but nevertheless it is thought that there is a closer tie between children and their mother than between them and their father, and that, because of this, the blood tie between descendants of the same parents is thought of in a significant sense as originating from the mother.

This belief is illustrated by three statements. The first of these is frequently used to illustrate the close relationship between, for instance, first cousins, that one of each of their parents is 'from the same womb'; secondly, there is the related statement that the father has less to do with the children than the mother since 'he throws them out of his belly' (τὰ ρίχνει ἔξω ἀπὸ τὴν κοιλιά); and thirdly there is the cynical expression, again frequently used, to the effect that you can be sure who is the mother of a child but by no means so certain of his father: 'One mother, many fathers' (μία μάννα, πολλοὶ πατεράδες).

In one of the most crucial aspects of life, therefore—that of the bearing and nurturing of new representatives of the family—it is the woman who is thought to play the more significant part, and this aspect of her role, that of motherhood, is reinforced by the infrequency with which the man is in the house and the fact that on account of this the upbringing of a child in its younger years is left almost entirely to the mother.

The woman therefore is thought to have a double role, both physical and metaphysical, for it is she who makes of the house a sanctuary for the living and a memorial for the dead, while she herself is the matrix from which succeeding generations spring. This expressive aspect of the woman's role was beautifully phrased one day by an old man who had received a village woman and myself into his house, but was unable to find anything to offer us to eat. He was distressed about this, but when his wife came in and produced bread, cheese, olives, and wine, set out on a table-cloth with clean napkins, he said, 'Look, when the woman is here the house is a garden.' And the importance of the woman's part in guarding the ritual life of the house was summed up one day when a woman, who had been weaving rag rugs all day on the first day of the Christmas fast, was blamed by two villagers for the fact that the same day her husband accidentally cut his hand on his axe. The comment in this case was: 'The man goes out with an axe, he cuts wood, or he ploughs a field, but the woman in the house must keep the saint's day.'

It is because of these various strands of relationship between the woman and the house that it is not enough merely to say that the woman is necessary to the house, so much that she *is* the house—that she embodies by her actions the symbolic aspect of the house, and, as such, represents in her own person the history and continuity of the family. It is because of this that not only is the word 'house' (σπίτι) used interchangeably to denote either the physical structure or the family who live or have lived in it, but may also be used to indicate the mistress of the house. This last point is illustrated by the phrasing of the statement that a man should consult his wife before deciding to go away on a journey: 'One should ask the house.'

In this way a woman's absence from the house is contrary to her role, not fundamentally because such absence is taken by the community to indicate adultery—although it may be so represented—nor again because her absence is seen to cause practical chaos in the house, but essentially because such absence is recognized to be in itself a sort of spiritual infidelity, an action damaging to the unity of the house which, without the woman, falls apart. Economically and symbolically, unity and harmony are constructs from which, because of the nature of the temporal world, humanity is continually falling away. The continual reconstruction of this harmony in the home can take place only through the agency of the woman, and because of this she must continually be present: 'Without the housewife', the villagers say, 'the house cannot function' (χωρὶς νοικοκυρὰ τὸ σπίτι δὲν γίνεται).

The symbiosis—a partnership between equals—which is seen to be attainable in symbolic and moral terms by the partners of a marriage in this society, is also seen in the practical situation which conditions it. In this situation the lack of spare cash, the narrow margin of existence, the dependence of the house on the physical work and skills of both partners, and the division of labour according to the broad classification of man/forest, woman/house, all contribute to a marriage contract which is based on a total mutual interdependence. Thus the symbolic union of marriage is echoed on a thoroughly practical level, where one partner quite literally cannot do without the other. This aspect of the binding nature of marriage in these conditions is recognized and approved by the villagers, who compare unfavourably the cash economy of more urban areas and the consequent increased independence for both men and women, with their own situation in which the man is 'bound' (δεμένος) to the woman and she to him, whether they like it or not. And several explanations given to me for there being so few divorces in village life were based on the practicalities of the division of labour: the woman is dependent on the physical strength of the man for working the farm which provides her livelihood, the man cannot leave his wife even if he wanted to, because then he would have no one to cook, bake, and wash for him, and he would be unable to find another wife if he was known to have already deserted a former one.

In contra-distinction, however, to the dignity which can be achieved by the woman who observes in all its integrity her marriage role, the dishonour of a woman who fails to observe it is correspondingly great. Lack of shame, in the matter of literal unchastity, or in any of the related fields of trouble-making, excessive gossiping and quarrelling, carelessness over prescribed social and ritual obligations, or slovenliness in the house, are all means by which the woman's baser nature may break through the restrictions of role, and, becoming active in the social world, preclude her from the possibility of perfection described above. And because she is so much more deeply implicated in the house than is the man, the catastrophe to the house if in fact she does fall is correspondingly greater. It is because of this that it is said that while a bad man is bad for the house, a bad woman destroys it utterly; and that 'One-storeyed houses, many-storeyed houses, and cottages with tiny windows, are lost on account of women' (νόγια, κατανόγια, καὶ κατὰ παραθυράκια, ἀπὸ τὴν γυναίκα χάνονται).

It is plain therefore from this that the state achieved by the married woman who faithfully observes her role is very different from that to which she is as a female by nature inclined. For while in her nature she holds the seeds of the greatest corruption—a lack of intelligence and a predisposition to sensuality—she is seen in society as a being who is virtually synonymous with the house and holds together by her own social self-discipline and religious dedication the security of the most important social group, the family. She has, in fact, by virtue of submission to her role—of continually repressing her baser nature by means of modest conduct, hard work, and total fidelity to her husband and her house—achieved a state of being in which she has transcended this nature and become able to create with her husband a relationship of equals. While man creates the woman conserves, and in this partnership she becomes the pivot of the house and a person whom I once heard referred to, by a man, as 'a second God'. Nevertheless it must not be forgotten that this equality is not one whose criteria are those of power and authority, for in this field, as we have seen, the man is unalterably superior; it is one whose criteria are those of life and the symbolic significance of generation. And paradoxically, this symbiosis, the perfect marriage relationship of this society, is attainable only on condition that the woman bows to her husband's authority and remains inalienably faithful to him, for only by means of subduing relentlessly her own nature and submitting to his protection and authority can she conquer the evil elements in her nature and rise above their destructive potential. If she does this, she can achieve a state in which, though subordinate, she is not inferior, and may become perfect in her own domain.

Marriage is thus the only relationship which makes possible for woman the transcendence of her nature which is a part of her social and metaphysical heritage. While girls and unmarried women with good reputations are treated as underprivileged but neutral members of society, and widows as dangerous and disruptive embodiments of the darker powers of feminine nature, to the married woman alone is given the charter to mobilize her nature in all its aspects, including that of its sexuality, and thus to tame and conquer those elements by which society is threatened.

It is this conception of the capacity of woman to transcend her own evil potentiality, if she is placed in the context of marriage, that accounts for the stress placed universally on marriage for a woman. This is taken quite specifically to be a divine ordinance: 'God wants you to be a housewife', they say, 'and to have a family', and in some contexts the importance of having children is seen as the duty of mankind to propagate 'God's people' (τοῦ θεοῦ πλάς'). However, because the mobilization of the total nature of woman is a necessary condition to its eventual taming by sexual shame and to its transfiguration into the ideal figure of wife and mother, marriage is an estate which is fraught with danger as well as with promise. Not only are the standards of responsibility in the ritual as well as the social sphere much more exacting for a married woman than for an unmarried girl, but the temptations to various kinds of sin are much more prolific. This conception of the risks attendant on the purification of feminine nature is voiced in the popular expression, 'If you get married you damn yourself' (παντρεύεσαι, κολάζεσαι), a state which is seen as being involved both with sexuality and with the broad range of sins that will inevitably be committed at times by the new wife—cursing her children, quarrelling with her in-laws, failing to observe the fasts, and so on. There is, therefore, an ambivalent attitude towards the release of feminine nature in marriage, but this ambivalence is due not to a feeling that this release is improper, so much as to an awareness of the severity of the role and a fear of failure within it.

Thus the house takes on yet another symbolic aspect, for in the context of the house feminine shame can be expressed in the pro-creation of a family and in obedience to a husband, and sexuality therefore transmuted into a symbiotic relationship between husband and wife and harmonized with the highest human ideal. In society, however, the reverse applies, for here the masculine and feminine sexual principles are seen in opposition to one another, and the virility of man to exist at the expense of the shame of woman. On the level therefore of what is considered the most dangerous agent of evil in society, that of sensuality, the conflict between members of unrelated groups is total, and sexuality, instead of being the means of achievement of a symbiotic relationship between man and woman, becomes the focus of deepest antagonism between them.

It is because a woman can only be redeemed, if it may be put like that, by her total dedication to her house and family, that her loyalties on marriage are transferred almost totally to her new home.

The physical aspect of life in such a society contributes to this transference. A woman who must bake, cook, wash, and clean for her own house, must look after the children, feed the hens, graze the goats, cultivate the garden, and carry water—all of which activities are time-consuming and relentless in their endless recurrence in her scheme of priorities—finds that even when she lives in the same village as a mother or a sister she is very restricted in the amount of time she has to see them, and may spare time only for an occasional service such as baking or washing when there is sickness or emergency. When the villages of two members of the same elementary family are separated by any distance, two sisters may see each other perhaps only once or twice a year. In addition to this physical aspect of separation from the family of origin by marriage and incorporation into another house, there is the related aspect of feminine fidelity according to which the woman is expected to take over completely the loyalties of her new family by marriage, and to support, in case of conflict, the interests of her husband against those of her parents and siblings. To such an extent is this the case that it is even said that a girl has, before she is married, only a 'temporary mother' (προσωρινὴ μάννα), since the woman with whom she will spend most of her life and to whom she will give most of her obedience is her mother-in-law. Women therefore who leave the house at marriage are inevitably separated from their families of origin by a double compulsion—by the practical and ritual considerations that inevitably attend their involvement in a physically separate house and farm, and by the moral duty to transfer their loyalties totally to their new family.

In the case of a man, however, the superiority of the male principle brings it about that after marriage he may remain ideally identified with the interests of his family of origin, and this is not only ideally but practically the case when he brings his bride into his parents' house to live and serve them as their 'daughter-in-law' (νύφη).[1] In earlier times there were sometimes as many as three married sons living with their wives and children in the one-roomed house of their parents, pooling their efforts in the common cause. However, on the growth of more people than the house could hold—presupposing in one case the extension of the family to include more than sixteen members—or on the development of excessive friction over the deployment of labour or the allocation of resources, the extended family would begin to split up; while in the present day this separation is anticipated, and the extended family never consists of more than the parents and one married on with his family. In the event therefore of a man creating his own family entity in a separate house, he also is affected by some of the

---

[1] νύφη has the primary meaning of 'bride'. But it takes on the connotations of 'daughter-in-law' when used as a term of address by the senior couple in a house to their son's wife. In some houses still in Ambéli, Νύφη is always used, rather than the name, to address such a woman, even after many years.

factors which affect his wife's loyalties, and he inevitably becomes alienated to some degree from his family of origin by his duty to his new family, and by the location of his interests in his new house and in the land which he must cultivate independently to support it.

Where, therefore, the house has been split up by marriage or emigration, the group loses its exclusive nature according to which every member's good is absolutely identical with that of all the others, and is instead related to the wider community by those very members which it once incorporated unconditionally in itself. In the same way as the identity of the group is projected into the outside world by its kinsmen, so also the hostility, which is a given characteristic of the outside world, may threaten the group even through its own members, if those members are now part of that outside world. To leave the house, therefore, for whatever reason—whether it is to marry and set up a new and independent group, or to emigrate—is to create a different and ambivalent situation in which influences and interests opposing that of the group of origin may come to bear upon those members who have left it, in a way that cannot happen while the group is united in the same house.

Just as the house is not merely a place to live in, but a monument to the past, a sanctuary for the present, and the repository of the hopes for the future, so the family is not an end-stopped unit, but part of a continuum which stretches back to the level of great-grandparents and forward into the unknown generations to come. It is partly because of this that male children are particularly valued, since not only are the boys traditionally 'in the house', that is to say at least one son remaining in the house with his bride to look after his ageing parents and to inherit the house when they die; but also it is through the male line that 'the name is heard again' and the passing generation gains renewed life. The fact that this life is not considered to be a purely vicarious existence, but as in some sense a positive way of defeating death and continuing in the descendants the significance of individual life, is illustrated by the comment of a woman of fifty-two years of age on her grandson Christos: 'I am now as far as little Christos. We live as far as little Christos'. The significance of this phrase in pointing the part played by the male line as opposed to the female will be understood when it is made clear that Christos has a younger sister, Tassoula, who was not mentioned in this context.

While it is the male line into the future which protects the family from extinction in the temporal world, so it is on the whole the male line stretching into the past which is principally thought of when the ancestry of the house is being called to mind. This is not because the women of the family are considered unimportant in the process of generation, for as has been shown it is here that the feminine principle is thought to be paramount; but because of the dominant character of male activity in all social and economic life, it is with the male principle that the reputation of the family is associated, and with which the history of the house and land is pre-eminently involved. There is a very specific sense in which the past history of the family is linked with the land for it is from the male side of the family that the bulk of the land is inherited, and the particular aspect of possession which makes land so precious to the Greek villager, over and above that of sheer material wealth, is the implication of that land with his 'grandfathers', who toiled in it and made it what he possesses during his lifetime.

The family therefore in its work on the farm as well as in its life in the house is continually implicated in its own history, and it is to a large extent this identification of the family land with the labour of its ancestors that, in addition to material considerations, gives to the villager's love of his land a particular passion and involvement. For while many of the more conscious categories of village thinking are influenced by an attitude to the earth which tends towards exploitation or domination, the villager's feeling for the land is in fact deeper than can be explained through sheer material necessity, or the knowledge that the land is 'undying' (ἀπέθαντος) and therefore proof against the fluctuations of the political and economic world.

A significant factor in the villager's thinking about his land is indeed economic, and if any family were assured of a field better than one they were being asked to give up, they would relinquish it without objection. This is because loyalty to the family is seen less in terms of sheer attachment to family history as in terms of the duty of each householder to maintain, and if possible improve upon, the material prosperity of the living family which he builds upon the labour of his ancestors: and in this case the exchange of a poor field for a better one is clearly an act which consolidates rather than undermines their toil. But at the same time the double notion of loyalty both to the labour of the 'grandfathers' and to the economic good of the living family overlaps in a different way, for because each family knows exactly the history of every field and the labour that has gone into it, and because it derives its identity principally from its relationship with its progenitors who acquired and worked these fields, it comes to identify what is its own with what is good. Unless therefore it is demonstrably untrue, the family has both practical and emotional reasons for thinking that its own fields are better than those of anyone else, simply because it is its own forebears and none other who have worked them, and because it is with itself rather than with any other family that these fields are now involved.

The villager's relationship with his land, therefore, which in general he sees as given to him by God with the rest of material creation, he sees in particular as given to him by his forefathers, not only because he has inherited it from them but because it has been cleared, cultivated, planted, and tended by their hands. It is because of this that quarrels over land generate a particular intensity, for people contend not in the cause only of the land itself but in the cause literally of the solidarity of the family continuum which will be impaired if the work of the forefathers goes for nothing and passes into the hands of strangers.

The family, then, is more than a unit drawn together for economic and social reasons. It is a part of a whole way of thinking in which the individual draws his validity from the group and from the strength of his role within the group, and from his position in the kindred both past and present. This identity is linked with the land—which expresses the values and to a degree represents the lives of those who acquired and worked it—and the name, the house, and the whole social history of the family. The house is a microcosm, the most positive social and religious world of the villager; in it are found in their fullest expression the masculine and feminine principles for creation and conservation, while the house itself with the hearth and the woman at its centre has its parallel in the cosmic process of generation. The harmony, order, and generosity of the cultivated earth are reflected in the house, revealed in the full store rooms, and expressed particularly in the customs governing hospitality, while the love and mutual trust which bind the members of the family together are reflections of the divine values of love and peace which are those of the sacred world. It is thus to this central nucleus of Greek village life, the house and family, that all the most exterior features of society must be referred, for it is around this nucleus that all other components of society cluster.

The house, therefore, and the symbolism of the house with its pattern of ideal roles and its vision of the perfect society, is a reality which stands at the very foundation of Greek village life, and provides the villager with a positive dynamic which counterbalances, if not outweighs, the destructive nature of so large a part of intra-community relations. It is from this sense, always, of the integrity of his own family, the strength of his own identity, and his position in the microcosm of his own house, that the villager engages with the outside world, in the process, as he sees it, of preventing his rightful honour from being stolen from him by an envious community.

VII

THE SOLIDARITY OF THE KINDRED

In the last chapter it was described how the positive values of village life are centred within the family and articulated principally by means of the chief masculine and feminine roles within it. Outside the family, however, relationships with the community tend to be negative, contrasting radically with those within the family and differentiated from them chiefly by the fact that their basis is not mutual trust and interdependence, but suspicion and competition. As the blood links, originating in the family, 'in the same womb', disperse through the community and the ties weaken, so the mistrust, which begins to take root as soon as any member of the family leaves the house, strengthens. At the extreme limit of non-relation the situation is one which is the reverse of that obtaining within the family, and instead of love, the dominant relationship is one of hostility, or as the people themselves define it, hatred ($\mu\tilde{\iota}\sigma\sigma\varsigma$).

Paradoxically, however, this hostility may be related primarily to the very exclusiveness and positivity of the family that has already been referred to; for it is the coherence and solidarity of this group, the exclusive nature of the love and trust that is found within it, the genuine sense of honour and integrity which are experienced by members of the same house, that create conditions in which the reverse of these values are experienced in dealings with the outside community, and in which competition and jealousy become the way of life between the different groups.

The particular intensity of this competition is related to the double sense, discussed earlier, in which honour is experienced in this society. In the sense in which a family's honour is experienced as its own participation in the values of the sacred world which it takes as its model, this honour is something of which the family remains convinced even while the fortunes of its general reputation may rise or fall; and because of this knowledge, each family is absolutely committed to the cause of reaping the social rewards of its own virtue. In the sense, however, in which honour is experienced as good reputation, this reputation is held only in relation to the community in which the family is set. Here therefore it becomes an essentially relative notion, involving the wider community and a hierarchy of prestige.

The combination of these two senses of honour—that is to say the recognition by others of the family's sense of its own worth—produces extreme competition, for in these circumstances the preservation of honour becomes a question not only of acting with honour but of defending that honour against a number of other families who are all trying to take it away. The characteristic competitive structure of community relations in rural Greece is the result.

Broadly speaking, then, the villager's social world consists of two antithetical types—that of his house and family where he can rest in the security of mutual confidence and affection, and that of the outside world where he must be continually on his guard against the hostility of others, and where he must struggle constantly for pre-eminence and recognition. In practice, however, this sharp differentiation between the two worlds is modified by a number of relationships which fan out from the family and into the community, linking the different family groups to each other in a number of different ways. Chief of these is the blood relationship; secondary relationships are created through friendships (based on proximity, expedience, mutual co-operation), through the spiritual kinship of godparent or wedding sponsor (κουμπαριά), and through marriage. These last must not be taken necessarily as categories totally separate from blood relationship, since the original blood tie is often reinforced by such considerations as proximity or the necessity for mutual aid, and deliberately consolidated through marriage and spiritual kinship.

Kinship in Ambéli is reckoned according to the system of cognatic descent, that is to say descent that is traced equally through both the father and the mother. Thus a man's kindred is a category of relations including all kinsmen on both his mother's and his father's side to the level of the third ascending generation, or great-grandparents, and laterally to the degree of second cousin. The ancestors preceding the great-grandparents are recognized generally as a part of the history of the family, but are not, except in the case of a person with exceptional memory, thought of by name or linked specifically with the living generations. This upper boundary of the kindred arises therefore as a natural process in time which depends on the memory of each generation, and according to which the more distant progenitors of each family are subsumed under a general category of 'ancestors' or, more literally, 'great-grandfathers' (παραπαππούδες). Laterally, the definition of the kindred as extending to the degree of second cousin is more arbitrary, since this definition depends not on a natural process of forgetfulness, but on a definite acceptance of a point at which a relationship determined by blood converts into one which is between strangers, and one therefore at which marriage is permitted.

It is thus a feature of the kindred that only siblings have a kindred in all respects identical with each other, since only siblings share the same four pairs of great-grandparents from which their own relatives are descended.[1] In this sense, therefore, the kindred is, for each individual, a precisely defined category of relationships which divides his kin from strangers, and which holds its own canons of loyalty and obligation. A villager's 'close relations' are the members of his elementary or extended family, his first and second uncles and aunts, his first and second cousins. In the reckoning of relationship, the stress is always on the original elementary family, on the 'same womb' from which any blood relationship originates—first cousins are described as being closely related because their parents were siblings and from the 'same womb', while second cousins are described as being closely related because their parents are first cousins and therefore 'like siblings' (σὰν ἀδέρφια). This stress on the origin of relationship always in the preceding generations is voiced also in the case of second cousins in such a phrase, 'The kindred endures from our parents' (το σόϊ βαστάει ἀπ' τοὺς γονεῖς μας). Beyond this point, however, kinship is said to cease, and at the degree of third cousin or third uncle and nephew, people are described as having 'un-kinned' (ξεσοϊσανε) and can marry.

Since the blood relationship is essentially thought of as a tie originating in the same womb and weakening gradually as the strength of the bond is dispersed among following generations and new marriages, this abrupt 'un-kinning' which takes place between

---

[1] '. . . since any particular kindred comprises descendants of four pairs of unrelated great-grandparents, only the sibling group which is central to this kindred is related to all its members.' J. K. Campbell, *Honour, Family and Patronage*, pp. 46–7.

the children of second cousins, and between one person and the child of his or her second cousins, does not harmonize with what the villagers actually feel on the subject. The result is that while advantage is universally taken of the permission for marriage after the second degree of kinship, and to that extent the outer edges of the kindred are kept distinct, there are many contexts of village life in which blood relationship is thought to persist long after the technical kindred has merged into the community of strangers.

The very fact that 'close relations' (*καλὸ σόϊ*) is the term used to encompass the whole range of the kindred implies that relationship, though less close, persists after the degree of second cousin. For relations who are especially close, that is to say fit to be trusted with the care of a small child or with the negotiations for a marriage, the word 'exclusive' (*ἀποκλειστικός*) is used. The frequency also with which a man enumerating his kindred will take his description into the marriages and activities of third and even fourth cousins testifies to his instinctive belief in the lasting strength of the blood tie; and, indeed, if village lore is to be believed, there was once a time at which marriage was prohibited up to and including the seventh degree of kinship—a piece of knowledge which is quoted concurrently with the saying, 'The blood lasts up to the seventh degree of kinship' (*στὰ ἑφτὰ ζινάρια βαστάει τὸ αἷμα*).[1] It is in accordance with these beliefs that the marriage between, for instance, a man and the daughter of his second cousin, which is not uncommon and which is permitted by the law, the Church, and by village custom, is referred to by many of the villagers as ill-omened, and as being the reason for any illness, misfortune, or untimely deaths in that particular family.

On several occasions I have heard third cousins, or a man with his third nephew, referred to as 'kinsmen' (*σόϊ* or *συγγενεῖς*), a statement which, when queried, was modified into 'distant relations' (*λίγο σόϊ* or *λίγο συγγενεῖς*); and a sentiment which illustrates well the popular emotional conviction that blood relationship persists after the technical limits of relationship have been reached, finds expression in the idea that one of the distresses of a

---

[1] The *ζινάρι*, properly *ζωνάρι*, is the word used for the belt which on the old costume winds several times around the waist. Here the word is used metaphorically for the single revolution implied in one degree of kinship.

very long life is that the old person is forced to witness his descendants intermarrying.

Another instance of the way the villagers regard relationship, in addition to their understanding of the formal kindred, may be seen in the notion of *katameriá* (καταμεριά), where blood relationship through affinity is implied. *Katameriá* is in this context a dialect expression for which it is difficult to find an exact translation. In Ambéli I have heard the word used for the old system of pasturing the oxen, in which context it plainly means 'all in the same place', and in the context of marriage the meaning is very much the same. It is likely in fact to be related to the word καταμερίζω, 'to divide up in proportion', and to imply here the state of being separated into the correct grouping. In the village explanation, marriages that are *katameriá* are those contracted between members of two kindreds which are already joined once or more by marriage but in which the movement of men and women is always in one consistent direction. This is to say that while, for instance, two male first cousins may marry two female first cousins, it is not proper for a man to marry the (female) first cousin of his (female) first cousin's husband, for in this case the initial movement of a woman, A, to her husband's family is reversed when another woman from the man's kindred is taken back into A's kindred. Such a man is said to have 'turned round' (γύρισε) in order to take his wife—a term which is used commonly to indicate an inauspicious action—and the use of this phrase here indicates clearly that in facing the wrong way, backwards and not forwards, the man has turned again to seek a wife from those that are in a certain sense seen as being of his own blood. This prohibition also applies to second cousins.

It would be a mistake to compare this notion too closely with that of incest, for such marriages are in fact contracted from time to time, and although they are looked on by the older people with disapproval, they are not regarded with horror; but one may infer from what still persists of the idea of *katameriá* the idea that blood once passed into a family in marriage extends in some way to the furthest degree of close kinship, that of second cousin. Marriage between families thus related through affinity is permitted, but the demands of kinship must be observed to the extent that once an affinal relationship has been set up by a woman being taken into a man's kindred, a similar passage of men and women must be maintained.

On the subject of the marriage of two siblings from one family with those of another, however, village opinion is still rigorous, and united. Sister exchange is absolutely prohibited, and the marriage of two brothers from one family with two sisters of another is only permitted if the wedding takes place on the same day. Again, the explanation is that the blood must not 'return' again to its own family. There is an additional explanation which carries the same significance as the return of the blood, and may be said to be a reinforcement and reinterpretation of the same fact. This explanation, given in answer to the query as to why such marriages are prohibited, occurs most commonly as the rhetorical question 'How can affines marry?', and implies that the preservation of the correct relationships with the community which guard the integrity of the family, depend to a great extent on the observance of correct roles. In confounding the role of affine (in this case indicating the man's brother's wife's sister, and the woman's sister's husband's brother) with that of husband and wife, the correct relationship is lost and the family itself thrown into confusion. It is relevant to add here that the shock to the village mind of second cousins marrying is partly due to the fact that second cousins cannot become affines, and in this context a story was told me of a woman who, after the secret marriage of her son to the daughter of her first cousin, answered her cousin's greeting of 'Affine!', with, 'Affine! What affine? We are cousins.'

Finally, mention must be made of the joining of two kindreds by marriage as it is understood to be a union of two social groups, unrelated to any esoteric notion of the intermixture of blood.

The binding nature of the marriage contract is such that on marriage a person, whether man or woman, takes on the whole of his or her spouse's kindred, and the cousins, aunts and uncles, nephews and nieces of the one become the same of the other, and are referred to in the same terms. Thus 'my cousin' can mean either 'my own blood cousin' or 'my spouse's cousin', and so on. Only within the elementary family are differences of relationship between the stranger to that family and its own descendants preserved in the kinship terminology, with the words κουνιάδος (fem. -α) for brother- (sister-) in-law; ἀδερφός (fem. ή) for brother and sister; πεθερός (fem. -ά) for father- (mother-) in-law, and πατέρας and μητέρα or μάννα for father and mother.

This equivalent adoption by each partner in a marriage of the spouse's kindred is a principle basic to the symbiotic nature of the marriage roles, and is modified only, not denied, by the principle mentioned earlier that the wife's loyalties should, when occasion demands, defer to those of her husband. This bias in favour of the husband's kindred used to be very pronounced, as is illustrated in the earlier use of Ἀφέντη (Master) and Κύρα 'Σύ (Mistress, lit. Mistress You) by a woman, in addressing her husband's brothers and sisters, and his first and second cousins. However, since these are terms of address rather than terms of reference, they indicate more the wife's subordinate position in a kindred with which she has ultimate total relationship, rather than her placing in a different type of relationship altogether. And the relative rather than the absolute nature of her subordination is shown also in the recent tendency to level out this particular expression of respect, and the words Ἀφέντη and Κύρα 'Σύ are now hardly ever heard in Ambéli. The only more traditional form of address, indicating the subordinate relationship of a wife to her husband and her husband's family and kindred, which is still used daily in some households in the village, is the term 'νύφη', 'daughter-in-law' or 'bride' rather than the name.

While to a partner in a marriage all his or her spouse's kindred become relatives, the parents-in-law have a much more limited relationship with their affines. Co-parents-in-law address each other reciprocally as συμπέθερε (from συμπέθερος, fem. -α, affine), and the son- or daughter-in-law's siblings, as well as his or her uncles, aunts, nephews, and nieces, are all also technically συμπέθεροι of the parents-in-law, but this form of address is rarely used in this context in the present day, and the relationship thus created is now indeterminate.

The siblings also of a partner in a marriage have similarly limited relationships with their brother- or sister-in-law's kindred. The principal affine is referred to as the γαμπρός (groom) or νύφη (bride), the sister's husband's brother and the sister's husband's sister, brother's wife's brother and brother's wife's sister, as συμπέθεροι, as are the parents of the groom or the bride; but while the rest of the brother- or sister-in-law's kindred again are technically affines, this reckoning finds no reflection in the kinship terminology or in social relations, and in these contexts the term συμπέθερος is never used.

A special relationship is that between the husbands of two sisters, who are known as μπαντζανάκια, and between the wives of two brothers, συννυφάδες, although this relationship is one which denotes more a type of comradeship which may or may not be the basis for a stronger liaison, rather than determining any sort of system of mutual obligation.

Finally, all the aunts and uncles of a particular kindred receive the new member into their kindred technically as 'bride' or 'groom', but more specifically as 'nephews' and 'nieces', in evidence of which may be quoted the delighted comment of an old man at the engagement party of one of his first nieces—'Look how many nephews and nieces I've got!' To which somebody replied, 'In this way the kindred increases.'

Broadly speaking, then, the relationship through affinity is one that only has real significance for the two extended families thus united; more peripheral members of the two kindreds involved may recognize a distant affinal relation as a matter of courtesy, or of interest, but this relationship has little bearing on the nature of social encounters of day-to-day life, where such an affine will be regarded as a stranger. The primary reason for this is that in all the various loyalties which arise through a man's ties with his family or families (that is to say his own, his family of origin, and his wife's family of origin), and with the close relations linked thereto, a distant affine necessarily has little claim to his time or to his affection. In addition to this is the fact that, as a result of perfect confidence existing only in the house, no real degree of confidence can normally exist anywhere at all except through the blood tie. While, therefore, an affine may be called upon to find out about a proposed marriage, or to carry through some delicate piece of business, the origin of that trust lies always in fact in the blood relation through whom that affinity has been created. Such trust therefore is never placed in 'affines' as a category, but only possibly in that particular affine who is joined in marriage with the close relation in whom primarily confidence is placed. It is in accordance with this that the villagers say that only very close relations are used for arranging marriages.

Apart from such instances, relations between close affines are again those of courtesy rather than mutual trust. A man will always seek help from his kinsman rather than his affine, if he can, though he may turn to the latter for minor assistance if he has nowhere else to go.

From this brief description it can be seen that the kindred holds two contrary characteristics which both tend towards solidarity. First, because of its formal nature, the kindred circumscribes a specific range of relations from whom support may be expected; and secondly, in its indefinition at the outer edges of kinship it provides an ever-extending relationship with the outside world which gives the villager a conceptual and emotional framework within which he exists as part of the wider community.

To take the first point first. The support which is experienced between one member of the kindred and another is a vital element of social life in that it significantly minimizes the degree of hostility which every family meets outside the walls of its own home. However, even among close kin, outside the elementary or extended family, this support is not categorical, and in each case the support which is expected and given is subject to a number of considerations all built into the particular circumstance.

Broadly speaking, the structure of sentiments within the kindred is as follows: within the elementary family, within the same house, there is said to be complete mutual confidence, and jealousy, the canker of society, not to exist at all. One of the reasons for this is that since the individual is so deeply identified with his house and with the group, to envy anyone within the group is tantamount to self-destruction. Between first cousins also, especially between those who have grown up together, there is a deep bond of affection and mutual loyalty, and though jealousy between such cousins may exist, the tendency is for those who feel jealous to suppress any manifestation of this out of shame. Between second cousins such mutual confidence is greatly diminished, and it is said that although second cousins should not betray one another, they frequently do. The same degrees of affection may be said to go with first and second aunts and their relationships with their nephews and nieces.

Thus the institutionalization of relationships within the family may be said to extend to those of first cousinship, where the proper relationship is one of loyalty and support, and where shame prevents what personal emotion may prompt. However, a proviso must be made as to the regularity even of this relationship, for the very existence of such an emotion as jealousy between first cousins reveals again the potential degree of fragmentation within the kindred, as a result of the exclusive concentration on the family. Because of this, and because within the cognatic system it is impossible for one person to do the right thing by all his relatives, it is customary to find other criteria, in addition to those of kinship, determining the degree of loyalty to be found between one related family and the next. And it may be that one of the purposes of the link of spiritual kinship (that contracted between an individual and his relatives with his godparent or wedding sponsor and his relatives), being in former times largely created between people who were already related, was to consolidate and confirm a liaison which in itself was liable to schism. It is only since 1950 that, with the shifting of ambition from aims within the village to those outside it, the emphasis in these relationships has begun to change from kinsmen to unrelated people in the wider community in positions of economic or social power.

As well as spiritual kinship, the criteria for loyalty include, importantly, proximity. Where siblings live in the same village, or, still more, in adjoining houses, their children grow up together 'like siblings'. Such relatives, if they do not quarrel by reason of this very proximity, are usually very close. Conversely, as in the separation of family groups on removal to different houses, the distance even of one neighbourhood of the village from another can, by rendering contact more infrequent, be significant in lessening the degree of mutual support; the distance of one village from another can be still more important, and that caused by emigration very serious. Except in the case of quarrels, however, such distance does not undermine the basic affection between kinsmen; it merely prevents the steady consolidation of such a relationship which is one of the villager's main supports in his daily life.

Other criteria for cementing the bond of kinship are similar to those involved in proximity—co-operation over the fields, the harvest, the need for a companion on a journey, and so forth—for they are relationships of mutual need and can build up into a reciprocal relationship of love and service.

Kinship, therefore, outside the family, must not be seen as a definitive criterion of relationship on its own merits, so much as the essential basis of a relationship of mutual obligation which may, or may not, develop from it. The obligation which draws such kinsmen together is not only that which dictates a positive relationship between those who are related by blood, but also that which excludes a man from asking help from any but a kinsman. That help, once given, requires repayment when reciprocal help is needed, and it is on this basis of mutual service, loyalty, and protection that the relationship between kinsmen is built up.

The solidarity resulting from the indefinition of relationship at the outer edges of the kindred is of a different type, and is one in which the individual is related by innumerable, if tenuous, links to the outside world, rather than one in which he may expect support from a precise category of kinsmen.

The arbitrariness of the cessation of the kindred at the degree of second cousin, and the feeling, however faint, that 'blood lasts to the seventh degree of kinship', act quite definitely to perpetuate the idea of relationship far beyond the accepted limits of the kindred. To the degree of third cousin and third cousin's children this sense of relationship is one that carries with it a certain degree of expectation, and a visitor to a village where he or she has no other close kin will go to such a cousin's house and be received not as a total stranger but as one who, however distantly, is of the same origin. However, this positive social relationship is normally of little practical significance in the villager's life, and it is on the conceptual and emotional level that the infinite extension of kinship into cousinhood of remote degree is most important, for here it provides the villager with an extroverted social stability which links him to the wider community, and complements the more introverted stability which he finds with his own family in his sense of his continuity from his ancestors and his perpetuity in his children.

The cognatic kinship system, therefore, at the same time as casting an exclusive emphasis on the family and defining a formal category of blood relations, also brings it about that the individual through his kindred is related in ever more minute ways to a vast number of other families scattered throughout the surrounding area. The differentiation between the kindred of the parents and that of the children simply increases the complexity and range of these relationships for the various families involved, for although practical links of friendship and obligation tend to be kept up more with relations of the children than relations of the parents, there is also a sense in which the direction of loyalty is reversed and in which children 'honour' their more distant relatives on account of the closer relationship which these hold with their parents.

While certain characteristics of the kindred are conducive to the solidarity of relationships within the kindred and between those of the kindred and the wider society, there are also, implicit in these same characteristics, tendencies which can lead directly to schism and conflict.

The chief of these tendencies has been mentioned already as the concentration on the family which, because it creates a proliferation of more distant relationships all originating 'from the same womb', necessitates also their consolidation by other ties simply because they lie outside the elementary family. However, since the individual's categorical rights and obligations are all to his family, these outweigh, in the last extreme, all the loyalties owed to his kinsmen in other families. It follows that for members of the same kindred there exist in many situations two standards of behaviour centred on the two poles of loyalty to family, and loyalty to the kinsman. Where these two loyalties conflict it is likely that that of the family should triumph, leaving the disappointed kinsman with the bitterness of betrayal to add to the loss to his self-interest; and it is for this reason that some of the most bitter quarrels in the village are between the same kin.

There is another aspect of the kindred which makes for a certain confusion in the interpretation of the rights and obligations attached to kinship. This is the fact mentioned earlier that in any kindred the focus is taken from a group of siblings which is itself only a sub-group of the basic social unit—the family. Since in any one family group it is only siblings who share the identical kindred with one another, it follows that there exist within the elementary family as many different categories of the kindred as there are generations represented in that family. Looking back into the past this distinction between the generations is of little practical significance, since the ancestors are incorporated into the general history of the house and remain symbolically if not practically relevant for the generations who have dropped out of living relationship with them. As regards the lateral degrees of relationship, however, the redefinition of the kindred with respect to each group of siblings is very important, for it means that between each generation and the next, one degree of lateral kinship is lost: the second cousins of the parents are no relations of the children, and the first cousins of the grandparents are no relations of the grandchildren. Thus while the formal kindred remains quite clearly defined for each individual, the fact that the children's kindred is different from that of the parents and that the focus of the family is chiefly directed to the children and their welfare, means that the relationship between a man and his kindred may change as his children grow up and look for support to their own close kin. Again, therefore, the possibility of two standards of expectation and obligation is created, with the same potentiality for disappointment, jealousy, and hostility, which in many cases acts against the ideal solidarity of the kindred.

The fact, also, that blood relationship needs to be consolidated by other criteria, means that even within the network of first cousins there can be considerable variation between the degree of affection and assistance given between them, and this variation increases in the remoter degrees of kinship. In such a situation it may be seen that the criteria of correct behaviour in a given circumstance are often confused, and often give rise to a conflict of interests and loyalties.

Finally, the same principle applies also in the case of relationship between third cousins, even though these are not technically kinsmen, for once again a double standard of expectation and obligation is implicit in the possibility of the two definitions. This situation brings it about that while one man may for instance act against his third cousin as if he were a stranger, the injured party is doubly offended because it is his 'kinsman' who has thus damaged him. It was in illustration of this situation that one man said to me, 'In Ambéli we hate each other. Why? This is a small village, here we are all more or less kin with one another. If someone damages you, you think, "That is my kinsman who has stolen my pine." So the hatred grows.'

Relationships through affinity tend not to generate any particular pattern of hostility, simply because they do not generate any particular degree of mutual confidence or expectation either. The one exception to this is the area in which expectation is high, and the possibility of disappointment therefore correspondingly great— the expectation of parents for their children's happiness and advancement.

It was explained earlier how it is the business of a match-maker to persuade each family that they are getting what they think they deserve—the best. Normally, after marriage, knowledge of the various imperfections of the other is accommodated easily into the growing marriage relationship. However, there is one principal case in which this progress may be hindered or disrupted, and this is when the groom's parents live with their son and his bride. The person on whom, in this case, all depends, is the mother-in-law. If she is 'good' (καλή), then all is well; but if she is 'difficult' or 'aggressive' (ζαβή), then discord follows. Popular village imagination tends usually to represent the mother-in-law as the latter, certainly as the rival of the new bride for power in the house and for her son's affection, who puts too heavy a burden of work on her shoulders or who tells tales (false or true) about her to her son, which may make him beat her. Where this is indeed the case—and there are various instances in Ambéli past and present which show that such a situation is by no means rare—relations between the mothers-in-law can degenerate rapidly into quarrelling and mutual recrimination. This pattern of hostilities, however, depends on the chief circumstance of the newly married couple living with the husband's family. With the decrease of this custom, this source of friction is also subsiding.

Although, therefore, it is true to say that within the kindred, as in other circumstances of village life, the greater the degree of affection and expectation the deeper the resentment and antagonism if something goes wrong, it is definitely true also to say, as the villagers do, that 'Kinsmen mean support' (οἱ συγγενεῖς εἶναι ὑποστήριγμα).

There is one respect in which the expected level of behaviour between kinsmen approaches that of a categorical obligation, and this is the prohibition of gossip about them to strangers. It is accepted that a person's practical resources are limited, and that since the first call on his time, money, or material possessions is by his family, there may on occasions be little left over for others. It is with this knowledge that every family tries to be as self-supporting as it can, and it is only in cases such as illness or emergency, or the rare need to be absent from the village for some festival, that calls on close relatives are made for such things as baking, cooking, looking after the animals or the children. However, the one commodity that costs nothing is the loyalty of preserving the secrets of kinsmen against the curiosity of the rest of the community, and to gossip about such a kinsman is an act of deepest betrayal. The occasion in the village when a woman was struck by a relation by marriage, a first uncle, because she had spread tales about his daughter, her husband's first cousin, was judged by the community to have been just, for she was 'closely related' to the girl about whom she had gossiped, and had therefore had no business to say anything.

The way in which kinsmen must be loyal to each other in the matter of gossip is threefold—they must not reveal their secrets, they must back them up in any deceit or evasion they think fit to practise, and, particularly, they must not speak evil, true or false, about them. These obligations are largely kept—except in the case of admitted hostility—by first aunts and uncles, first cousins and closer relatives, since, as was stated above, these relationships are to a certain extent institutionalized and it is a matter for shame if they are violated. But even in these relationships there can be a certain variation as to how the demands of loyalty are interpreted, owing to the combination, in each case, of all the different strands of obligation and self-interest. Between more distant relations this type of loyalty is even more a matter of individual circumstance.

Even though the preservation of the secrets of close kinsmen is one of the crucial values of this society, the fact that the original centre of loyalties between siblings and parents is later fragmented into different houses, each with their own different categories of close relations, means that even between members of this original family the circle of loyalty is not closed. Not only do people love to gossip, but they are also, in a sense, obliged to, since the prescription for loyalty between kin means not only that one kinsman should preserve the secrets of another, but also that he should not exclude such a kinsman from his confidence. Thus son may speak to mother, mother to her sister, sister to her husband, or godparent, and so on. This is one of the causes for it being inevitable that once a secret has been let out of the house it is likely eventually to reach all the community by one means or another.

One aspect of the kinship system which prevents it from providing a totally reliable channel of information is the fact mentioned earlier that not all relatives are on the same terms of mutual affection with each other. A story may therefore spread, but with differing degrees of veracity according to the way in which, in each encounter, the speaker balances his loyalties to those he is speaking about with his loyalties to those he is addressing. Thus the possibility of doubt as to the different interpretations of the same story remains, and the subject of the story retains some degree of autonomy.

The first two categories of loyalty therefore—the non-revelation of secrets and the perpetuation of lies on behalf of a kinsman— while they are in essence categorical, are effectively incomplete ways of preserving another person's secrets. As regards the question of slander, the prescription for loyalty is less ambiguous, and it is rare for close relatives up to first cousins to indulge in such a thing, although second cousins are said to do so more often.

In addition to refraining from gossiping themselves, kinsmen also support each other simply by their presence, as this in itself helps to prevent the gossip of others. There is an expression frequently quoted by the villagers, 'You can't shut the mouth of the community' (δὲν μπορεῖς νὰ μπαλώσεις τὸ στόμα τοῦ κόσμου), you cannot stop people gossiping. However, not only is it true that the more relatives a person has, the fewer people there are to gossip about him, but also the very fact of having relatives tends to limit the gossip when they are about. If they are powerful relatives, so much the better. The young widow of the village, about whom at one time there was a flood of gossip, said several times to me that when her brother came back from the Merchant Navy the community 'shut up'. This brother has the reputation for being quickly roused to anger, and his very presence in the village curbed, though it did not end, the talk. This particular type of protection is normally limited to the family, and to its male members, since the deterrent to the gossiper lies chiefly in his fear of violent retribution from that quarter. It is very unlikely in the present days of fragmentation of the kindred and legal sanctions against violence that any but a brother or a father would involve himself violently in such a situation, and even then not all have the temperament for such an action.

The presence of kinsmen may also support a woman as regards her treatment by her family of marriage. A girl who had married a fellow villager was, while she lived in Ambéli, moderately well treated by her husband, but now, living down in the valley in another village, it is said that he knocks her about continually.

Although her neighbours do not like this, being non-related they dare not take the liberty of intervening; were there relatives there, however, the husband would be ashamed to treat his wife as he does, in front of them, unless he were prepared to embark on a lasting quarrel and suffer the inconveniences that such a quarrel at close quarters would involve. In such a case, a type of support, involving as it does the moral solidarity and combined disapproval of one group against an individual of an opposing group, and not presupposing violence, may be expected from the kindred as a whole.

Kinsmen of all categories can in general be expected to give a person good advice, to tell them of the reactions of the community, and to guide them in the way of correct, or at least sensible, behaviour. Non-kinsmen cannot be relied upon to do this, but are rather suspected of deliberately giving bad advice so that the subject of that advice then makes a fool of himself and they can 'laugh' and enjoy themselves at his expense.

Important, too, is the ability of a kinsman in another village or a different situation to give advice in business negotiations and information about possible sons- or daughters-in-law, to provide links with possible patrons, and generally to act as a link of communication with the outside world.

It is clear, therefore, that in the non-material but very practical world of what might be termed moral support, a villager's kinsmen are vital to him. Concerning the support due in financial or material terms to a kinsman, such support is limited severely by the narrow margin of resources and the pre-eminence of the family. In cases of emergency, however, people turn to their closest relatives for help, and it is rarely refused, for no one will ask even from a relative more than it is in their power reasonably to give. In the case of long-drawn-out hardship each family looks to itself again, for it is admitted that, while one is obliged to help those kinsmen who turn to one in cases of sudden need, the main resources of the family cannot be continually drained even by a married brother or sister, whatever their situation. One married woman in the village, whose husband was ninety-two and of whose three children two were insane, had one married brother and two married sisters in the village, and yet, except for occasional help at the harvest or in time of sickness, she and her one healthy daughter had to manage on their own.

Relationships between kinsmen who are in different houses,

therefore, whatever the affection between them, are subject to the law of reciprocity, simply because the total resources of the families concerned cannot stand anything else. On the basis of mutual obligation—the return in kind of help once given—the giving of such aid may become a working relationship. Thus in the normal day-to-day ordering of life the material support given to kinsmen is one that is self-regulating, according to the capacity of each to receive, and to give, such help. This type of relationship is one that involves, perhaps, a loan in time of need, or making a stable available for a few hours to an animal while the owner goes by bus to one of the nearby towns; help in the fields at times when more hands are needed, or some shopping done for someone who has not time to make the journey down to Kateríni. Since all villagers prefer, and unmarried girls are obliged, to do everything involving excursions from the village in company, relatives will arrange to go together to shop in Kateríni, to collect winter fodder for the goats, or in summer to watch them as they graze; and within the village they may collaborate over their washing, they will cook and bake for each other in times of sickness, and eat together on festivals or name-days.

Lest it should be thought that relationships between villagers are exclusively confined to kinsmen, it must be said here that this is not the case. Groups of unrelated girls will go together to collect wild greens from the fields, to go to Kateríni, or, before a saint's day, to clean out one of the little churches that are around the village. The alliances that are seen in the groups of men who attend the various cafés are formed as much through friendship and political affiliation as through kinship. This type of flexible comradeship is an important part of village life, and shows that although hostility dominates the generality of relations between non-kinsmen, it is not to be found inevitably in every single such relationship. Yet it remains true that for the vital necessities of life only kinsmen may be depended upon, only close kinsmen may be trusted.

The corollary of this is that somebody with no, or few, kinsmen is in a very difficult position. One woman with influenza one year had to go out in the snow collecting fodder for her goats because 'she had no one to go for her'; and regarding another woman whom I wanted to help in some way, I was told, 'Let others do it, her kin, her daughter-in-law, her sister'—an ironic reference to the fact that she was childless and had quarrelled with her brother, her only close relative in the village. In a situation where relationships, through mutual aid, gain their first impetus from relationships through blood, those outside this circle are, except for possible occasional help, left to fend for themselves.

Within this relationship of mutual aid, the crucial element is that everyone should do what he can. When, therefore, physical capacity breaks down, no offence is caused and the relationship holds. Help refused, however, when it could be given, is evidence of lack of care, or even an indication of hostility, and the relationship wanes accordingly. There are occasions, even within the family, when someone unable through age or sickness to contribute much to the well-being of the family, is rejected or resented, and an old widow complained bitterly to me that her son and daughter-in-law, with whom she lived, had no longer any use for her because she was old and could not work and 'ate bread'. In other cases, however, families with old parents or parents-in-law or with crippled siblings show them varying and sometimes great degrees of affection and consideration, accepting their incapacity as a fact of nature and the will of God. It is, however, significant that it is only within the family that the positive dynamic engendered within the house is sufficient to sustain a relationship when a lack of reciprocity threatens to undermine it. Outside the family, particularly towards the outer edges of the kindred and especially with regard to non-kinsmen, an imbalance in the relationship of mutual aid is almost invariably damaging, and when mutual co-operation lapses the relationship lapses also. Because, in the present day, the area of mutual co-operation has shrunk, vigorous relationships, which were once dispersed throughout the kindred, have shrunk correspondingly. It is consistent with this that one woman, answering my question as to why she would not seek company, on a certain emergency journey, from some distantly related person in the community (for she had few close relatives) answered with a variant of a familiar formula, 'Some help, but another will say to you, "I have no need of you, go yourself".' It is consistent also with this situation that villagers are frequently heard lamenting the diminished solidarity of the kindred in terms which are the reverse of those quoted earlier in this section: 'Kinsmen no longer support one another' (τώρα συγγενεῖς δὲν ὑποστηρίζουνε).

7. Sowing the Broad Beans

While it is on the whole the more distant range of relations within the kindred which tends to lapse from its sanctioned relationships, there is one main issue which is responsible for fragmentation of relationships between much closer relations—first cousins and siblings. This is the question of the inheritance, or the sale, of land. Where the inheritance has been, or is thought to have been, unfairly distributed between the legatees, or where one legatee claims land which another thinks to be rightly his own, there can arise lasting and bitter quarrels. Such quarrels are not easy to settle, for it is universally accepted in the village that the person who receives an unfairly large proportion of land is nevertheless perfectly entitled to keep it, even though relatives who take offence and quarrel over it are commiserated with. The onus therefore is on the offended party to abandon his stand, and this is often not found to be possible. Over the sale of land, however, which by-passes a close relative and transfers the land to a more distant one or to a stranger, the problem for the original landowner is even more difficult to solve, for here it is a question not just of a disproportionate allocation of land within the family, but of the family as a whole being deprived of land which passes for ever into the hands of a collateral branch, or of strangers. The comment on one man who had sold his land to a stranger was, 'What a sense of honour! He had a brother and yet he went and sold his land to Mitzos', a comment which voices village opinion in general on this subject. Yet when the question is asked as to whether someone should really sustain a financial loss by selling cheaply to a brother what he could sell at a better price to someone else, the answer is more equivocal—'He *should* sell to his brother, but . . .' Once again, therefore, we see two incompatible standards of behaviour where a man is torn in two totally opposite directions, between the interest of his family and loyalty to his brother.

Finally, as regards the type of confidence that can be placed in relations concerning matters of sex, it is commonly agreed that between first cousins there is absolute trust, since they are 'like siblings', although even then the community does not like them to rag around together (καλαμπουρίζω) too much, while between second cousins a high degree of propriety must be maintained. A certain amount of confidence may, it is said, be placed by a woman in her brother-in-law if he has children, for here the presence of children to whom the sister-in-law is first aunt draws the links of kinship closer and allows for a greater degree of trust. But between relatives by marriage who are more distantly related there can be placed no confidence at all.

The relation of spiritual kinship (κουμπαριά) is one which in this society is very important—in the case of godparenthood it is theoretically even more important than blood relationship—yet it is one in which the type of strains present in kinship are even more apparent.

The relationship is entered upon when one person, a man or a woman, becomes either the sponsor at a marriage, or the godparent at a baptism. All those who are united in spiritual kinship are known reciprocally as *koumbáros* or (fem.) *koumbára* (κουμπάρος, fem -α) except for the direct relationship of godparent/godchild, where the godparent is known as νονός, his wife as νονά, and the godchild as ἀδεξιμιός (fem. -α) or βαφτιστήρι (n.). The relationship is closest between the two parties directly involved, and their immediate families; but all in the direct line of the two people concerned—the parents, first aunts and uncles, siblings and children—are in fact *koumbároi* with each other, although between such more distant *koumbároi* the form of address *Koumbáre* is not always used.

Of the two types of spiritual kinship, that of godparent is of a higher order than wedding sponsor, although the two types of relationship are closely linked in the village mind, and a 'proper *koumbaros*' (κανονικὸς κουμπάρος) is one who has acted both as sponsor at the wedding and godparent to the first child. This person then has the right to be the sponsor at that child's wedding, and to baptize the first child of that union, and so on. If for any reason he does not want, or is not able, to exercise this right, he is entitled to pass it on to a close relation of himself or his wife. Thus it is traditional practice for the sponsor at a wedding to be already the godparent of the groom, and the significance of the 'crowning', which is performed by the sponsor, is not only in that it reveals and completes the mystical union of marriage, but also in that, by enabling that union to come about, it also enables children to be born of that union. Since the sponsor is indispensable to the 'crowning', and therefore to the birth of children within the spiritual law, it is appropriate that the first of these children falls to him to baptize. Thus the mystery inaugurated by the sponsor in the marriage service is completed at baptism, a necessary sequence of events which is expressed by the villagers in the saying that a *koumbáros* crosses his hands at the wedding and must uncross them again at the baptism. This refers to the fact that at the crowning the sponsor holds the fillets or crowns over the heads of the bride and groom, with his hands crossed, right over left. He changes these fillets over three times, and finally places them on the heads of the couple.

The deeper importance of the relationship of godparent over that of wedding sponsor is a reflection of the emphasis placed by tradition on the spiritual life. Every villager, when asked why baptism is a greater mystery than crowning, will answer that the godparent 'puts the oil on' (βάζει τὸ λάδι), or, more explicitly, 'makes him [the child] a Christian' (τὸ κάνει Χριστιανό). This act, it is said, makes the godparent even more important to the child than his own parents, for though through his parents the child is born into the world of the flesh, through the godparent it is born into the world of the spirit. When it is remembered how deeply the villager is aware of the ubiquity of the demons and the inevitability of sin in the world in which the child is born, it will be seen how vital an act is this symbolic linking of the defenceless infant with the victorious world of Christ. The relative strength of the relationship of godparent when compared with blood relationship is illustrated also in the use of the term of address 'Godparent', or '*Koumbáre*', rather than that of the kinship terminology if the godparent is also a blood relation; and also in the prohibition on marriage for the godchild with any of the godparent's children, his or her siblings, and with any of the godparent's other godchildren.

The relationship of godparent is highly prized for two reasons. First, as the villagers put it, 'for the mystery' (γιὰ τὸ μυστήριο), and secondly, 'for the relationship' (γιὰ τὶς σχέσεις). To 'make the child a Christian' is an action carried out, as they say, 'for the other world' (γιὰ τὸν ἄλλον κόσμο) or 'for the soul' (γιὰ τὴν ψυχή); and illustrating this there is a popular custom which decrees that when a person dies the belt which they wear—in older times the long *zinári* (ζινάρι)[1] which wound several times round the waist—must be fastened or unfastened according to whether or not they have had godchildren. If they have godchildren this belt is fastened, but if not then it is left loose and dangling. The significance

[1] See p. 145 n. 1.

of this was explained to me as being the equivalent of a person going with torn clothes, shamed, before his Maker. But it is plain also that this unloosing of the belt, which is in this case, like the dance, a symbol of generation and of the passing on of life, represents the failure of the person concerned to pass on to others the kingdom of the spirit—his failure, in fact, to do in spiritual terms what he should also do in the flesh, and that is to have children. It is, then, for the sake of the soul that the traditional greeting to a prospective godparent going to a christening is 'May you reach a thousand' (*νὰ τὰ χιλιάσετε*), and because of this that even the poorest people will eagerly strive to be a godparent, even though the christening in these days costs them not less than a thousand drachmas, or about £15, in the clothes and necessary articles for the child.

Although in the villagers' eyes the 'relationship' is ranked second to the 'mystery', the relationship is nevertheless very important, and it is the desire of families to be, in spite of all the opposing tensions of society, on good terms with one another, that prompts overtly many of the instances of spiritual kinship in the village. In older times, when the solidarity of the kindred was stronger, it was on the whole the relatives, rather than strangers, who became *koumbároi*. Often, indeed, it was the same relative who was preferred, and there is one case in the village of a certain man who baptized all his sister's eleven children. The present trend towards the dispersal of these relationships among the wider community reflects both the diminishing value placed on the kindred, and the growing awareness in the village mind of the advantage of having patrons in the outside world. These patrons are on occasions of real advantage to the villager, and there are various tales of considerable aid given by a godparent for the education and general furtherance of a particular child. However, the inevitable self-interest in either side of the relationship makes it likely that any real dependence on a *koumbáros* in a financial sense is bound for disappointment, and the realism which informs the villager's attitude to his *koumbáros* is illustrated in the following comment, voiced during a discussion of possible godparents—'It's not so important; he's not going to feed me and I'm not going to feed him.'

The obvious value placed on social relations through spiritual kinship, however, does not alter the essential priorities. Spiritual kinship is not, as it is sometimes represented, a mere form which is used to initiate or to confirm a desired social relationship; it is itself its own *raison d'être*, the final cause of its own existence. The fact that it results in important social alliances is merely a reflection of the high value in which such kinship is held. It is almost certainly for this reason that the custom in Ambéli and the surrounding district is for the godparent to supplicate for the child, never for the parents of the child to ask anyone, even a relation, if they will baptize it. The gift that is freely given without having been sought tends to be given for the sake of a relationship. The nature of the gift in this case may well be unimportant; what it expresses, vital. The gift that is, by invariable custom, always asked for and never offered is plainly one which holds its own intrinsic and pre-eminent value. Spiritual kinship is one of these; and even in the present days of weakening spirituality and greater emphasis on patronage and material advantage, the custom of seeking rather than accepting to be godparent still symbolizes this traditional value.

In spite of the custom of perpetuating spiritual kinship, once inaugurated, with the same family, there is still within this custom latitude for the exercise of personal choice. In the case of the death of the godparent and his or her spouse by the time the god-child comes to be married, the sequence is broken, and although a son or a daughter of the godparents may be asked to be sponsor, it is equally likely that the choice will fall elsewhere. Traditionally, it is the godparent of the groom rather than of the bride who is sponsor at a wedding, but again in the case of the death of his god-parents the groom may pass the selection of sponsor on to his wife. Also important to the flexibility of these relationships is the fact that it is only the first child which is traditionally the spiritual child of the wedding sponsor; every subsequent child of the marriage may be baptized by someone else. It must also be mentioned that the custom of perpetuating spiritual kinship in the way mentioned above is not always observed, and the family concerned is always free to insult—for so it is interpreted—the family of its godparent by preferring another family in a situation in which the former should by rights be accepted.

The question of *katameriá*, which has already been discussed with reference to marriage, is also relevant to the creation of spiritual kinship, and it is considered inauspicious, although it is occasionally done, for such kinship to be reciprocal. Once the relationship of godparent has been created between two families it should continue in the same direction, and a return baptism from anyone in the direct line of the related pair, i.e. parents, siblings, and children, is considered unlucky, for in this case 'the oil turns back' (*γυρίζει τὸ λάδι*) and can result in misfortune or death. This has been cited to me as the direct cause of the death of a child several years ago who was baptized by the brother of its grandfather's godson. 'It wasn't *katameriá*', I was told. 'Nikos baptized the child, and, look, within a year it was dead.' Further evidence also for the power latent in spiritual kinship is seen in the belief that ill luck or death overtaking a child is due to the godparent; and even though such responsibility is seen as lying in an involuntary property of ill chance rather than in deliberate malice, the death of one child is enough to cause its godparents to be reticent about asking to baptize another in case the same thing should happen again.

In spite of the central symbolic content of spiritual kinship, the essentially objective and non-contemplative nature of the villager's philosophy causes him to accept the mystery, once performed, as having been confirmed, and from then on the godparent's responsibilities towards the child, and vice versa, are almost exclusively social.

Apart from the aspects of direct patronage mentioned above, a good relationship between *koumbároi* is greatly valued in a society where it is only some type of 'relationship' that can override the traditional pattern of hostility between people who are not related by blood. Such *koumbároi* will be frequent visitors to each other's houses, will support each other in quarrels, gossip, and lawsuits, and will mediate perhaps in some situation where non-related people would hesitate to interfere. One may give the other a loan, if he is in a position to do so, and in general will join in the various reciprocal arrangements for mutual aid that are found normally only between kin. It must be stressed, however, that spiritual kinship offers an opportunity for relationship only: it does not provide the relationship itself; and just as in kinship the relationship needs to be consolidated by other criteria, so much the more in spiritual kinship between non-kin the relationship needs to be reinforced by other types of expediency and a great deal of goodwill on both sides.

The reason for spiritual kinship collapsing, as it often does, lies once again in the exclusiveness of the family and in the nature of self-interest always to refer back to it. Whereas with kinship the self-interest is inevitably implicated with other members of the same origin, in spiritual kinship where there is no accompanying blood tie, there is only self-interest to keep the relationship together. Where this self-interest dovetails between the two families, the relationship prospers, but where there is a discrepancy between the expectation on one side and the understanding of obligation on the other, total breakdown can occur. Spiritual kinship thus tends to be a highly volatile relationship, unable in many cases—even with the reduplication mentioned above—to withstand the tendencies to fragmentation that continually operate in the community outside the family.

The problem of reconciling expectation with obligation, of preserving the relationship at the same time as keeping a firm hold on family resources, is one which every individual solves in his or her own way. One such case, however, is indicative of the types of strain involved in such a situation, and the means taken to resolve them. In this case a widow in Ambéli had as her son's godfather a shopkeeper in Kateríni. He, being a merchant and moderately well off, was in a position to provide her with services such as marketing her wine, organizing a purchase for her from any shop to which she was unable to go, lending her money, and so on. He did not, however, carry his patronage so far as to sell her items from his shop at a reduced rate, and his goods were even, so she said, more expensive than at some others. But in return for his services, and for the sake of good relations, he expected her to do all her shopping at his shop, which it was plainly uneconomic for her to do. This situation was resolved by the use of a vast amount of tact on the part of the widow, who bought items from him on occasions so as to keep him content, but who also shopped secretly at other places—calling at his shop when he was closed, or telling him that he was away when she urgently needed to make some particular purchase. In this case the interest of the two of them militated towards a perpetuation of the relationship, for it would have damaged his reputation to lose a client, and would have deprived her of at least a minimal source of dependable help from a person of some means. Concealment, trickery, and lies, however, were essential in the maintenance of this relationship if the honour of the shopkeeper and the finances of the widow were not to be threatened, and in this context such duplicity is evidence, not of moral failure but of a creditable intent to maintain a positive relationship which would, with the introduction of greater honesty, be bound to fail.

There are, on the other hand, many cases where the clash of two antipathetic poles of expectation can lead to total failure of the relationship, and in Ambéli it is a common source of grievance that a certain *koumbáros* has not given the support which it is thought was due. There is a case where a godfather has taken his godson to court for the alleged theft of some trees, and they now never speak to each other; and another case where a *koumbáros* is involved in a bitter and enduring quarrel with the man whose marriage he sponsored and whose first child he christened. All these quarrels are caused by one of two things—either divided loyalties, or an interpretation by one individual of the obligation owed him by his *koumbáros*, which clashes with his assessment of the obligation which he himself owes. Such discrepancies of interpretation, lacking the ballast of the blood tie or of a strong will to keep the relationship alive, are inevitably very frequent in spiritual kinship, and it is because of this that there is a popular saying which runs: 'Where spiritual kinship exists, there friendship is lost' (ἐκεῖ ποὺ εἶναι κουμπαριά, χάνεται ἡ φιλία).

VIII

THE PURSUIT AND CONTROL OF FAMILY INTEREST IN THE COMMUNITY

THE particular nature of this society depends upon the interrelation of three characteristics which have already been discussed. These are the exclusive and dynamic nature of the elementary family; the fact that relationships between the different families consist largely in the struggle for reputation; and the particular evaluation of human nature and the perfect society as understood by the villagers, which results in the value system of honour and shame and the definition of the ideal roles.

Because it is the nature of the elementary family to have an unconditional claim over the loyalty of its members, this family solidarity involves its members in behaviour to the outside community which is the reverse of the behaviour normal within it, and imposes on its members the obligation to defend it often at the expense of loyalty to kinsmen. Between unrelated families the normal and accepted relationship is one of competition and suspicion, which often breaks out into active hostilities. Very existence, therefore, in such a society, is often a matter of self-preservation, and such preservation is seen as the necessity to look after 'τὰ συμφέροντα' (sing. τὸ συμφέρον) or self-interest. Like honour and shame, συμφέροντα is a word which translates clumsily into English, for, because the individual is so crucially identified with his family, the emphasis of such interested behaviour is not the self only, but the group. However, with this proviso, this rendering as 'self-interest' is the most accurate available, and will be used in the following pages.

Because self-interest in this society involves this inevitable concentration on the house and family, and because the family is the sacral centre of society as well as being the group which provides the individual with his sense of purpose and identity, this self-interest is seen not only as a social necessity but also as a moral good. Self-interest thus becomes a value in itself, and it is this value, rather than any notion of a disinterested ethical obligation to another, which in one way or another is the deciding factor in most of the situations making up village life.

As has already been argued, there is a sense in which the possession of honour within the family is something which is considered by each family to be already a fact, and the acquisition of a public reputation for honour is simply a question of the public vindication of its innate virtue. The pursuit of self-interest has an identical motivation, for in this pursuit each family is simply striving, in the sphere of material advantage and financial gain, to achieve the success which it thinks is due to it. Competition and jealousy between the separate houses is extremely intense, therefore, because the different families compete not only psychically over reputation but also materially over their practical interests, and because each family is totally convinced of the justice of its own cause.

In spite of the moral value given to self-interest, it is plain that unchecked pursuit of this value by any family would result in anarchy. Two factors in the structure of the community prevent this. The first is the fact that each family does not pursue its own self-interest in a vacuum, but in competition with all the other families in the community who are all doing the same thing. One family, therefore, automatically provides a check to the unlimited self-seeking of another, and the varying degrees of hostility, which include not visiting, not speaking to, speaking ill of, and finally outright quarrelling, all provide sanctions against other families by which one family may prevent too great an infringement of its rights.

The second factor is that although the villagers are realistic enough to allow the basis of repute to lie in a fairly minimal adherence to the ideal value of social responsibility in all situations, the theoretical strength of this value persists in all situations where criticism of others is relevant. It is a value according to which not only does a man not murder or steal in order to further the good of his family, but he does not lie, cheat, or infringe the rights of others either; and because every family wants to be able to judge adversely and to laugh at the actions of other families with which it is in competition, it is this standard to which it appeals when it is passing judgement on them. In an effort to avoid the shame of being laughed at, the different families of the community all adjust their actions in some way to take account of this extreme standard against which they are being judged. The self-interest, therefore, of the community, which takes the form of criticism and mockery of others, helps to balance the self-interest of the individual houses, which takes the form of direct self-seeking by whatever legitimate means are available.

The existence of these two standards—the ideal standard which is appealed to in criticism of others, and the partial standard which is the only one possible in practical terms—causes a good deal of tension and counterpoint in society. It is impossible for a villager to give unconditional loyalty to his family and at the same time to be scrupulously correct in his dealings with others, and yet according to the ideal standard this is what is required of him. It is also impossible for self-will and sheer personal desire not to conflict, even in a society as rigidly structured by role as this one, with the morality to which he is ideally meant to conform. The result is that the villager lives in a world in which he is caught continually between the frying-pan and the fire: on the one hand he may risk a brief abandonment of his family interests, on the other a quarrel with his neighbour; over a certain matter he may have to choose between disobliging an aunt, or not telling the truth to a first nephew by marriage; he may compromise his self-esteem if he allows someone to steal a pine of his and thus make a fool of him, but on the other hand to involve in a lawsuit for the sake of a trifle is also ludicrous. Although the pre-eminence of the family and of the male line within the family are the factors which influence predominantly all decisions in which such choices have to be made, this does not automatically save the villager from causing offence elsewhere, and there are many situations in which roles come into conflict with one another and where it is personal inclination and the immediate pressure of the situation rather than straight appeal to the moral code which have to bring about a decision.

Although in this society there exist these factors which make an infringement of the ideal value system inevitable, there exist also other factors which resolve the conflict at a point long before it becomes a threat to the system itself. One of these factors is paradoxically the very same characteristic of the moral code which gives rise to the conflict of loyalties mentioned above—that is to say its rigidity. For this, at the same time as producing a situation in which it is impossible for the individual always to do right, produces also at the same time a variety of possible standards of conduct from which he can choose, and in this way creates a system of behaviour which in fact has considerable flexibility. Thus since, in any one situation, the individual involved has a number of differing loyalties to deal with simultaneously, and since he cannot accommodate all his loyalties in a single action, he is left with an area in which he is, within limits, autonomous. The same ambiguity, therefore, which is found in the conflicting pull of loyalties in a given situation, and which often makes it impossible for one individual to do right by all parties, also gives that individual a chance for self-justification by appeal to any one of the various values held in the same scheme. The individual, in other words, can manipulate the system for his own ends, and all villagers are in fact past masters in the art.

The second way in which the pressure of community standards on the individual is minimized, is to be found in lying—a practice so prevalent in this society as to be an institution. Here, the individual does not appeal to alternative standards within the value system to justify his action; he simply denies the action altogether. Lying, like the manipulation of the value system mentioned above, is also a talent indispensable to village life, and one which is almost universally possessed.

It is plain, therefore, that by these two means—by the lie and by the latitude for a certain freedom of action in any given situation—the system can in many cases be accommodated to the individual when the individual finds that he is unable to keep to the highest requirements of the system. And, drawing from this, it seems that two generalizations may be attempted. First, that any society which insisted rigorously on the literal and consistent attainment of its highest values would inevitably break against its own rigidity, and that because of this there must exist, in a society where individual behaviour cannot always accord with ideal behaviour, institutionalized ways of getting round these values without actually defying their validity. Here it is the very rigidity of the moral code causing it to break into numerous particularities when applied to the complexities of social life, which gives the individual considerable latitude for personal choice within it. The second generalization is that every sanction carries with it its counterpart, and that where there exists a sanction there will exist also some means for avoiding it. The fact that people inevitably offend against the code and that this, if discovered, is inevitably penalized by a hostile community, makes it also inevitable that some escape route will be devised. In Ambéli the community is avid for the discovery of lapses and swift to mock them, but the individual (or the group) counters this by continuing to a certain extent in his own way while developing an extreme ingenuity in deceit. Thus personal weakness and the latitude for personal choice are accommodated in a system of extreme severity; the individual is not crushed, nor is the system shattered.

One result of this situation is a continual interplay of accusation and self-justification, either of which is, in its own terms, extremely powerful, since the accusations are made with reference to the ideal standard, while the self-justification appeals to the other more relative values which are implicit within the same scheme.

An important element in this type of self-justification is the fact, already mentioned, that the practical morality of the Greek villagers has often very little to do with their awareness of sin. The perfect life, the paradigm for mankind, they see as the life of Christ; but although they are aware that their lives match up to this model in very few respects, this awareness neither spurs them to greater efforts to improve the moral quality of their lives, nor does it plunge them into despair. Caught as they are in a system in which lying, quarrelling, gossiping, envy, jealousy, and hatred seem to a large extent to be inevitable, they accept their sinfulness as part of the *status quo*, as a thing to be philosophically accepted rather than to be fought against or worried about. This acceptance in no way compromises their understanding of sin, and it could on the contrary be said that the very clarity of their vision of perfection as represented in the life of Christ and the figure of the Mother of God is a chief element in the clarity of their perception of their own faults and therefore in the fatalism with which they accept their own sinful situation. This attitude was well illustrated by a man who walked away and chatted to some friends while a sermon was being delivered. I asked him later why he had not stayed to listen, to which his answer was: 'I knew what he would say: he would say, "You mustn't quarrel, you mustn't tell lies, you mustn't swear"—but I know that the next time the mule treads on my foot I'll curse it, and the All Holy Mother of God too. So what is the point in listening?'

On the whole the villagers are more concerned with the faults of others than with their own, and they drop naturally into a frame of reference involving the ideal standard when they evaluate their neighbour's actions. Not unnaturally, when they are evaluating their own actions, it is the relative standard of practical social life which is invoked. Eaves-dropping, lying, gossiping about neighbours, inventing scurrilous explanations of events—all common occurrences in village life and all accepted among friends as being a perfectly legitimate way to keep up in the endless business of defending personal secrets while finding out those of others—are sharply condemned by those who happen to be suffering from these things at the time. 'Is this the way people behave?', they ask, indignantly (῎Ετσι κάνει ὁ κόσμος;), referring unconsciously to the standard of the perfect life; while of course it is exactly the way that people do behave, and exactly the way the person making the complaint will behave himself, a moment later, if the situation arises. However, there are rare moments in which the knowledge of the reality of their faults is phrased by the villagers in terms in which they associate themselves with the reverse side of the divine standard—with the reality, as they see it, of the human situation. 'That is how we are made' (εἴμαστε πλασμένοι ἔτσι), they say sorrowfully, in explanation of a particularly blatant piece of self-interest on the part either of themselves or of someone else; and here it is clear that while their attitude to their own sin resolves personal conflict, it does not obscure the reality of the divine standard against which they are sinning.

The same sort of dichotomy is observable throughout the whole pattern of social life. Quarrelling, for instance, for those involved in the quarrel or in the interests of those quarrelling, may be a vital aspect of social survival, while for those who are uninvolved it is a matter for laughter. The attitude of both participants and onlookers in a quarrel is of course determined by what the quarrel is about, and there do occur situations in which everyone recognizes that a quarrel cannot be avoided. But on many occasions those who are involved in a quarrel can be mocked by others simply for their indulgence in it, for lacking the type of self-control and intelligence which would keep them out of trouble; whereas those quarrelling will justify their actions with passion, and refer to standards within the value system which apply to obligation, personal honour, self-interest, and the rest. Again, although the house must be

protected against others, there is a sense in which to come into
conflict with others is in some way damaging to the house and
compromising to honour. Because of this, while there are those in
the community who ruthlessly defend their grazing rights against
others and are relentless in their demand for compensation if
strange animals trespass on their land, others are reluctant to press
for compensation except in extreme situations, saying, 'I am
ashamed to' (ντρέπομαι). Here again two standards are seen to
exist simultaneously—that of generosity on one hand, which is
admired, and self-interest on the other, which is necessary. The
same difficulty applies in the matter of lawsuits, where the advantage of protecting the honour of the family in terms of self-esteem
and not being made a fool of must be weighed against the ideal of
magnanimity, not to mention the possible mockery of the community and the inevitable waste of time and money which frequently outweighs the material advantages gained from such a
case. In each case, the line which divides generosity from stupidity,
self-interest from meanness, defence of honour from lack of self-
control, is so tenuous as to need redefinition by the participants and
the onlookers in each particular situation.

In addition to the different standards which coexist within the
value system, there is another dichotomy in village thinking which
is brought about by the change from traditional to more modern
values. Those who live 'according to the old way of thought' (μὲ τὸ
παλαιὸ μυαλό) are strict in their condemnation of engaged girls
who go on short trips to their fiancé's village; while nearly all of
those who actually have girls to marry and find that it is almost
impossible to find a bridegroom to accept a girl without first
taking her as his fiancée to his own village, bow to the inevitable
and allow them to go. There are those in the village who think that
an unmarried girl should not even greet an unrelated man with a
'Good morning', because, 'If you say "Good morning" one day,
you will say more the next, and more the next, and so you fall into
evil'; while those men who come back to the village for a few
months' holiday from their country of emigration think that girls
who behave with elaborate modesty, such as not answering when
they are greeted, are behaving like animals.

This dichotomy does not only operate between people of different mentalities; it sets up a double standard within the mind of
every individual. According to the older values, for instance, to be

a landowner was to be a householder (νοικοκύρης), a person of status. Today the community prefers offices and 'letters' (γράμματα), or education, and longs for release from dirty clothes and calloused hands; and yet there are still contexts in which a pride in farming and a recognition of the value of land persist. Another example of this ambivalence occurred in a conversation with one old woman who said to me that people had become cunning, or 'sharp' (as the word πονηρός is in this context more properly translated), and that this was good; but, when challenged, said that in the old days the community was on the whole simple or innocent (ἀγαθός), and that that was good too. The central point of both these evaluations is the concept of progress, the advancement of the family. Someone who is 'simple' is innocent of evil thoughts, of trickery, and because of this he is easily taken in. Such a person, in the old days when the individual families were more involved with the prosperity of the community as a whole and when purity in the eyes of God was thought to be a positive protection against evil, was on the whole a blessing to his family. In the present day, however, when the advancement of the family depends increasingly on single-minded and solitary pursuit of self-interest in material terms, such innocence becomes merely a liability, and the ability to spot the sharp practice of another, and if necessary to outwit him at his own game, becomes increasingly admired.

Many other instances of this type of confusion may be quoted. The fact that it is undoubtedly good that the men of the village have gone, either temporarily or permanently, to other countries, 'to better themselves' (γιὰ τὸ καλό), is asserted by the older people of the village even as they compare the old age of their parents, surrounded by their descendants, favourably with their own lonely and increasingly helpless state. Scientific discoveries are also looked on with mingled doubt and admiration—according to one way of thinking to meddle with the moon is to blaspheme and pollute a region of special holiness; according to another, it is obviously 'good' to extend man's knowledge of the universe and to exploit it for his use.

This simultaneous subscription to two irreconcilable values is evident to some extent in all the villagers, though it is more pronounced in the older people. It forms a paradox which they all become aware of at times, and none is able to resolve satisfactorily, although the increased comfort and prosperity of recent years always provide an overriding argument in favour of the present situation. To this conviction is added, in the younger people, an unquestioning faith in the scientists, economists, and politicians (ἐπιστήμονες), who have made these discoveries which have changed our social destinies, and who are so clever that they must, it is assumed, know where they are leading us.

In addition to possible reference to these varying values—to the ideal and the practical, the old and the new—there also exists the possibility of simultaneous appeal to one of a number of values which cannot be categorized in this way. A typical example of this was the insulting reference by one woman to another concerning her daughter's pregnancy by her second cousin, as a result of which she was compelled to marry him.[1] To this the answer was, 'She did it by herself. Was *I* to blame?' Of course, according to the values of society the conduct of a daughter reflects on the parents who have brought her up; but the counter-argument, in appealing to the indubitable fact that mothers do not always know what their daughters are up to and cannot always control them, was an argument which has its own particular logic, and was as a means of saving face acceptable to her kin and supporters. Another example, relating to accusation rather than to self-justification, occurs in two statements made at different times by one woman about another: 'Do you know what Athanasia has suffered? Her husband once put her head down on the fire-place and threatened to cut it off', and, 'Do you know what a terrible gossip Athanasia is? Her husband once banged her head against the fire-place to teach her not to gossip so much.'

It is in this world of conflicting and often totally contradictory evaluations that gossip, quarrels, and lawsuits are carried on, and it is in the continual reassertion of the values according to which each particular action is carried out that the justification of self and the condemnation of others find continual play.

In earlier days this situation used to be highly combustible, with a large number of powerful families living at close quarters and competing over land, women, and reputations; and threats of violence, fights with knives and fire-arms, and occasionally killings, formed part of the way in which the village ran its own affairs. However, with the beginnings of prosperity in the early 1950s and

[1] See pp. 93 and 223.

the increase of bureaucracy centred in Kateríni, Chalkis, and Athens, feuding and violence as an accepted way of settling differences of opinion began to be abandoned, and serious violence in the village is now virtually non-existent. Recourse to the law-courts of Kateríni is still frequent—so much so, in fact, that the villagers of Ambéli have a reputation for spending most of their time and all of their money there—but in spite of this the basic ways in which control is kept on the still potentially explosive situation in the village is not by recourse to criminal or civil law, or to violence, but by an internal system of informal control.

The last murder to take place in the village was in 1959, when a man was killed in an ambush by a fellow villager as the outcome of a quarrel of two years' standing.[1] For this the murderer is still in prison, and as a result of it his family left the village within the week. The swift departure of the family indicates that at the time the fear of reprisals from the murdered man's family was still great, and as recently as 1968 the young widow of the village voiced a fear to me lest her brother, who was very hot-tempered, should get to know of certain malicious rumours concerning her, and take violent revenge on the family from whom the rumours originated. On the other hand it is generally accepted now that not only do most of the villagers lack the temperament to risk long imprison-ment on account of violence or murder for the sake of family honour, but also that such an action would lead more to the des-truction of the family than to its maintenance. It is safe to say, therefore, that, except in abnormal circumstances, violent action by the villagers in defence of their interests now no longer occurs, and because of this, legal proceedings against any villager initiated by the authorities are now limited to the odd occasion of a forest fire. In such a case the fact that the forests are subject to public ad-ministration even though they are privately owned means that any damage to them is a matter for the State as well as for the private owner involved.

Other legal proceedings in Ambéli are all matters for criminal or civil law, and as such are to be seen more as an extension of local quarrels rather than as an impartial search for justice. These law-suits are usually concerned with ownership of land or trees, tres-pass, and access to fields, though they are sometimes caused by cases of assault, threatened assault, or abuse. In such situations,

[1] See pp. 4 and 67.

recourse is had to the lawcourts of Kateríni (*Εἰρηνοδικεῖον*), where lawsuits are conducted at the rate of, if necessary, up to about fifty a day, and where it is the avowed intention of the legal machinery simply to settle the situation, rather than to come necessarily to a just conclusion. To take the matter to the higher court in Chalkis (*Πρωτοδικεῖον*) is very rare, for there, even though the proceedings are more detailed and there is more chance for the truth to emerge, the prevalence of false witnesses and the inevitable complications of ownership in a system of land tenure such as that of Ambéli[1] make it all too likely that even there justice will not be done and that a great deal of money may be lost even by those who are in the right. In normal cases, therefore, there is no further final arbitration on any particular quarrel which the villager seeks, beyond that of the Kateríni lawcourts.

Even though the legal procedure in this court is known by all to be an inadequate way of finding out the truth of any situation, it is paradoxically just this inadequacy that enables the villager to accept the verdict, even though it may go against him. This is because by the time a quarrel over boundaries, for instance, has reached the court, the actual facts of the case, if they were ever accurately known, have become involved also with a host of other grievances, and the case becomes then more concerned with vindicating the honour of the rival parties than with the actual piece of land over which the whole thing started. Since the intention of such a court is to settle the quarrel rather than strictly to extract the truth, it is then open to those who win the case to boast how right has triumphed, and to those who lose to assume an air of injured innocence and resort to the oft-used phrase: 'When did you ever find justice in the lawcourts?' This is of course by no means to say that the material advantage or loss which results from a lawsuit is unimportant to those involved; but that since the particular intensity of quarrels of this sort is generated not only by material self-interest but by the identification of the individual with his property and his relative prestige in the community, the inadequacy of the legal mechanism in these cases allows him to maintain his self-esteem and defend his reputation, even while losing his case.

The sanctions which are applied by the lawcourts (usually a choice between a fine and imprisonment) are therefore not by any

[1] See Appendix II on Land Tenure.

means inevitably limited to the guilty party; and, indeed, recognizing that in matters of this sort there is often no clear-cut line to be drawn, the court frequently divides the penalty equally between litigant and defendant. Thus since it is known that both parties stand a good chance of losing, the penalties of the court appear less as a punishment for the particular crime that was committed in the village, than as a sanction against allowing the quarrel to progress to such lengths that the court becomes involved. The sanction is against quarrelling as such, rather than against the specific act which started the quarrel.

Other types of organized sanctions are limited. There is no resident policeman in the village, and though there are four types of civil servant, three of these have virtually no part to play in the structure of social control in the village.

Being a purely administrative figure, the president of the local council has no authority in the conduct of local village affairs in so far as these lie outside the sphere of the council and the edicts of the National Government with regard to propaganda and subversive political activities.

The function of the priest also in village eyes lies outside the sphere of moral exhortation, being one which is essentially mystical and ritual, and the priest is seen predominantly as the guardian of the mysteries of the Church and the means by which the liturgy and other holy offices are enacted. Apart from this, while it is thought that ideally the priest should also be a pillar of respectability and moral discretion, it is recognized that in the structure of daily village life it is virtually impossible for him to be this. The priest therefore is respected for the role he plays in the religious life of the villagers—for being the priest; but he is not given credit for any special moral pre-eminence, nor is it seriously expected that he should attain to it. The answers from two women, on being asked why the priest did not try to settle quarrels and to make the village live more peaceably, made his moral position as regards the villagers' daily life quite clear: 'If he came and said to us, "You must love one another and stop quarrelling", do you think anyone would listen to him?', and, 'Him? He's worse than us!'

The sphere of influence of the teacher is limited to the children and has no effect on village life as a whole—a situation which seems to contrast with earlier times when general illiteracy made the teacher a unique and potentially powerful member of the village community.

The only sanctions, then, which are applied within the village by an official, are the fines which are imposed by the village guard on his own initiative for damage done by straying animals, and as a result of this system the villagers are on the whole careful about keeping their animals off other people's crops. Such a man is known to be partial in his assessment of damages, since he is, like everyone else, involved in his own alliances and enmities; but although his judgement on any particular matter may be questioned at the local office in Kateríni, this is never done, on the grounds that this would cause him thereafter to hunt the offender mercilessly for every little trifle. Since such offences as dogs not being kept tied up, or hens being allowed to stray into other people's gardens, are continually being committed, it is within the power of the village guard to harass quite seriously the life of an enemy, and for this reason people prefer not to challenge his office too deeply.

Briefly to be mentioned here also is the body of ten men which used to be known as T.E.A. (*Τάγμα Ἑλληνικῆς Ἀσφαλείας*) but is now under the present regime named T.E. (*Τάγμα Ἐθνοφυλακῆς*) who are all armed and who are called out to keep the peace in the event of national danger. These men, known supporters of the Right, were called upon in April 1967 at the time of the *coup d'état*, and again during the attempted counter-coup headed by King Constantine in December of the same year, but are otherwise indistinguishable from others of the community and so far have had no cause to use their latent authority.

Since, therefore, organized sanctions from a civil authority are relatively rarely invoked, and even the verdicts of the Kateríni lawcourts are taken into the general network of village quarrels, the sanctions which enforce social order and conformity to the value system in the village are informal and diffuse. Mockery (*γέλοια*) has already been cited as chief of these, and has great power to enforce conformity to the accepted values because it can arise from the entire community (making the exception always of those close supporters of the person who is mocked), and because its effect is to deprive the one mocked of that which he values most, his reputation. Other sanctions, such as the quarrel (*μάλωμα*), and the taking of umbrage (*κακιώνω* or *παραξηγῶ*), which are exercised by one individual or family against another, are also effective in enforcing a certain type of correct behaviour; but these, because they are individual and not communal, are feared less than general mockery, and also are less effective as a means of enforcing social control because they are used consciously to forward personal ends which may or may not be coincident with the highest values of society, rather than unconsciously to exact conformity to the highest ideal.

The motivation behind mockery is chiefly the desire to increase personal reputation, and a sense of self-esteem, at the expense of another's. As such, mockery springs from the same complex as curiosity, slander, accusation, quarrels, and so on. However, an inseparable element in this inflation of self-esteem is that, as they say, 'people like to laugh' (ὁ κόσμος θέλει νὰ γελάει), and this must be taken literally not just to indicate that people like to increase their reputation by destroying that of others, but also that people like to amuse themselves. Making fun of others is, given the wit and vividness of expression that these people possess, an unending source of real humour.

The total sanction implied by the word 'laughter', therefore, while being institutionalized as a general and predictable reaction by the community to certain types of offence, is not a formal type of satirical wit, but a generalized form of comment. In the case of malicious rumour it is very often a matter of chance as to whether it is believed or not, but because 'people like to laugh', they often find themselves quite capable of suspending their disbelief in the cause of their own entertainment. And where a particular action is no longer a matter for speculation but for outright judgement, mockery is inevitable from all but the close supporters of the person concerned, and, as it is said, 'All the world laughs' (ὅλος ὁ κόσμος γελάει). To avoid this painful and humiliating experience people will go to considerable lengths, either in conformity or in concealment, for as it was succinctly put to me, 'In the face of laughter one is ashamed.'

The particular power of mockery to destroy reputation lies in the relation of reputation to the respect of others. As has been argued, a man's reputation is granted to him by others—it is an external evaluation of an inner condition. For as long, then, as this evaluation is withheld or denied, a man's reputation ceases to exist. Sheer disapproval where it is not combined with mockery may yet be combined with a type of respect, but mockery and respect cannot coexist.

It follows from this that mockery must be analysed as being directed not against the human situation as such so much as against the individual human behaviour within the situation. Poverty, catastrophe, bereavement, ill luck, lack of judgement in business or farming are, in themselves, not funny, but are, even when they happen to an enemy, part of the human situation in which all find themselves. In this general context, because all the villagers realize that they too are in the hands of a fate which may dictate to them also a sudden reverse of fortune, they are not inclined to judge too harshly the situations of others. It is because of this that while the young widow, frequently blamed for her husband's death and gossiped about in comments such as 'Do you know what Voula is? She killed her husband with her wicked talk', is nevertheless even by her enemies sometimes sympathized with as they say, 'Misfortune overtook her, the poor thing.' The loose girl of the village, however, in whose case the situation and her behaviour within the situation are virtually synonymous, is never referred to in these terms, but is, at best, dismissed pityingly as 'the simple creature' (χαϊβανάκι).

In its extreme form, as judgement and condemnation, mockery is an index of how far the person has fallen away from the ideal. It follows therefore that where the roles are strictest and so where deviation from them is likely to be most apparent, the mockery will be the greatest.

It is for this reason that a widow, particularly a young widow, is the outstanding figure in the community who by reason of her role is the most open to mockery. In this case they laugh, not at her role, for her role protects her from laughter, but because any deviation from her role indicates that she is finding herself incapable of putting up with her situation. In a system of values such as the one described above it is virtually impossible for a woman in a widow's position not to deviate from the highest standard expected of her, and, in addition to this, she has the added misfortune of representing in an active form the most subversive element in society, that of sensuality. In her figure she epitomizes the sexual conflict between unrelated men and women, and as such is desired by all though available to none. She herself is known to be awakened to a sensuality which is neither controlled nor satisfied by a man, and in whom therefore quarrels, nervousness, bad temper, and excessive hostility are as indicative of sexual frustration as any kind of flirtatious behaviour, too much talk with men, and visiting strangers' houses.

It is in fact almost impossible to act such a role perfectly, and because of this it is frequently said, 'People laugh at widows' (τὶς γελᾶνε τὶς χῆρες). If a widow goes visiting the houses on a name-day, people laugh and say, 'What business has she got, to go round the houses looking for a man?', and when, after seven years' mourning, the young widow of Ambéli began leaving off her black stockings in summer time, the ironic comment from one woman was, 'Perhaps she wants to marry again.' When her field caught fire in the summer, this was immediately taken up in bawdy innuendo: 'Voula's field caught fire and she had terrible trouble putting it out', and speaking about her to a woman who was, *soi-disant*, a friend, I was told: 'Voula's all right, but—she's a widow.' In such a society where every slightest action has its significance and where correct behaviour is the vital pointer to a proper sense of shame, the severity of the widow's role (and in particular that of a young widow) and her relation to the sexuality which provides one of the chief sources of wit in the society make her a continual topic of speculation and mockery. As Voula said to me, referring to a particularly scurrilous story about her which was providing great amusement in the cafés: 'People want to laugh. Those who are my own kin won't believe, not any of them, but those who aren't turn it so that they can laugh.' And although in the normal course of events the old topics of mockery drop away from public interest and new ones appear, the widow they have always with them, and, with reference to her, new sources of mockery, real or invented, continually appear.

Although in respect of widows by far the greatest mockery centres round the young ones, that is to say those under fifty or so, even the older widows are not exempt from scurrilous comment. One widow of sixty-three who lives by herself told me that the community would laugh at her if she visited the houses on a name-day, and after the school-teacher had gone to live in her house for a few months it was said to me in an undertone by one woman: 'Xanthi's all right now, she's fixed herself up with the teacher.' However, the very fact that it was in principle permissible for the teacher to live in her house indicates how sharply the mockery attached to widows drops off after they have become, as they say, 'old women'.

I have dealt with mockery in relation to widows at some length since this is an extreme example of a situation in village life which consistently attracts scandal. A situation giving rise to still more scandal than that of a young widow is that of an immoral girl, but since this is an abnormal situation in so far as such a girl has, by her behaviour, put herself 'apart from the community', rather than as the widow being within the community but still open to mockery, it does not provide such a varied illustration of the way mockery works.

It was as a preventive mechanism that mockery is plainly the most effective agent for social control. 'Don't do such and such,' children are told, 'people will laugh' ($\gamma\varepsilon\lambda\acute{a}\varepsilon\iota$ $\acute{o}$ $\varkappa\acute{o}\sigma\mu o\varsigma$); one frequently hears people rejecting a possible course of action because they say people will laugh, or because they say, 'I am ashamed to', which amounts to the same thing. People are scrupulous in observing the niceties of relationships with those with whom they wish to remain on good terms—for instance sending round a plate of food in return for a gift previously offered, in case, as was said to me, the giver of the gift should laugh and say, 'Look at her, she doesn't know anything.' People will try to avoid quarrels, women and girls will be meticulous in their public deportment, private eccentricities will be sternly suppressed for fear of the community's mockery.

Mockery is incurred also not only by extreme deviations of behaviour but by anything that is out of the normal. People always go to church in their best clothes, feel compelled to have at least one new dress a year, try to conceal any extreme evidence of poverty—such as selling any of their rugs or dowry articles—for fear that people should laugh at them. It is in these cases that mockery is seen to cause not only emulation in a positive sense of the highest ideals of society, but also a rigorous control over behaviour in the minutest details. An example of this is seen in the behaviour of a woman who married into Ambéli from another village and has a beautiful voice, although she will never sing except at special festivities because she says, 'People will look at me and say, "Listen to the woman from Kastaniá singing" ', a comment which achieves the double aim of poking fun at her both for singing, and for being a stranger from a poor village. Another example of the way in which simple events are used as ammunition for mockery is seen in the self-reproach of a woman who on her way to a nearby village failed to notice that an embroidered blanket had fallen off her mule. Turning back to find it she said, 'I hope no one else finds it because they will laugh and say that we couldn't even get to Perachóri without losing a blanket.'

As a corrective measure, mockery is effective whenever a person is involved in a course of action from which he or she may draw back without losing face—as for instance in the case where a woman in mourning for her first cousin wore a dark yellow headscarf because it was more becoming to her, but changed it to the correct dark brown after she heard people were laughing at her. In many cases, however, such as for instance during a quarrel or the negotiations for an engagement, values such as self-esteem or self-interest and so on can all create a situation from which in spite of the mockery of the community it is impossible for the principals to withdraw. Here a conflict is created between the interests held in the particular situation with regard to the other party, and those which concern the community as a whole, and this particular conflict is beyond the power of mockery to resolve. It is in such cases, as well as in cases of an action discovered by the community which cannot be undone, that mockery becomes purely punitive.

Instances of punitive mockery occur in, for instance, the derision with which the entire community, with the exception only of her parents (for her first uncles, aunts, and cousins had long since given up the unequal struggle to be loyal),[1] viewed the behaviour of the girl who was notoriously lacking in shame; the scandal that swept the village when an engaged girl went to stay in her fiancé's house for periods of a fortnight at a time; and the gossip that inevitably accompanies a quarrel—in particular quarrels in which people have come to blows.

Even though mockery is a combined expression of disapproval and laughter, there are times when other values in the system cause a distinction to be drawn between these two elements. In situations for instance in which one person makes a fool of another, both parties may be said to be subverting the social order, one because he is exploiting, the other because he is allowing himself to be exploited. But because of the value placed, especially in the

---

[1] Even her cousins say of this girl that since all the advice they can give her is useless—because she pays no attention to it and even goes and tells the man concerned what they have said—they can do nothing else but laugh with the rest of the community.

present day, on cleverness (ἐξυπνάδα), and because of the centrality of stupidity (μονρλάδα) to the quality of shamelessness, it is, when it comes to the test, nearly always considered more admirable to be clever, in the sense of cunning (πονηρός), and to practise deceit, than it is to be stupid, in the sense of simple (ἀγαθός), and to think no evil. In cases, therefore, such as when a man managed to seduce a girl by means of promises of marriage and a trail of deceit, or when someone amused himself by (so it was said) arranging marriages for a friend of his and then breaking them, while the community's disapproval was aroused by the deceit, it was the fact of the leg-pull (κορόϊδο) which caused the most laughter. Indeed, such a man is said to say, 'What need have I of the community since I've found such easy game?!' Mockery therefore in cases of this sort chooses stupidity rather than cunning as its target, and thus, while being the predominant sanction, is not automatically invoked by every offence against the social code.

Mockery is also not an absolute sanction in the sense that even when the fear of mockery has failed and mockery itself is called down on some wrong-doer, it does not last for ever. The community gets weary and 'looks for other things to laugh at'. Honour is not normally lost, only damaged, and with the focusing of the community's interest on newer topics the old victims of the mockery have time to heal their wounds and look round for likely targets themselves.

Finally it must be emphasized that in spite of the pre-eminence of mockery as a means of social control, it must not be seen exclusively in this light, for since it is motivated by competition and hostility and since its overt motivation is not in fact a desire to secure the good life in the community but the need to find entertainment and to increase the mocker's sense of his own self-esteem at another's expense, it can become a double-edged weapon. There is a point at which the desire to mock gives rise to false stories about other people, and at this point mockery ceases to be an agent for social control and becomes yet another manifestation of hostility within the community which itself needs to be controlled.

Closely related to this search for laughter and the search to avoid being laughed at, is the double phenomenon of curiosity and secrecy in which all members of the community are trained from early youth.

Since everyone automatically suspects everyone else of concealing faults or of trying to deceive them in some way, it is the business of every family to find out as much as they can about others
by whatever means are available. Eaves-dropping, questioning,
checking the answers given by some with those given by others,
angling for information in various kinds of unobtrusive ways, are
all common means in this battle for knowledge that is never
ceasing. When there was doubt in the village as to whether an
engagement had been finally agreed or not, one woman incited me
to greet the family concerned with the phrase 'With health!' (*μὲ
γειά*), the proper formality on any auspicious occasion, in order to
see the reaction. Unwisely I did this, and the news was all round
the village in a few hours, together with the woman's cautious
answer, rejecting my greeting, 'We haven't arranged anything yet.'

Information is sought not just about the truth of events, but also
about the truthfulness of people regarding those events. A man
from Kateríni who brought some suitcases up for me one day on
his mule was seen in Ambéli by a villager, who later said to me: 'I
asked Thanassi what he had been doing—I knew of course—and
he said, "I've been taking the stranger up to Ambéli"!' A woman
one evening asked me where I was going, and I answered, 'To
Anna.' 'To eat?' 'Yes.' Later I found out that she had already
known that I was going to eat there, and that her question was
designed to find out whether I was going to lie rather than what I
was going to do.

The various kinds of motivation that can prompt questions of
this sort are well illustrated by the question invariably asked of
everyone who has seen a village girl's fiancé—'Is he good?' (*εἶναι
καλός;*), meaning 'What's he like? Is he well off? Is he good looking?' These are: (a) that they are curious about the man; (b) that
they are curious to know how one will react; (c) that they want to
hear that he is not good so that they will have something to talk
about, and (d) that they want to catch you out and get you to say
that he is not good so that they can then go to the person concerned
and make trouble.

In such a community, discretion in general obviously becomes a
paramount virtue, and discretion as regards the family, vital, and
for this reason children are trained in a secrecy which is all the
more essential because it is continually being tested by the outside
world, who see in a child's possible unwariness a good source of

information as to what is going on in the fastnesses of other houses. One evening I was in a house and the paraffin ran out, and the eldest boy, a child of eight, was sent to the café to get some more. As he was going he was told, 'If anyone asks you where you're going, say you're going to feed the animals. Say nothing else, see?' And when he returned he was asked by his mother: 'Who was in the café?' He told her. 'Did anyone ask you what company you had tonight?' 'No.' And a similar example occurred when two other women and I were sitting telling fortunes from cards, and the son of the house, aged ten, returning after a visit to another house, was asked, 'Did they say, "What is your mother doing?"' 'Yes,' he answered, adding ironically, 'and I said, "She's sitting playing cards".'

It is not just from a hostile community that secrets are kept, but also in certain cases from close kinsmen who are not in the same house, simply because it is recognized that complete security does not exist outside the family. However, the fact that relationships consist in telling people things about oneself as well as about others means that all but the most vital secrets eventually get confided to a relative, and it is this fact that causes the break-up of an otherwise intransigent situation in which curiosity and secrecy meet head on. Thus the lines of communication are kept open, and the sanction of mockery given the means by which to take effect.

It must be stressed here that loyalty to friends and kinsmen is an important value, and that, although there are innumerable cases in which someone promises faithfully not to say anything and then immediately goes and tells people, it is certainly not the case that in this society there is no lasting loyalty to anyone outside the elementary family. But what tends to happen, even where there is such loyalty between the people concerned, is that since information tends to be exchanged rather than given freely, since people can only gain credit for knowing things if they prove that they know them by passing them on, and since all in this community enjoy discussion of the events around them, they find it very difficult to guard a secret with complete fidelity. News about proposed marriages is often passed on in this way, with no idea of conscious betrayal, from mother to aunt, for instance, or to a relation by spiritual kinship, and so outwards through the community. Details of other events also tend for the same reasons to become disseminated piecemeal, in hints and comments, even though loyalty is observed to the extent of the information being angled with reference both to the family it concerns, and to the person who is receiving the information. Factors influencing what is said to the latter include the relationship of that person to the family about whom the information is concerned, the relationship of the family to the giver of the information, the amount and accuracy of the knowledge that that person is likely to have already, and so on. Over one match-making, for instance, the woman who was the sister of this particular girl's sister-in-law told me that the marriage was as good as arranged, and the only doubt in the girl's mind was whether the bridegroom was tall enough; at the same time she told her aunt that the negotiations were likely to fail because the girl did not like the positioning of the bridegroom's house in relation to the town. Months later, after she had quarrelled with this girl, she told me that what had prevented her from getting married was that she was so fat and ugly. While all these explanations might have had a grain of truth in them, the real explanation —if one is to believe most people in the village long after the event—was that the dowry offered by the girl's family was not large enough.

Confiding in friends is an even more dangerous process than confiding in relatives, because the extreme flexibility of this type of relationship makes it likely that the friendship will sooner or later suffer a setback or come to an end, and when this happens the secrets entrusted to either party when the relationship was good are all revealed, with a good deal of exaggeration and accusation, to an interested community. And even during the course of friendship the relationship may in general be unstable enough to provide no real security, while deep enough at moments to encourage the giving of confidences. One example of this occurred in the betrayal by one woman to another of a friend whose son shared with hers the same boarding house in Kateríni. This woman had become pregnant but did not want everyone to know, because she was preparing to have an abortion. However, she unwisely told this friend of hers who, within a few hours, was saying to someone else, 'Chrysanthi has eaten something. Something has happened to her. She's eaten too many beans.' And, on receiving no response to this, insisted with meaning, 'Something has happened to her, *I* think.' When I remonstrated with her over this blatant piece of mischief-making, she said, 'Chrysanthi is a fool. If she didn't want people to know she shouldn't have told anyone.' This is, of course, the literal truth.

Secrets must be kept not only by words but also by actions, for the public nature of village life makes it such that the villagers read the lives of others from signs and indications much as a hunter tracks an animal by its prints. Rice being bought at a shop indicates meat for a meal and therefore probably a visitor for lunch; a strange animal tied up outside means perhaps a prospective bridegroom for the daughter of the house; a girl away with her goats for longer than the customary time means an illicit rendezvous in the forest. The fact that appearances are taken to indicate the reality— that, as was said earlier, it is as important to be seen to be honour-able as it is to be honourable—means that excessive care must be taken not to give the wrong indications even though the action behind these indications may be perfectly innocent. It means also that if a secret is to be protected, false trails must be laid to side-track the curiosity of the community even before it has been aroused. A case in point is that of the priest who was acting as match-maker for a particular family. The prospective bridegroom was a mason from a nearby village, and so as to give the village nothing to speculate about, the two went to the café and there began to talk about prices and materials for reconditioning the church. After a while the priest got up saying, 'Come to my house and we'll discuss the matter further', and, relating this to me much later, said, 'So we deceived the community and they realized nothing.' It is relevant here also to mention that in Greek the word for 'to deceive' is the same as that meaning 'to laugh', $\gamma\epsilon\lambda\tilde{\omega}$, and may be interpreted freely as 'to have the laugh of'—an interesting indication which makes the connection between lies, deceit, mockery, and laughter still more apparent.

It is plainly only a short step from concealing secrets and causing people to make false assumptions about one's actions, to actually telling lies, and the phrase 'You can't live without lies' ($\delta\grave{\epsilon}\nu\ \zeta\tilde{\eta}\varsigma\ \chi\omega\varrho\grave{\iota}\varsigma\ \psi\acute{\epsilon}\mu\mu\alpha\tau\alpha$), which is universally current in the village, accu-rately sums up the situation.

The villager, therefore, finding that he lives in a world where it is impossible for him perpetually to live up to the high require-ments of the moral code, finds instead that very often his first concern is not how to keep up to these requirements, but how to fall short of them and not be found out. This is in fact difficult, because the curiosity of the community is such that any violation of the code is likely to be discovered unless the cover-up is fool-proof, and even then lies about matters important enough to be of interest to the total community are, in the last instance, usually revealed. But even in these extreme cases the wrong-doer's elaborate and whole-hearted attempt at concealment does do him some good, for his continual protestations of innocence, his probable accusation of someone else, and the fact that he will be supported in whatever he says by his close kin, will enable him to cast a smoke-screen over the proceedings and to preserve to some extent at any rate his self-esteem, if not his reputation.

Lies are not used only to conceal offences against the value system; they are used in all the various occasions of social life in which they are thought to be useful. They are used in order to trick an informant into giving some information which the questioner needs; they are told in order to take revenge on an enemy; to make trouble; to avoid giving offence; and are even used purely for fun as a sort of esoteric entertainment of which an example follows later. Nevertheless, in spite of the prevalence of lies in this society, and in spite of the concept of truth which accommodates such lying into the demands of the value system, lying is itself subject also to a form of social control. Since within this system of honour and shame there exists also an ideal code of behaviour with reference to which lying, cheating, gossiping, and so on are all considered undesirable, these things are, within the framework of the values in which they occur, self-limiting. The inveterate gossip is disapproved of, the incorrigible liar is no longer believed, the cheat is made to feel ashamed. In this way these are all mechanisms which carry their own sanctions, and which therefore, when they are in danger of causing a greater disruption than society can bear, simply collapse under their own weight. Not only is the lie an ineffective way of sheltering the liar from the community's mockery but also the community, although it likes to laugh, has a good deal of common sense and tends to know roughly the likelihoods of each situation, even though the standards according to which each person judges that situation will vary in accordance with his particular alignment at the time. So neither the defensive nor the slanderous lie has unlimited power, and, in the case of the latter, the network of kinsmen and supporters around any particular victim of slander helps to produce a situation in which an equilibrium between the victim and the community is kept.

Lying is thus a phenomenon which is built into the structure of social relations, and is a vital safety-valve for the tensions that would otherwise accumulate under the pressure of an ideal code and the eagle eyes of an inquisitive community. And the way in which the villager personally relates to his lying, being culturally conditioned by the same context that produces the lie, produces no disharmony between himself and his understanding of his own honour. In spite of this, however, it is not that the villager is unaware of the difference between telling the truth and telling a lie—as is revealed by his use of the phase 'I told a lie' ($\varepsilon \tilde{\imath} \pi a \ \psi \acute{\varepsilon} \mu \mu a$). It is that truth for him has many manifestations, and a lie on one level may legitimately be accepted as a way of revealing a truth on a higher level. It is, if one may put it like this, the appearance (which may be contingently false) revealing the reality (which is essentially true). The villager knows he may be sinning as he lies, but he is certain also that his enemy of the moment is a far greater liar then he. He knows that the truth is a value, and that according to the standards of ecclesiastical exhortation he 'ought' not to tell lies. At the same time he knows that absolute truth is to be found only in Christ and in the divine world on which human life depends, and that the nearest he can get to this absolute truth himself is by means of his house and family which enshrine and reflect, albeit in an imperfect and fragmented form, this absolute. He is therefore compelled, by the overwhelming reality of his daily experience, to count lying as a sin far more venial than that of failing in the defence of his house or in the particular social and spiritual values with which his house is, temporarily or permanently, involved.

Although the number and inventiveness of the lies of this society prohibit their classification into watertight compartments, they fall for the main part into a series of types. The following analysis therefore adopts such a method, even while it is recognized that in certain instances one type of lie will overlap with another.

One of the principal lies is that told to conceal some failure of an individual or his family to live up to the highest requirements of the social code. These failures can be intentional or unintentional, and encompass a vast range of social action. Minor but deliberate lapses include such things as being forced to sell some household article in order to raise ready cash; or skimping, through overwork and great haste, on the proper procedure for baking, cheese-making, cooking, or washing. Such lapses are, if possible, kept concealed from the public, for every woman knows that the over-critical eyes of outsiders will seize on any chance to laugh at her for not being able to manage her house properly. A different type of failure, intentionally committed out of personal desire and impatience with the restrictions of the value system, consists of such things as casting beans or playing cards in order to tell fortunes, gossiping about someone or betraying a confidence, behaving unchastely, failing to observe mourning customs or breaking a religious prohibition, and so on. On one occasion a woman boasted to me of how, by urging on her horse, she had left behind a party of people on their way to Kateríni, and had been the first to greet a new baby. All things being equal, the first person to do this is normally taken as godparent, and this woman was duly accepted. However, the woman's brother-in-law's un-married sister had been in the party, and the woman herself had by the girl's mother been put in charge of her. In leaving the party therefore she had committed a double sin, in breaking the com-pany (παρέα), a thing normally never done, and also in failing to chaperone this girl adequately. A quarrel of gigantic dimensions blew up afterwards, and the next I heard of this story was the woman indignantly informing me that it had not been possible for her to remain behind with the party because she had a high-spirited mare and had not been able to hold it. This story she put out to the community also, and was supported in it by her close relatives.

Lies to conceal unintentional failures are also common, and occur frequently in situations relating to match-making, where an attempt by a son or a daughter of the house has failed, and more rarely in situations where a man's ego has been wounded on account of rejection by some woman. Carelessness, loss, or un-intentional stupidity are also always, if possible, concealed. The question of marriage is a particularly sensitive one and crucially associated with family honour, especially as regards girls, for since the points on which an engagement stands or falls are the beauty and reputation of the bride and the size of the dowry, the failure of a girl's attempt to marry impugns both the honour and beauty of the girl and the economic stability of the house. In the event, therefore, of a girl being turned down, the effort is always to make it known that in fact the girl has turned the man down—he was balding, he had sunken eyes, he had scaly hands, the bride would have had too much work to do, the gardens were too far away, and so on. If, however, the community cannot be prevented from finding out that in fact it was the man who had turned the girl down, it is then said that someone in the community slandered her unjustly.

A third category of lies is those attacking others by false imputation. The power of this particular sort of lie is considerable, particularly with respect to questions such as marriage, simply because, as has been argued already, a woman's reputation is not something she possesses by virtue of her being honourable so much as something she is given by the community by virtue of the fact that she is seen to be honourable. The community then is always at liberty to say, as two women did of an apparently virtuous girl who had just got engaged, 'She pretends to be good.' And indeed in a community where the expression 'How do *I* know what *she* is?' is so frequently heard and so representative of the truth, it is easily seen that this distrust of the motives and actions of others is a genuine phenomenon which is related to the fact that the honour of another is not as apparent to the individual as his own honour, and that therefore anything might in fact be true of that other even though nothing is actually manifest.

This basic scepticism about the characters of others, the necessity for a girl's behaviour to have been more than impeccable if she is not to have even one slanderer, and the general desire of the community in any event to mock, causes a situation in which, so they say, not one engagement can take place without someone slandering the particular girl involved. I was told: 'If they can't say that the girl has been with a man, if she stays inside all the time, they will say that she is lazy, or that she is ill. If she goes out and talks to people in the road they will say that she is loose and that she talks to all and sundry. Something can be found, even if the girl is an angel. Why? People want to laugh. They break the engagement and they sit back and say, "*Now* what is she going to do?" '

The slanderous lie automatically breeds a further type which is that to avoid trouble or quarrels. The essence of gossip is that it is behind the back of the one gossiped about. Face to face that gossip becomes an insult, and a quarrel is then inevitable. The form that such gossip takes is often, for example, for two women, A and B, to criticize a third, C. Later, on reflection, A for instance realizes either that the other will probably betray her, or that she has in her hands a good means of stirring up trouble, and for either reason or for a mixture of both, will go to C and tell her all that has been said, imputing it all to B. The excuse given for this sort of report is a spurious loyalty of the order: 'You ought to know that . . .' In any event, C will then go to B and confront her with it, on which B, if she does not want a quarrel, will either deny having said anything, or else say that A said it all.

This situation has a number of permutations, but this is the basic pattern. The value of the lie here is that if everyone lies enough about what has been said, or who has said what, no one will have to apologize and the subject of the gossip will be relieved of the necessity to have a quarrel with either. She will in her own mind come to some conclusion as to what she thinks the truth of the situation is, but the denial of all parties to have said what has been said will calm down the situation until time has passed and the whole thing been forgotten. Everyone's face will have been saved, and 'words', the real consolidator of quarrels, will not have been said.

It may be seen from this that in one incident there may occur various different types of lie, and that the categorization attempted here must not be taken as exclusive. In the situation described above the impetus for repeating to a person what has been said about him by another is not always an instinct for self-protection against a similar accusation, but often the sheer desire to make trouble; and this kind of report is often bedevilled by the fact that the person reporting it may have invented a great deal. As such, this type of lie may be included under the previous heading as a type of slanderous lie.

This type of lie, that to avoid trouble, often occurs also when an individual finds himself in a situation of conflicting obligations —for instance the obligation to help a neighbour at the same time as preserving some commodity for the use of the family. In a situation such as this, therefore, it avoids insult to a neighbour and preserves the owner's reputation, as well as serving the family's interest, to say that there is none left, rather than that there is some but that she will not give it. The same situation also occurs in reconciling a proper sense of obligation with self-interest, as I saw when going with a certain woman to another village, when just as we were leaving, another woman asked us if we would wait while she went and fetched something she wanted us to take with us. 'We'll be going next week', said my companion, and the other woman was satisfied. Later I asked her, 'Are you really going next week?' 'No.' 'Then why say so?' 'It was a lie. You can't tell the truth all the time.' 'What will you say to her next week?' 'I'll say I changed my mind.' 'Did she know when you said that you were going next week that you were lying?' 'No.'

Self-interest takes a more illicit turn when it comes to a question of lying for material gain. Cheating on a deal, pretending a mule is younger than it is, is justified according to the idea that cunning is one of the virtues of a clever man and a good provider, and on the grounds that everyone cheats everyone else, the clever man cheats the stupid, and that's the way the world goes round. However, cheating, out of the context of a financial deal, simply to acquire something without giving some sort of return, is not considered admirable, and stealing is something which is now regarded with universal disgust and condemnation.[1] Giving false witness at a trial, however, comes under a different sort of judgement. As has been said earlier, by the time a quarrel over boundaries has reached the court, the actual rights and wrongs of the case have become deeply confused, and the case is much more concerned with vindicating the honour of the rival parties than with the facts of the original dispute. Giving false witness therefore, in so far as a man is laying claim to land that is not his own, is simply part of the general struggle for prestige, and as such is, of course, never admitted by either party, and continually indulged in. There is, however, a sin involved, not because the false witness is attempting to take a man's rightful property from him but because he has to lay his hand on the Bible and take an oath which he has no intention of keeping.

There are also lies for sheer concealment, with no particular

[1] This is to say theft of movables. 'Theft', or appropriation, of a field or a pine and, by extension, of wood, is in village thinking a different kind of offence, and one of the last types of the lawlessness of the old days still to be validated by customary village practice.

motive except a love of secrecy and a fear of the unknown power
of the community. The need for the lie here, as in other cases, is
generated not so much by the love of lying, as by the need for
secrecy in the face of the ruthless curiosity of others. If no one
asked what people were doing, there would be no need to lie. But
since everyone always asks, for instance, children what their
mothers are doing, from childhood up people learn to counter
with a convincing lie. This confuses the inquirer at the same time
as avoiding the insult—'I won't tell you.'

This lie to conceal is allied with the lie which is told purely out
of mischief, to confuse the authorities (as in the case of the man
who, when asked for information on a certain piece of land that
had been sold for 15,000 drachmas to someone he did not even
know well, said, on the spur of the moment, '5,000 drachmas'),
or to have private fun at the expense of others. I was an onlooker
at an extraordinary joke where one woman, Dimitra, pretended to
steal some flowers belonging to another woman, Frossou, and
where the two of them elaborated on this action over a period of
days to see if a mutual relative living next door would come and
betray her. 'If she doesn't come,' said Frossou, 'I'll say, "I wonder
who can possibly have taken my flowers? I had two pots here
before, and now there is only one." ' I asked what was the proper
course of action for this woman to take, and was told, 'Not to
speak at all, if she is good.' Of course she did come running round
straight away, and the apparent victim of the theft pretended to be
very angry and went round to everyone saying how awful it was
that Dimitra had come and taken her flowers without asking her.
Dimitra's scornful comment on the whole thing afterwards was
'Thus we make fools of them all.'

There was, however, an additional motive for this joke, and
that was as a way of resolving a situation in which two people
wanted the flowers but in which only one could have them.
Dimitra was Frossou's second cousin, whereas the other woman,
the one who figures in the betrayal, was Frossou's husband's
sister. It was therefore in favour of the latter that Frossou's
obligation lay. Since she did not want to give the flowers to her,
but preferred to give them to Dimitra, they concocted between
them this way round the situation, as a result of which, as Dimitra
said, 'I kept the flowers and my aunt didn't take offence with
Frossou.'

Finally there is a very large category of lies which are undertaken out of absolute necessity—those told in defence of a friend or a kinsman. Here the obligation, though not categorical, is strict, particularly if good relations need to be maintained. The community will try to find out certain things from one person about another, and there are often only two courses open in such a case—to betray, or to lie. Only one example need be cited here, and this concerns my going down to Kateríni to tape-record two women singing some church music. These women were at the time in the second year of the five-year period of prescribed mourning for their mother, while, for thirteen years previously, custom had prohibited them from any secular singing, as after a five-year period of mourning for their father's death, their mother had been taken seriously ill and had remained so for the eight years until her death. By this time it was natural that they should have got impatient with some of the customs of formal sorrow, and since they were both good singers they sang me, in a low voice so that no outsiders should hear, a number of demotic songs. On my return to Ambéli I went to supper with a certain family, who asked me where I had been. I answered that I had been to Kateríni to tape-record Anna and Zoitza singing the Petition to the Mother of God (*Παράκλησις*). Immediately, scenting scandal, they asked, 'Did they sing you any songs?' 'Of course not', I replied in automatic defence; 'they are in mourning.'

This last type of lie—the lie as part of the network of friendship and obligation—is far-reaching and extends into the field of official relations and patronage, carrying with it the built-in understanding that a friend supports one's interests, right or wrong. Non-support in many cases equals in the other's mind non-fulfilment of an obligation; at the very least it is important for a friend or relation to conceal if necessary the actions of those he is friendly with, and to support them in their particular version of any incident in which they are currently involved. A friend who fails to do these minimal things is no friend.

Some structural implications of the lie as it occurs in Ambéli may therefore be summarized as follows:

The lie reconciles the need of the individual to be an individual and to break the code on occasions, with the need for subscription to the moral code which is vital if the code is to survive. In this case, actual violation of the code does not question or invalidate it, because verbal subscription to it reaffirms its centrality to village life.

Where the lie conceals some unavoidable failure of the family to live up to the highest requirements of honour, it acts as a mediator between the situation of the individual and the code of the community.

Where it occurs as a denial, overt or implicit, of intent to offend, it acts as a mechanism to break a deadlock without violence, and by minimizing the totality of the confrontation it allows both parties to escape from the situation without either quarrelling or compromising their honour.

Finally, the lie as a mechanism for sheer concealment for the sake of concealment, or in the cause of non-betrayal of a friend, serves a vital function in reconciling the need for individual families of the community to lead a private life, with the sanctions (curiosity leading to mockery) which must operate if the moral code is to have force.

It would obviously be unrealistic to argue that the lie has a solely constructive function in Ambéli, for, as many of the examples quoted above show, it is responsible for a large measure of disruption, quarrelling, and unhappiness. However, it is true to say that even in the case of the most vicious lying, that of slander, it is possible that the need of the individual to put himself or herself above the reach of even the most malicious enemy is a factor which helps to maintain behaviour at something approximating to the high standards that society ideally demands. And it is also incontestable that, given the other components of society, the lie plays a vital part in mediating relations between the individual and the community, and that in doing so it helps to promote the continued validity of the moral code of honour and shame which would otherwise either break under its own inherent contradictions, or be broken by the villager's inability to conform to it.

IX

GOSSIP, FRIENDSHIP AND QUARRELS

THE medium by which all these quarrels, accusations, counter-accusations, self-justifications, lies, and innuendoes reach the community, is that of gossip, although gossip is a term which may be by no means limited entirely to discussion of these things. Gossip is both the means of mockery and the mockery itself, although it is not only these.

Although the word used in Ambéli for gossip is one which is used generally in demotic Greek—*κουτσομπολιό*,[1] its connotation extends in the village beyond the dictionary definition[2] where it is linked solely with criticism, accusation, slander, and speaking ill of others. In Ambéli, gossip implies almost any discussion of other people's actions behind their backs, for it can, according to the context and the intention, cover speculation, hypothesis, and the search for information, as well as condemnation and abuse. There are of course varying degrees of gossip—some, including slander, so blatant that the gossipers themselves recognize at the time what they are doing; others more fortuitous and more dependent on circumstance and interpretation for their classification as 'gossip' rather than as 'conversation' (*κουβέντα*). However, because of the public nature of life in the village, a great deal of the talk is about other people, and a great deal of this talk about other people is termed by them, if they get to hear of it, as 'gossip', even if it is not directly concerned with criticism and abuse. It is helpful also to remember that because the individual draws his

---

[1] *κουτσομπολιό*. One possible etymology is given by Ν. Π. Ἀνδριώτη, Ἐτυμολογικὸ Λεξικὸ τῆς Κοινῆς Νεοελληνικῆς, Athens, 1951, as being from *κόψω* to cut, and *μπολιάζω*, to graft, thus meaning the cutting up and piecing together of reputations. In my opinion, however, a more likely etymology is from *κουτσός* meaning lame, and *μπολιάζω*. *Κουτσο-* is often used as a prefix and the compound it forms is invariably given the implication of being limping, imperfect, deficient. If this etymology is right, then gossip implies a false or one-sided piecing together of conclusions.

[2] Δ. Δημητράκου. Μέγα Λεξικὸν τῆς Ἑλληνικῆς Γλώσσης, Athens and Thessalonika, 1951, s.v. *κουτσομπολ* (ε)*ιό: ἐπίκρισις τοῦ ἀλλοτρίου βίου, ἔμμεσος κατηγορία, κακολογία.*

identity more from his relevance to a particular group than from his own essential individuality, the concept of talking about others must be extended from the concept of an individual talking about other individuals, to that of a member of a group talking about other members of a group.

The essentially pejorative nature of apparently innocent talk in Ambéli is the result of the continual battle between secrecy and curiosity that is waged between the various families, for where there is a high value on secrecy, any attempt to violate this secrecy is seen as a manifestation of hostility. This was clearly shown when the second cousin of a girl who had just got engaged was sharply criticized for 'gossiping about her relation', when all she had done was to be overheard asking someone whether they had seen the bridegroom. The explanation of this criticism, however, lay in the fact that the girl's question was, as indeed are all questions of this sort, deeply disingenuous. In this case there had been considerable speculation about the dowry and the strength of the relative interests within the family, since it included the girl, the parents of the girl, and a married son who, it was thought, was trying to prevent too much money leaving the family. Other potential bridegrooms had apparently been lost to this family because of lack of agreement over the dowry. The fact that the girl was not only very fat but also twenty-seven years old, which is old for marriage in Ambéli, added to the degree of speculation and malicious comment that inevitably accompanies any negotiations for a marriage, and all the village was 'bursting' to find out exactly what was happening and why it was happening and what inferences could be drawn about it all. Any further piece of information, therefore, was avidly sought so that it could be added to those facts already garnered and the entire picture slowly pieced together. In such a situation any inquisitiveness about the bridegroom could be interpreted, and rightly so, as a heavily loaded question.

Because gossip is against the interests of those talked about, it naturally takes place behind their backs. Where criticism is given as personal and considered advice it is quite a different phenomenon, and hostility expressed directly to the person concerned is an insult (προσβολή) and is recognized as such, for the innuendo which is subtle enough to be made directly to the person concerned without giving grounds for offence does not occur here as a feature of gossip. Such insult in Ambéli invariably results in a quarrel. But while it is one of the normal advantages of gossip that it enables free criticism of others while avoiding quarrels, there is always an element of danger in gossiping, for, as has been shown already, few people are totally dependable and things usually tend to leak out somehow. In addition to this, the community is not lacking in people who reverse the normal privacy of gossip and, having taken part in a critical or scandalous conversation about someone else, then go straight to the subject of the conversation and repeat what has been said.

There is one sub-distinction of gossip which must be made because the villagers themselves make it, and that is the distinction between the main body of gossip, and slander (*κατηγορία*). The word 'slander' is most frequently heard in the context of match-making, where the act of slander consists in going deliberately to a third party and speaking evil of the man or the girl concerned. It is also heard, though less frequently, in cases where one person denigrates another to a third party from a different village, where the motive behind the slander is more likely to be an unconsidered manifestation of competitiveness, or even an inclination to wit, rather than particular intent to damage. Slander therefore refers to deliberate and gratuitous abuse of a fellow villager to an outsider, or to talk which has specific intent to damage, rather than to the ramifications of scandalous reference that crop up in so many intra-village conversations. Slander is recognized as being particularly vicious and is thought of as serious since it involves the conscious will to harm another human being.

Slanderous innuendo is not classified as such by the villagers, and when they refer to it they think of it more as a type of gossip than as slander—as a fault rather than a sin. It is a method useful in a society where everyone feels the need at times to denigrate others but where most wish to avoid the repercussions which can accompany such denigration, for by innuendo the speaker may sow the seeds of doubt while not actually implicating himself or herself in the act of slander. Some people are brilliant at it. An example of it has already been given where reference to eating beans was an indication of pregnancy. Another example occurred on the occasion of a girl from Ambéli marrying into another village. Talking to someone from the girl's new village, a woman from Ambéli commented: 'You've taken the best girl from us, the

best. She's a good girl that one, the best of them all.' The tone of
voice she used was not one of outright irony, nor even one to
invite disbelief, yet in spite of this the falsity of the statement was
beyond doubt; and in fact the speaker had told me some time
earlier that this particular girl was thought by everyone to have
had an affair with a fellow villager who had then gone overseas.
The sort of comment also, such as 'Poppy has gone to Kateríni
with the teacher', is one which may be defended by the speaker
as innocent, and yet which holds all the overtones of slanderous
accusation.

The character of gossip in Ambéli is determined by the various
features of the society—the nature of the value system, the
importance of a limited number of roles which express these
values and which provide ideal standards of behaviour, the privacy
of the home, the publicity of communal life, the intense relevance
of every member of the community to every other member, and
the unceasing competition for reputation. It is consistent also
with these conditions for gossip that it is an activity indulged in
pre-eminently by women.

   This is not to say that men do not gossip, nor that a man may
not be known as a 'gossip', but that the spheres of activity and
leisure in which men pass much of their time are not so conducive
to gossip as are those of the women, and that therefore their ability
to gossip is more limited. The café is indeed a place where much
information is exchanged and learned, but because of the publicity
of the café it is not normally a suitable environment for the detailed
discussion of this information which is a vital part of gossip, and
which takes place in the privacy of the home. After this detailed
examination it may happen that a subject of gossip, if it is suffi-
ciently interesting, is taken by the men back to the café where it
will reach the dimensions of a general discussion when those most
intimately concerned with the incident are not present. Thus there
are occasions on which the men take over from the various individual circles of gossip and provide a kind of community judgement. However, the fact that the male range of interests includes
business, economics, and politics, and that the men's experience
has in many cases included active service and travel abroad, gives
to their conversation a flavour which removes much of it from the
sphere of gossip; while the women, thrown by the nature of their

lives and interests on to the resources of their immediate sur-
roundings, are inexorably channelled into observation and
criticism of their neighbours. Men gossip, but women are thought
to do nothing but gossip.

Gossip is not only encouraged by the social environment in
which people live: it is made inevitable by it, and it is in fact more
or less impossible for any group of women who share a common
background and a number of mutual acquaintances to meet and
talk for any length of time without falling into it. The vivid
memory and graphic mind of the villager, coupled with a natural
philosophy which sees the working of superhuman forces or a
supernatural law revealed continually in the doings of others, give
to talk even about neutral subjects the remorseless tendency to
turn into talk about personalities; and this was well illustrated by
an incident in which the priest, meeting a few women going to
spend the night in a chapel dedicated to the Mother of God,
scolded them roundly and told them that they had no business to
celebrate Her feast by gossiping the night away in the chapel.
The women protested that they were going with the utmost piety
and had no thought of gossiping at all, to which the priest replied:
'What do you think you'll do? You don't know how to chant,
you'll do nothing but gossip.' They continued on their way,
grumbling and indignant, but, five minutes after they had settled
down in the chapel with some women from another village, conversation about various personalities and events began and only
ceased when the talkers fell into an exhausted sleep some time
after midnight.

It seems therefore a mistake to explain gossip, as has been
done,[1] in terms of fundamentally 'purposive behaviour', since the
motivation of gossip is not always conscious and does not always
lie in a 'purpose'. Gossip in Ambéli is a socially determined way of
talking, and this is a fact about gossip more fundamental than the
fact that, within this way of talking, certain very specific ends
may be achieved. It must also be added that in a society where
there is no cinema, no chance of dressing up and 'going out', no
concerts, books, theatres, or television—in fact no form of prepared entertainment at all, except for a radio which not all houses
possess—it is natural that people should instead derive their

[1] See R. Paine, 'What is Gossip About? An Alternative Hypothesis', *Man*
Vol. II, No. 2, 1967, pp. 278–85.

entertainment from the human comedy around them. One characteristic about much of the gossip of Ambéli is that it is very funny, and a characteristic of the people who indulge in it is that they have an acute wit and a great sense of the ludicrous.

Because gossip is inevitable, people often find themselves gossiping when they did not intend to, and are much more conscious that 'others' gossip than that they do themselves. Relatives do gossip about one another even though they should not, and so do friends. The offence to the one gossiped about may be great, but the gossiper is often at the time unaware of exactly what he or she is doing, although sometimes belated awareness of the enormity of what has been said may cause the gossiper to go to the person to whom they have gossiped and beseech his or her silence. 'The words escaped me' (μοῦ 'φύγαν τὰ λόγια), is the justification often given on these occasions. It is only the categorical obligations of family ties that unequivocally defeat the process of gossip in which the villagers normally find themselves caught up, for, in the context of the family, an act of disloyalty to the family is an act of disloyalty to the self, and therefore for anyone to gossip about his family is tantamount to self-destruction.

The fact that people are often unaware of the degree of malice in their conversation, or of the inevitability with which innocent conversations will turn to gossip, does not, however, mean that they do not realize in principle that gossip nearly always accompanies any group; and in cases where their own self-interest or reputation is at stake they are highly sensitive to the dangers of interested parties meeting and talking. Everyone in fact knows that sooner or later everything gets talked about, usually with derogatory inference, and with 'a lie or two added as well', and although they take what care they can to prevent such talk, and are likely to receive specific news of it with fury, they accept in principle the inevitability of gossip about themselves, as about others, with philosophic resignation. One day I had heard that certain people were suspecting me of having had influence with the judge in a particular lawsuit, and of having got the defendant off with a light sentence. The grounds for suspicion were that I was on good terms with the defendant's wife, and that I had attended this particular lawsuit. I was complaining about this to the young widow, who suffered a great deal from gossip herself, and I said that it was all very difficult. 'It's not difficult', she answered. 'It's how it is. People like to talk.'

Since, in such a community, everyone knows everyone else so well, people know exactly where to go to extract certain bits of information, and they know equally well the danger points of the community where a leak could be fatal. It is along the lines of relationship or friendship that the gossip channel normally runs, and precautions where relevant are duly taken, such as warning someone, 'Don't tell Artemis, because she will tell Maria and Maria will tell Ioanna and Ioanna will tell everyone else';[1] or, 'Don't tell Maria, because she will tell Petros and Petros will repeat it in the café, and Vassili will hear it and repeat it to his mother, and then there really will be trouble.'[2] Alternatively these weak points may be used by someone who wants to circulate some bit of information, as the following example shows. This conversation concerned a particularly scandalous assertion about the fiancée (from a village in the plain) of a recently engaged villager from Ambéli:

Panayiota: 'It doesn't matter if you tell people, only don't say it came from me.'

Aliki: 'I won't tell anyone, and of course I won't say it came from you.'

Panayiota (finally, in desperation): 'Tell the community so that the whole village may learn.'

Aliki: 'I'll tell Ioanna, and then everyone will hear about it. I'll say that it came from the plains, that I learned it in another village.'

As can be seen from the above examples, there is no one specific gossip channel, except for the ever-recurrent Ioanna who can be relied upon to tell everybody everything. However, there are certain patterns of relationship which are known about, and there are certain dependable sources of information to which people may go when other informants fail. People will go to the godmother, or aunt, of a girl thought to be thinking of an engagement, or perhaps they will go to Vangellio, the lame dressmaker, who never gets out of the house but who is on good terms with many of the villagers and who learns the news as soon as anyone. Once a secret

[1] The gossip channel here runs: listener to friend, she to another friend, friend to second cousin, second cousin to the community.

[2] The gossip channel here runs: listener to friend, she to her husband, husband to the general public in the café, and son to mother. Both this example and the former one are direct translations of warnings given to me not to divulge a certain piece of information.

is let out of the family there is little chance that it will not, sooner or later, be circulated among the entire community. This fact, irritating as it is to those who wish to keep their affairs private, is nevertheless made use of by them when they wish to find out about others or to circulate their own version of a particular event.

It is in the privacy of the house that most gossiping is done, or, in summer and autumn, in little groups that gather round the doorways. The occasions for gossip outside the house used to be much more frequent than they are now, since the old way of life involved many processes of work which entailed the gathering of groups of people. The threshing of the wheat has already been mentioned; at the mills in the ravines men and women would talk for hours waiting for their flour to be ready or for a rug to be properly steeped and felted; the long processes of cleaning and carding wool, spinning and twisting it, would be done, in the colder weather when farm work was less demanding, by groups of women who would sit until late at night around big fires which would be lit in various neighbourhoods of the village. Here also they would work on the endless preparation of dowries, telling folk tales, relating village lore about herbs, cures, and divinations, discussing the histories of the past, and the dramas of the present. There was a lot of work to be done and many people to do it, and they did it in company. In the present day, more sophisticated techniques of work, the loss of so much of the population, and the increasing isolation of the families from one another bring it about that, except in the cafés, it is becoming more and more rare to find groups of unrelated people meeting and talking. However, one such occasion still persists: the eventual encounter of every member of the village with every other at the fountain. Here the men will pass by briefly to water their animals, but the women will gather, waiting for their water jars to fill, to rinse their washing, to clean their vegetables, and beat their rugs free of mud and ash by the method known as 'thumping' (κοπάνισμα). In 1966, after an exceptionally dry summer, the water in the cistern which lies behind the water sources had almost dried up, producing only a small stream from the centre channel. Here everyone would have to wait for up to half an hour to get one bucket of water, and for nights on end could be heard the chatter of women, the sloshing of water, and the scrubbing of brushes as the entire village, little by little, cleaned out the old wine barrels ready for the grape harvest. Thus in the present day it is the fountain alone which provides the women with the means of meeting and chatting with people whom they would not otherwise encounter, and private discussions of some length are possible between two women if there are no other people around, especially if they block up the water channels so that the water does not deafen them, and stoop down low over their work, talking rapidly in quiet voices.

One way or another, therefore, although the pattern of work in the village does not favour the general and communal exchange of information in the way it used to, there are still opportunities, outside the normal pattern of visiting and friendship, for people to meet and talk, and they are opportunities that are fully used.

The inevitability of gossip in the restricted and intimate life of Ambéli, and the damage it does by severing relationships and fragmenting still further an already dwindling community, are acknowledged and lamented by the villagers who refer to it as the product of 'hatred' ($\mu\bar{\iota}\sigma\sigma\varsigma$, more properly translated here as hostility) and attribute it categorically to the work of the Devil. However, since it is thus recognized to be a manifestation of something which, if unchecked, would destroy the community, it automatically carries its own sanctions.

One sanction against excessive gossiping is simply the general disapproval of the person who gossips too much. To be called a 'gossip', however, is a common accusation in the village, since everyone gossips 'too much' in the opinion of others, and thus this accusation has little inhibitory effect. However, where there is a tendency for gossip to be too extreme or too implausible, the community laughter is not with the gossiper but against him, and this laughter, although it cannot control the inveterate gossip, undoubtedly acts to curb the tongues of those who are more socially sensitive.

A more effective sanction against excessive gossiping is the quarrel, for although gossip is by definition behind the backs of those gossiped about, it is not self-contained, and the hostility which gives rise to gossip, together with the indeterminate loyalties of extra-familial life and an ill-placed sense of amusement, also gives rise to the tale-teller. Reasons for betrayal are usually to make trouble—to stir the pot and enjoy the scenes that result, to make the one who has been gossiped about 'burst', that is to say be angry and aggrieved; or, as has been illustrated earlier, to cast the blame for gossip in which the tale-teller has had a part but about which she has suddenly become nervous, on to a third party. When this happens, the offended person will, if the type of gossip permits, go to the person who has gossiped about her and accuse her. If the inevitable denial of the gossip, or the attempt to throw the blame on someone else, fails, then a quarrel follows. These types of confrontation are very common in village life, and the only cases in which it is difficult for the object of the gossip to go to the gossiper, occur when the talk is about sexual misconduct on the part of a widow or an unmarried girl, for here the victim normally preserves more honour by remaining silent than by going and provoking a quarrel.

One final way in which gossip can get back to its victim is through a well-disposed friend or relative. However, since the object here is not to cause a quarrel but to inform the person about what is going on and to advise them of a proper course of action, the immediate furious reaction on hearing of such gossip is often, though not always, forestalled, and a quarrel avoided.

It is of course impossible to tell how far the fear of betrayal and reprisal limits the amount and the type of gossip. It is very likely that it inhibits the amount of scandal that goes on over negotiations for an engagement, though it does not totally check it; and it is likely too that it limits much really destructive gossip to the family group where each member is certain that he will not be repeated. To this extent, then, fear of a quarrel may be said to limit some of the more destructive types of gossip, either by quelling it entirely, or by confining it completely to intimate groups where it fails to develop into public scandal or to do any effective damage. However, this is only a very partial control, and the amount of people in Ambéli at any one time who are not speaking to each other testifies to the fact that the quarrel is as much a punitive as a preventive sanction in the case of gossip.

There is, however, a functional aspect of gossip which goes entirely unnoticed by the villagers but which is a significant element in keeping alive the sense of community and of preserving its highest values;[1] for although gossip springs from the competi-

---

[1] See M. Gluckman, 'Gossip and Scandal', *Current Anthropology*, IV, 1963, 307–15, and E. Colson, *The Makah Indians*, Manchester, 1953, for discussions on the functional value of gossip in society.

tion and hostility which exist between the different groups in the village, it relies for its expression on the common values and the shared history of the total community. These can be analysed under four heads.

First there is the effect of gossip to disseminate information about others, to judge them by appeal to and identification with the highest values of society, and to punish by ridicule those who deviate from those values. Secondly, while to evaluate and criticize people to their face is often insulting and results in a quarrel, the processes of gossip make such evaluation possible without open insult to the person concerned. Thirdly, the constant juggling with reputations and with the merits and demerits of other people's lives keeps the relative status of one person to another in continual flux and maintains the principle of equality. And finally, the act of gossip relies on a knowledge of past history, a common body of tradition, and a shared experience of life, and therefore unites in a positive relationship, even if only temporarily, those who gossip and mock with reference to these experiences and values. Groups of women who are thus gossiping are, in the act of division against others, reaffirming and re-creating the solidarity of the particular relationship which they hold with others in the group. For the duration of the gossip, the hostility which normally underlies relationships outside the family and circle of close kin is kept at bay, and friendship momentarily asserted by common identification with the ideal values of the community.

Because of the inevitability of distrust and one-upmanship recurring once these groups have broken up, it has been said that the friendship experienced by the people in these groups is only 'pretence'.[1] It seems plain, however, that in this society at any rate, this is far from the case, and rather that the temporary union of members of opposing families in common discussion creates a situation which, by extending the sphere of a common sympathy and by allowing affection beyond the normal confines of the family, allows not only a temporary reassertion of the society's ideal values, but a brief re-enactment of them. It is a situation which emotionally and socially is quite as 'real' as the hostility which encircles it; it might almost be said to be more real, for according to the people's own categories it is love and affection and trust which are the true states in which humans should live, and it is

[1] M. Gluckman, op. cit., p. 313.

only the work of the Devil which perverts them into competitiveness, hostility, envy, and malice. Certainly, from the point of view
of an observer both of these meetings and of the critical comments
about one another which often follow once the people have
separated, it is impossible to tell whether the friendship or the malice
is the more genuine. For while the meetings take place on the
ground of a common understanding of the hostility of others, and
a common experience of life and suffering and God and Fate, the
comments which follow take place on the grounds of the assumption of the superiority of the individual's family over everyone
else's, and his or her instinctive tendency to demonstrate this
wherever possible. Both situations represent a type of communion, one between members of society in general, the
other between the close-knit family group. It is not therefore
that the critical comment invalidates the mutual sympathy
which has just preceded it, but that those who are criticizing a
former companion are assuming a different basic situation—
one in which the paramount factor is their experience of
the separateness of their respective families rather than their
experience of their common situation in the face of life and
death.

The question of whether gossip is a constructive or destructive
element in society is not one, therefore, which has very much
meaning, for it is in the nature of gossip not to be completely one
thing or the other. The question is, rather, in what proportions are
the tendencies to cohesion or to fragmentation in gossip balanced
with each other at a given moment. In the case both of a society
that is getting stronger and of one that is getting weaker, it is not
that gossip changes its nature but that the balance of forces working
within it alters. As the community fragments and as the ambitions
of each family become more separated from that of the common
good and more related to the separatist values of the outside world,
so mutual co-operation weakens, the impetus given to gossip from
hostility begins to gain ground, the values to which gossip appeals
become weaker and more diverse, and the balance imperceptibly
alters from one in which it tends towards cohesion to one in which
it tends towards disintegration. In Ambéli it seems plain that
gossip has now, along with these other features of society, turned
into a more purely destructive phase, and this total situation is, it
seems to me, the social reality which underlies the villagers'

unanimous verdict that they have increasingly over the years
'fallen into hatred' (ὁ κόσμος ἔχει πέσει σὲ μῖσος).

The villager, therefore, however much he may long for a utopia of
universal peace, finds himself caught up in a system where friendship is, almost by definition, impermanent, and where it occurs as
an exception to the normal state of competition and suspicion.
Only within the family group can he rely on the close relationships
he desires and needs, and on an absolute union between his love
and his duty; outside this group he is nearly always in a more
equivocal position where loyalty to his family cannot be the
undisputed arbitrator of his behaviour. For much of the time the
villager manages his various relationships without causing these
different obligations to come into conflict with each other; but in
the case of such a conflict, each man's loyalty rests unquestionably
with his family and not with his friend, and the friend knows this.

Thus the inevitable placing of priorities on the self-interest of
the family rather than on the self-interest of the friend results in a
situation in which minor hurts are continually being inflicted
between friends. As long as the tie of mutual self-interest holds,
this tie is strong enough to make these neglects seem unimportant,
or at least to cause the offended person to control any violent
reaction. Such neglects are not in themselves a violation of friendship: they only become so if the partner in the friendship chooses
to treat them as such. When, however, mutual self-interest lapses,
the one element which is able to conquer the basic division
between the two people is lost and antagonism re-emerges, surging
back in a flood of accusations for past neglect and little insults,
and enlivened with a good deal of exaggeration. In both cases
each friend feels unjustifiably betrayed or accused, and has all
the impetus of righteous indignation to add fuel to the things that
each says to the other.

The reason for these friendships breaking in the way they do,
lies in the fact that they are essentially relationships of practical
expedience, and so they lapse when expedience lapses. This is not
to imply that these friendships are of a totally different order from
those found in societies where friendship is expected to be more
permanent; it is simply to say that in this society the relationship
between friends, lacking the dimension of insight and self-
knowledge which is given the chance to develop within people

belonging to more contemplative or more tormented cultures, takes place on the relatively simple level of the people's practical need of one another. The more permanent type of friendship found elsewhere is also concerned with mutual need, but these needs, being more concerned with deeper levels of the person, are more immune from the changes and chances of the purely social world in which they happen to be.

There are two chief ways in which friendship can lapse. One is when the external event which bound the friends together in the first place fails any more to be relevant. When such a liaison lapses the friendship lapses also—sometimes naturally and without a quarrel, and sometimes by means of a quarrel which works on the vacuum left by the absence of mutual self-interest. In other cases a difference of opinion occurs which proves to both people concerned that they can no longer rely on the other for help and support. This then becomes the subject of a quarrel, and the friendship is broken.

The impermanence of individual friendships, as well as being seen in its own terms, should also be seen in relation to the total system of which it is a part. Friends are necessary in such a community simply because it holds this tendency always to fragment into a number of self-enclosed and hostile groups, and because of this the quarrels do not on the whole diminish the number of friendships there are in the village, but simply effect changes of alliance within the over-all number. One man, for instance, having quarrelled with a café owner, went and made up a previous quarrel with the owner of another café so that he could still have somewhere to go; and a woman, having quarrelled with two relatives in turn, was forced to go and make her peace with the first in order to borrow an essential piece of equipment she needed for her loom. The friendship between the three women who were closest to me during the year and a half that I was in the village was in continual motion as one would withdraw from, or briefly quarrel with, another. This would be usually over some trivial piece of gossip, sometimes an over-curt refusal to help, occasionally a piece of what was termed 'stupidity'. However, they were all women who were for one reason or another effectively on their own, and could give each other a type of companionship they could find nowhere else, so the differences of opinion would, instead of destroying the friendship, simply redistribute the affection of the group for a few days until the whole thing had blown over.

The impermanence of friendship therefore makes for a type of tension and unrest in this society; but it also contributes towards a general stability in that it allows for a continuing system of extra-familial alliances, even while it prevents these alliances from entering into too extreme competition with the central alliances within the family. And the fact that friendships are exchanged among the community rather than actually destroyed means that the general proportion of alliances in the village remains more or less the same, even while the individual elements within the total pattern are in a continual state of flux.

Because of the element of mutual aid which is found in these friendships, one of the most obvious areas for friendship is the neighbourhood. Such a neighbourhood is primarily a group of houses in close enough relation to each other for their inhabitants to be described as neighbours—a description allotted according to a simple spatial definition whose criteria, due to the layout of the village described in Chapter I, are more those of proximity than ease of access. Being defined by the position of the houses, the domains of chiefly feminine activity, it is effectively a relationship between women.

Even in cases where there seems to be little convenient contact between two houses, physical proximity is taken to equal neighbourhood. For instance, two houses parallel with each other, separated by the width of a main path and a small garden, with the front of one looking on to the back of the other, were described to me by one of the inhabitants as having 'the same doorway'. In one sense the houses were separate, for all the activity of the house in front of the other was carried on in its own yard, out of sight of the house behind, and the women of either house used different paths to go to the fountain—so chance contact in the form of daily housewifely encounters was no more frequent than it was with the members of many other houses. But these two houses were in fact physically near each other, and their inhabitants were there-fore neighbours.

These types of neighbourhoods plainly do not form separate entities, but overlapping nuclei in which each individual house acts as the focus for the neighbourhood which falls within its radius. It follows therefore that at the edge of each nucleus there will be houses which occupy an equivocal position mid-way between neighbourliness and neutrality, and that the definition of neighbourhood is to some extent dependent on the particular disposition of the families concerned. Where the two dispositions are in conflict, either they will both ignore the possible claim to neighbourhood, or there will arise a situation in which the charge is evoked from one party to the effect that the other does not fulfil her obligations as a neighbour. This is likely either to evoke a denial that she is a neighbour, or at least a neighbour near enough to bother about, or it will prompt the sort of non-committal response which is often heard in the village in various contexts: 'Is she a neighbour? Isn't she? How do I know what she is?' In other words, since the obligations of a neighbour are fairly specific—not to quarrel, to be prepared to give help in a crisis, to lend the odd cooking implement or the use of an oven—an easy way out of failing to fulfil these obligations without loss of face is to question the assumption on which the claim to these rights is based. The way in which the houses are positioned often helps this indeterminacy, and helps to minimize the totality of the inhabitants' confrontation with each other.

Between admitted neighbours the situation is somewhat different. Where there is no difficulty about the relationship, any one house will accept neighbourhood between itself and up to three, four, or even five houses. Where there is a reluctance to admit neighbourhood by one or both parties, this neighbourhood may be reduced to a minimal acceptance of one or two other houses which cannot be ignored because they are adjoining or closely adjacent. The rights and obligations of admitted neighbours assume a definite relationship, although these obligations are never assumed to be so great as to involve serious inconvenience to the one who is asked to help. A neighbour is meant, negatively, to be one with whom you do not quarrel and who does not give you cause for offence, and positively one with whom you reciprocate in a tenuous relationship of mutual aid which acts against the hostility of the world in general and helps to counteract mishaps or emergencies in the house. A neighbour who refuses help without good reason, or who goes to a house to help and then gossips about what she sees there, is not acting properly. The fact that the latter is frequently done, and that a woman's closest neighbour is her closest observer and frequently abuses the fact, does not weaken the value ideally placed on this relationship. This is illustrated perhaps most clearly in the fact that when someone is doing a small service for someone else, the one who is doing the favour will explain her actions in the words: 'We are neighbours' (εἴμαστε γειτόνισσες).

Neighbourhood can itself induce good relations, but it is equally likely to give rise to, or increase, frictions which the two families concerned are unable to overcome. Quarrels between close neighbours are perhaps as frequent as alliances formed on neighbourhood alone. In these cases the breakdown of relations is openly admitted, 'Yes, we are neighbours, but what can one do?', implying that although this is not an ideal situation or even a proper one, it is not of crucial importance and simply one of the hazards of having a neighbour. She may be good or she may not. No one breaks her heart over such a situation, even though at the same time no one will accept responsibility for the rift and much anger may be expended on the failings in this respect of the other party.

The difficulty about this type of relationship is that it is one which, in essence, imposes a mutual system of rights and obligations between two groups of society which are fundamentally separate. Because the needs of the family always have priority over those of another family, especially if the other family is not related, the sheer fact of neighbourhood is seldom enough to prevent a serious quarrel on some other subject, or to cause a *rapprochement* between the parties after a quarrel has taken place. On the other hand where there is already a positive relationship deriving from another source, neighbourhood has a considerable part to play, for even between close kin the fact that two families live near to each other can significantly reinforce the existent ties through the continual contact of neighbourhood. Such relationships tend to be particularly long-lasting and are greatly valued, for a life in which nearly every moment of the working day is fully employed increases the value of a relationship which can be kept up independent of the necessity for special visits.

Neighbourhood therefore is an important relationship in a community where resources are limited and where the most obvious source for a certain type of help and companionship is provided by the person next door, but which affects community relations more through underlining existing relationships than through creating new ones. Where it does create new ones, it does so not as a single

effective force but as one of a complex of different criteria governing friendship, one of whose presuppositions is a relationship
of neutrality without conflicting interests. It tends therefore to act
towards unity or disunity according to the various pressures
involved, and is able, as a result of the basic indefinition of its
application, to adjust to many of these pressures without breaking.
Equally well the impermanence of so many of these quarrels is
such that the frequent violation of the code does not amount
to a repudiation of the code, but simply an instance where the
individuals concerned have been unable to live up to it. The
code itself as a viable moral guide and an ideal pattern for community relations is not threatened: it is simply disobeyed. Thus the
family is able to avoid sacrificing its own interests for the common
good, while still remaining ideally part of the complex of relations
which link the total community together. And when for whatever
reasons it finds itself able to be on good terms with another non-
related family living nearby, it will claim 'neighbourhood' as the
fount and purpose of its actions.

The expedience which is found in friendships within the village is
found intensified in the patronage alliances which link Ambéli
with Kateríni and the villages of the surrounding district, for here
the stress is less on the company and generalized loyalty of the
friend, and more on the sheer material convenience he or she
provides.

The business relationship in Greece owes its essential nature to
the Greek's basic conception of trade, not as the impersonal
exchange of goods for money, but the personal exchange of one
favour for another. One needs to have what the other has to give,
and because of this the relationship created by buying and selling
is not fundamentally one of condescension from the rich man to
the poor man so much as a reciprocal agreement for mutual
benefit. In the more informal type of patron/client relationship—
that is to say where this is concerned with buying and selling,
obtaining loans, and so on, and not with influence on the more
official levels of society—the relationship is essentially personal,
and one that is thought of as being between 'friends' (φίλοι).

However, friendship is in these conditions an even more delicate
matter than usual, and the balancing of generosity, a feature of
friendship, with self-interest, a feature of family solidarity, requires

a degree of tact and patience that is not always available. The theory is that everyone should gain, but in practice someone will usually think that he is losing, because since the relationship is not one of cast-iron obligation but of give-and-take according to the understanding of either, there is latitude within the relationship for infinite reinterpretation. The villager, for instance, may be torn between the demands of loyalty to his friend which compel him to patronize his shop, and those of sheer self-interest which prompt him to go elsewhere where the price is lower. This conflict is resolved in one of two ways—either he decides that his self-interest in fact lies in retaining the goodwill of his friend, and therefore goes to his shop; or else, as in the case quoted earlier, he goes somewhere else and pretends, if caught out, that he has not been, or that his patron's shop was closed when he passed by. According to how well he lies, how important the defalcation is, and how much the patron wants to retain his custom, the fate of the relationship is decided.

These business relationships therefore which characterize many of the ties between Ambéli and the outside world are, as are the majority of village relationships themselves, fluid rather than static, always susceptible to breakdown, always in need of building up and strengthening by fresh interchange of favours if they are not to fall into attrition. They are formed predominantly with kin— those of blood or marriage or spiritual kinship—though the formation of such a relationship is possible also simply through regular patronage of a particular shop, or because of the suitability of a certain business connection.

The question of contact with the world of officialdom, influence, and political power creates a slightly different situation, for where friendship occurs in a situation of economic or hierarchic inequality, the relationship becomes much more formal than that described above, even though in both cases the patron is spoken of as a 'friend'. In these cases the suppliant is spoken of (or speaks of himself) as having 'influence' (μέσα—lit. a 'means' or a 'way' of doing things or getting things done).

This is different from the simple business relationship between villager and shopkeeper where business dealings are conducted between two people of more or less equivalent status, for it involves the definite appeal from a man without influence not only in a particular matter but in a particular world, to a man with it.

The difference of status is tacitly or openly admitted, and as the man lower in the hierarchy begs the favour he is aware of the power of the man higher up to refuse it. The element of reciprocity, however, although diminished, still remains, for because these relationships exist either as part of the network of kinship obligations, or are created by the offering and acceptance of a gift, the two parties are from the very beginning linked in what is a partnership rather than a giving and receiving of charity. With the villagers of Ambéli these gifts are usually in kind rather than in cash, and consist of eggs, walnuts, a chicken, perhaps some fresh vegetables. However, whatever the gift—large or small—acceptance of it by the patron indicates a willingness to help which is not framed in terms of sheer condescension, but of the acceptance of an obligation and the intention to discharge it. It is a complex transaction which the word 'bribe' does not adequately cover, for it is still, essentially, a transaction between 'friends'.

The quarrels which so often form the disastrous ending to village friendships are seen by the villagers, as is gossip, to be evidence of 'hatred' and the work of the Devil. However, they are more sympathetic to the quarrels of the men than those of the women, saying, 'Men quarrel over their interests, but women over gossip.'

This, by and large, is true. Men's quarrels are chiefly about property—over ownership of field and forest; over boundary lines within the village; over access to fields which, because of fragmentation, often has to be through property belonging to someone else; over damage caused by straying animals; possibly over the taking of dead wood from someone else's land—an event so common as to amount to a system of reciprocal theft but which can still cause trouble if discovered; over a man's hostile witness in a lawcourt, or, alternatively, over his failure to agree to testify favourably. Quarrels over inheritance can be very fierce, and bitterness in these cases is increased by the fact that such quarrels are necessarily between kin.

It is often difficult to tell when trouble over one of these topics is the cause of the quarrel itself, or when such trouble indicates that advantage is being taken of a weak point in order to irritate or to damage someone with whom a quarrel has already begun; and the real motivation of such a quarrel may simply be, as it is meant to be with the women, sheer self-esteem. But self-esteem when displayed over self-interest—even over one pine or one square foot of land—is justified in a way in which women's quarrels on the whole are not, and it is because of this that men have got the reputation of being 'intelligent' in their quarrels, even when the apparent cause and conduct of the quarrel are very far from this.

Men are, in fact, very vulnerable to minor infringements of their self-interest and because of this it is not difficult for a third party to start a quarrel between two others which may last for years. Such a quarrel may be started by someone with genuinely good intentions, but equally well it may be started intentionally, for fun, or out of jealousy. It begins, for instance, by someone going to someone else and saying:

'That pine that Spiros is tapping used to be tapped by your grandfather—I know.' The recipient of this information then goes to the man who is tapping his pine and says, 'That's my pine you're tapping.'
'No, it's not.'
'Yes, it is.'
'No, I'm telling you, it's not . . .'

The degree of land fragmentation, the difficulty of verifying boundary lines, and the paucity of documents relating to sale, exchange, and inheritance all create a situation in which belief or disbelief of an informant in this situation is purely arbitrary. It is an ideal field for the trouble-maker and a frustrating one for the person with a genuine grievance.

Although certain quarrels over self-interest may seem to the outside community to be ill considered, basically concerned with sheer self-esteem, and therefore things 'to laugh at', it is true that men's quarrels are on the whole over material objects and therefore, to some extent at any rate, justifiable. Some men do take offence over small infringements of their self-esteem such as being prevented from leading the dance at a wedding or festival, or some joke being made at their expense, or thinking they are being cheated at a game of cards; but such offence is normally limited to the occasion itself, and unless linked with a graver cause for resentment, produces only temporary coolness. Insults hurled during the heat of the moment do not, as they do with women, give grounds for lasting offence, and the cause of the quarrel usually remains firmly rooted in the situation which first gave rise to it.

The constant identification of the men's world with self-interest and that of the women with gossip is illustrated in the comment made one day about a widow with one son who had quarrelled with a great many people—'What business has she got to quarrel? She hasn't got a family concern to bother about [the word used here was συμφέροντα—self-interest]; she hasn't got a man in the house.' The quarrels, therefore, even of women who are on their own and have no one else to protect their interests, are thought to be so basically conditioned by feminine irrationality as to be still essentially unconcerned with the true field of self-interest— the material prosperity of the house. And it is in fact true that this particular woman would have looked after her house better if she had kept quiet and attended discreetly to her business instead of flying off continually into frantic quarrels and furious accusation.

Women's quarrels, it is universally agreed, are over 'words' (λόγια)—which is to say that the resentment that rankles in the quarrellers' minds for years after the actual quarrel itself is normally not connected with the original incident but with the insults that accumulated during the heat of the moment. One description of such quarrels was given to me as follows: 'Women quarrel over nothing. They quarrel over who is first in the water queue, for instance, and five years ago when there was only one channel at the spring they would quarrel, and then, because they had once been friends and knew each other's secrets, after saying, "Harlot!", "Whore!" (πουτάνα, ρουφιάνα),[1] one would say, "You had a fair old time with such and such a person", and the other would say, "No, it was you," and they wouldn't speak to each other for years.'

At such a time, lies or exaggerations about the other person's behaviour are only to be expected, but the fact that every villager has close knowledge of everyone else's activities over the years adds considerable force to the basic accusations that are made. One quarrel, for instance, which originated over someone throwing her washing water in the wrong place so that it ran into her neigh-

---

[1] ρουφιάνα, a woman who connives at the adultery of another woman friend or who helps a man to seduce a woman whom, by trickery or friendship, she manages to influence. The insult also implies lack of chastity in the woman herself. This word is also used generally to indicate someone who goes around revealing secrets and stirring up trouble, but the more serious connotations of the insult are still implicit, and great offence is taken at its use.

bour's garden, culminated in one woman saying, 'You've eaten up our life, you whose daughters circulate the streets of Athens . . .'— referring to the poverty which had made this woman send her children to work in Athens during the civil war, and to the inevitable assumption of prostitution which accompanies such a step; and was answered by a reference to her own daughter's pregnancy by her second cousin, which had resulted in her dishonourable marriage to him[1]—'Why do you laugh when the laugh is on you, and in your own house your daughter had a bastard . . .' Plainly it is difficult to forgive such accusations, and forgiveness is consequently infrequent.

In addition to memories of past indiscretions and exaggerations of known weaknesses, words such as procurer, prostitute, and so on, form an indispensable part of abusive feminine vocabulary, and although almost trite as terms of abuse, are, because of their implications, lasting insults. Once a woman has lost her temper it is almost inevitable that she could call her antagonist a whore; equally well it is almost inevitable that, having been called a whore, the woman should respond with something similar. It is probable then that a grievance between the two will last for years.

The differences of opinion which sparked off the two quarrels just quoted are typical of the main causes of quarrels in Ambéli. In the late summer and early autumn the water at the fountain, which normally flows through three channels, flows rather slowly through only one, and tempers rise as one woman with only a small jar to fill pushes in front, too hurried to make an apology, or as another woman stands for twenty minutes filling up large containers. Inconveniences caused through neighbourhood are frequent, especially the tipping out of soapy water or rubbish in such a place that it finds its way into the neighbour's yard or garden; and the neighbour who observes all that is going on in the next-door house and gossips about it to her friends is particularly unwelcome. Trouble can also occur over the lack of fencing around gardens in the village or vineyards on the periphery, since straying hens and goats can do a lot of damage, although in these cases, since the damage is unintentional, it is not beneath the offender's dignity to apologize and to make reparation, nor beneath the offended party's dignity to receive it. Finally, tale-telling to husbands or mothers-in-law of a woman's behaviour, gossiping

[1] See pp. 93 and 177.

about moral lapses of any kind, or failing to observe proper discretion with regard to the lives of others, are all offences for which in the women's world the institutionalized form of retaliation is the quarrel.

Although quarrels occurring between whole families as a result of abduction, elopement, or infidelity used to be a feature of village life in past years, they are so in Ambéli no longer, although repercussions from such past quarrels may still be felt in the village from time to time. But quarrels arising through gossip and slander, through failure to discharge an obligation when it is required, and through the numerous small offences that accumulate during a lifetime's close acquaintance in hard conditions, come and go continually in the villager's world, and provide a background of permanent movement and drama which ruffles though it does not normally overset the work of each individual family and its abiding sense of its own integrity.

Some villagers, when not attributing quarrels to the working of hatred and the Devil, trace it to the difference of political opinion which consolidated during the civil war. This cannot be unequivocally true, for, given the structure of social relations in Greek village life, it is impossible to envisage a situation at any time in the past when quarrelling was not a major feature of social life; but it is undoubtedly true that the civil war sowed new hatreds even while it gained much initial ground from old ones. However, the concentration of the individual on his own family prohibits the occurrence of quarrels for reasons purely of political theory, and it is only when the interests of the party become, as they frequently do, identified with the interests of the house, that political commitment begins seriously to penetrate social relations.

The main political divisions in the village before the military *coup* of 1967 were between Left and Right, and were focused on the two main cafés. Here the staunch upholders of either faction would come in the evenings or on rainy days to talk or drink their coffees or play cards or backgammon, and their wives would do their small amounts of shopping in accordance with these political loyalties. However, not only did the lines of marriage often crosscut political divisions, but also the necessity in a small community of keeping the goodwill of the two possible patrons—the owners of each of the cafés. It therefore needed something more than sheer political loyalty to cause unvarying attendance at one particular café, or to become involved in a quarrel with anyone, and it was noticeable that the men who went exclusively to either one or the other café were those who had other, and more personal, reasons for doing so.

The history of the quarrel between the two café owners illustrates this, for although the two men were of different political parties, the quarrel was given its real impetus by the fact that while one family had lost a former high degree of power and prestige, the other was gradually gaining it. This quarrel became further extended when a niece of the left-wing café owner eloped with a man of a family deeply committed to the Right—a situation which developed into a series of lawsuits over land involving witnesses and supporters, and at one time a full-scale row in public when a judge and lawyers were called to the scene itself to try to effect a settlement.[1] Thus a large part of the village was caught up in the division. In this quarrel the significant feature was the accretion, on to the political division, of personal loyalties and interests, and these two factors combined to cause this particular quarrel to become for years one of the chief features of social life in Ambéli.

The above example is an illustration of the way in which people originally outside a quarrel can get drawn into it. The reason for this particular involvement was, I was told, 'Because it was a family affair over land'. In cases less deeply involved with such crucial personal issues, however, the defence of the house usually dictates non-involvement in the quarrels of others, and the normal feature of village quarrels is their containment within the houses of those involved. Whether or not a quarrel spreads to all members of the same house depends on the circumstances. Because of the nature of their quarrels, the men are meant to keep aloof from their wives' bickerings, while the women are meant to support their husbands in theirs. This support should not, though it often does,

---

[1] This is a legal proceeding known in the village as *Προσωρινὰ Μέτρα* (lit. nterim measures), by which instead of being adjudicated in the lawcourt with papers and witnesses only, the question is settled by officials of the court coming to the village in person and examining the situation for themselves. In fact both forms of legal settlement are officially known as *Προσωρινὰ Μέτρα* but the villagers distinguish between the two by referring to the latter kind only by its official name. This form of *Προσωρινὰ Μέτρα* is invariably more expensive than the other, and for that reason is less frequently invoked.

involve an extension of the quarrel into the women's world of abuse and insult, but simply a discreet loyalty to the husband's wishes and to his particular affiliations. In this situation the position of a daughter-in-law is particularly delicate because, although ideally her loyalties on marriage are transferred to the family of her husband, the emotional reality does not always support this. If therefore her in-laws quarrel with any members of her own family of origin or her close kinsmen, she is usually careful not to be seen speaking to them in case the inevitable conclusion should be reached that she was 'gossiping' about them.

Quarrels, therefore, like gossip, are built into the structure of social relations, and it is a very rare person who can consistently rise above the pressures towards open conflict with others. However, at the same time it must not be imagined that the villagers are puppets whose actions are totally determined by unyielding social forces. The situation is, in a sense, restricting, but within the general framework of extreme concentration on the family, a relative lack of insight which conditions the way people can relate to each other, and social relations which are dominated by jealousy and mistrust, the people have considerable freedom and a very great range and variety of self-expression. Within the same small village there are those who quarrel a great deal and those who hardly quarrel at all; there are those who are objectively speaking good neighbours, and those who are bad. Responsibility for quarrelling, as for everything else that happens in the village, does finally lie with the people concerned, and there are occasions on which they will exercise a good deal of self-control to avoid it. A woman once sent me to talk to another about a possible point of conflict, because she said that if she went herself she would be bound to lose her temper and say things that she would regret afterwards. Another woman, talking about a neighbour who let her washing water run all over the path till it smelt so bad that no one could pass by, said, 'We told her about it twice. But since she doesn't understand, what can we do? *Quarrel* about a thing like that? We go round the other way.' And the comment of a third on the foolishness of those who quarrel over trivial matters was, 'What did I do when Dhimos killed a goat and the blood ran all into my yard? I took a bucket and washed it away and didn't say anything.'

On occasions, however, when self-control is not adequate to

preserve good relations, but where an outright quarrel is not desired, it is possible to 'take offence', that is to say to be cool towards someone, perhaps to fail to greet them as they pass, or to stop visiting their house. Since nothing unforgivable is said or done, this is a situation from which both parties can quite easily and without losing their dignity take up their friendship again from where it left off. Such coolness does not usually last for longer than a few weeks, and is not considered to be very serious.

It is this sort of atmosphere, intensified, that dominates the relations between those who are in a state of being, as the villagers say, 'quarrelled' (μαλωμένοι). The quarrel itself is occasion for high words and violent accusation and self-defence, and for as long as the topic in question continues to be an active object of contention, these overt hostilities may recur, breaking out over the original topic or over a new disagreement founded on the old. However, the uselessness of such a course of action becomes obvious to all parties once the heat of the moment is passed, and the normal behaviour of two people who are 'quarrelled' is mutual non-recognition. Behind each other's backs both will be active in denigration, but face-to-face they will act as if completely unaware of each other's presence. Neither will visit the other's house for any reason at all, and some people, though very rarely, have shown such animosity as to preserve a quarrel after death, closing the shutters as the funeral procession passes by, and refusing to take the food for the dead at a memorial service.

While the situation of two people who have quarrelled is liable always to erupt into further trouble if for some reason they are forced to confront each other, the normal pattern of the quarrelling relationship is in fact ideally suited to keeping the peace in such a community.[1] For in this society, where quarrels are inevitable and contact frequent, one of the best means of avoiding further trouble between those who are on bad terms is for each to deny completely the social existence of the other. The fact also that quarrels are normally confined to the houses concerned, and perhaps even to the individuals within the house, means that there

[1] See P. Bialor, 'Intravillage tensions leading to conflict and the resolution and avoidance of conflict in a Greek farming community', *Acts of the Mediterranean Sociological Conference*, ed. J. G. Peristiany, Athens, 1963, who discusses the conduct of the quarrel in Vovoda, Greece, where the social effects are identical with those in Ambéli, and only the terminology is changed—ψυχραμένοι, 'being in a state of coolness', being used instead of μαλωμένοι.

exist, between the quarrelling people, neutrals who may act as intermediaries in any situation in which communication is needed with the opposing family, but in which a sense of dignity and self-esteem prevents it from being direct. This means of communication is very important in a society such as Ambéli where the isolation is such as to enforce a fairly high degree of interdependence even on those families who manage to be most self-supporting.

The ending of quarrels is something that happens unobtrusively and almost as a matter of chance. The official go-between to bring two quarrelling parties to an agreement is unknown in Ambéli, and an apology as such is never offered. Quarrels, if they do come to an end, do so simply because a combination of various circumstances makes the quarrel irrelevant: the two parties get tired of the situation, or have reason to need one another again, or the insults or hurts inflicted in the past lose their bitterness. Since the form that the chronic quarrel takes is that of not speaking, it is natural that the ending of the quarrel should come about through speaking, and the chief way in which someone may indicate a readiness to bury the hatchet is in offering, for instance, the traditional good wishes on some joyful event, or condolences on a sad one. Refusal of such an overture is always possible and is indicated by the failure to acknowledge what is said, while a brief acknowledgement reveals acceptance of friendship. Quarrels between women have several times been ended by the event of a death, where two women who normally avoid one another meet to wash and lay out the body, and are reconciled together in contemplation of the greatest enemy of all.

Men, it is said, patch up quarrels 'depending . . .' (ἀνάλογα), which is to say 'just as it happens', while women 'bear malice' (κρατᾶνε μῖσος). This does not mean that men do not very often continue in their quarrels for quite as long as the women, but refers more to the tendency of men to focus continually on the original cause of the quarrel and therefore to be ready, when this becomes irrelevant, to accept good relations again. Women, losing sight very quickly of the incident that first caused the trouble and dwelling furiously on the slanderous details that followed, find this more difficult. But for both men and women the quarrel ends in much the same way—a way which has been described to me as

follows: 'Time passes and then one day someone will say, "Good
day." "Good day." And they speak to each other after that.'

The relation of the ideal role of the men to their actual behaviour
in their quarrels is immediately apparent, for the ideal concern of
the man is the material defence of the house, and they quarrel over
those things which are necessary for this. Women's quarrels, however, appear to bring about the opposite situation from that ideally
required of them, since they are over 'words', and such words are
recognized to be powerful agents for trouble and destruction.
Nevertheless there is in fact between the quarrels of the women
and their ideal roles the same relationship as there is between those
of the men.

If, as has been argued, the fidelity of a woman to her ideal role
presupposes always a concern with the internal basis of her nature,
it follows that it is with this that her own integrity will be most
deeply involved, rather than with the material interest of the house
which is more the moral concern of the man. It is consistent with
this that while a man is most deeply injured when an attack is
made on his self-interest, a woman is most deeply injured when
aspersions are cast on her moral nature; and here it is significant
that the most unforgivable insults to a woman are always those
which imply infidelity or unchastity. Given, therefore, that quarrels
in this society are inevitable, it is inevitable that both men and
women will attack each other at their weakest point—that of self-
interest for the one, and of moral reputation for the other. It is
also inevitable that the reaction to each attack will be extreme. It
is, therefore, in spite of all appearances to the contrary, a logical
part of the woman's role and an aspect of her metaphysical defence
of the house that those quarrels with which she is most personally
involved are those concerning 'words' and 'gossip'.

PART III

X

PAST AND PRESENT

THE analysis of this society has, up till now, been carried out largely in terms of its traditional aspects, since it is these ideas which for centuries have dictated the forms of its culture and which, in however weakened or altered form, still provide the dominant ethos of village life. However, the entry in the present century of the Greek nation into the world of industry and commerce, and its gradual transformation from a subsistence to a consumer society, have had repercussions which have penetrated into the remotest corner of Greek rural life, and which have affected very deeply this traditional world view. The effect of this movement has been to change not so much the central elements of the value system as the ways in which they are interpreted; but this does not mean that this change is superficial, for it amounts in many respects to the setting up of new values which are often, although they are not always recognized to be so, antithetical to the old.

Communications with the outside world, and contact with its values, have been achieved in two main ways—war and emigration. The participation of villagers in the Balkan Wars from 1912 to 1914, in the campaign in Asia Minor from 1920 to 1922, in the Albanian campaign against the Italians in 1940, and later against the Germans in 1940–1, all tended to enlarge their horizons beyond that of traditional village culture. But it is emigration which has effected the deeper alteration to village thinking and incalculably changed the villagers' way of life.

The first significant instance of emigration was that to America at the beginning of this century. Many of the villagers of Ambéli were heavily in debt, others wanted to buy land, others to seek their fortunes permanently elsewhere—and several men left the village from 1905 to 1908, although most returned in 1912 at the outbreak of the Balkan Wars. Emigration also took place in the 1930s to America, but ended with the entry of Greece into World War II, and after that there was no further emigration from Ambéli until 1960 when there began the great exodus of young men to Canada, Germany, the United States, Australia, and Belgium, as well as recruitment of men for the Merchant Navy.

There was a great difference, however, between the earlier types of emigration and the later, for whereas in the former cases the migration ideally involved return, in the latter it was, and was intended to be, permanent. In earlier years the *émigré* went abroad in order to send money home to his wife and children, to buy land, possibly a house, or houses, returning eventually himself to take up his old way of life on a stronger financial basis; and while some did leave the village for good, these were only people who could not be supported on the land and resources available. Any-one, therefore, who was already established in the village, went abroad to secure rather than to abandon his inheritance. In the post-1960 emigrations, however, the focus has been the reverse, and not one of these *émigrés* had—or has—any intention of ever returning to live in the village. They come back periodically, to see their parents and to have a holiday, but they have no thought at all of taking up permanent residence in the village; and those who are forced, as some are, to return and stay for some months because of difficulties with their visas or work permits, are dis-contented and oppressed by what they see as the narrowness and lack of culture (ψυχαγωγία, lit. 'education of the soul', meaning in this context the frequenting of cinemas, nightclubs, dance halls and restaurants), and resolute in their determination to get away for ever.

The men who emigrate as bachelors usually marry Greek girls whom they meet either abroad or on a trip back to their village, and many of these couples then settle permanently in their new country, and one by one organize the emigration also of their brothers, sisters, and cousins. Of those who emigrated after they had married and settled in Ambéli, some have managed to leave their children with relatives and take their wives with them to work, and all intend, on returning to Greece, to abandon the village and buy a building plot near some relatively urbanized centre in the plains. While these people are abroad they send money to their parents and thus in a sense support the village, but this money is not enough to provide for a real continuance of the traditional culture; nor is it enough to establish a house: it is to keep two unambitious and undemanding old people from destitu-tion until they finally leave the village and go to live with a married son or daughter elsewhere. And although some men, though not all, send home money to help with their sisters' dowries, these dowries in fact also work against the continued existence of the village, for they enable the girls to marry 'well', into a different and, to however small an extent, more polished community. Thus while the tendency of the earlier types of emigration was in the long run to strengthen the village, the later type is destroying it.

This situation highlights some of the central aspects of social change and illustrates the positions outlined in Chapter III,[1] for while the earlier emigrations, taking place from a firm basis in village culture and a belief in its value, were a confirmation of that culture, rather than a challenge to it, the post-1960 emigrations took place from a village that was already losing confidence in its own inherited way of life—that had looked beyond the confines of its own culture and found what it saw attractive. The situation therefore arose in which the village the *émigré* left behind him perpetuated, because of its remoteness and isolation, a vital life in its traditional patterns; yet nevertheless at the same time it held the seeds of a totally foreign growth which was to flower, in the *émigré*, into a total disillusion with his rural origin. And while this disillusion did not compromise the commitment of those who were kept in the village by lack of opportunity to leave, it was an image of the failure of these patterns in the most crucial sense to offer fulfilment to an entirely new generation. Thus it seems that at some time around 1950 there occurred the beginnings of a deeply hidden but very central collapse of village confidence—a collapse which even by 1966 had not affected the villagers' sense of the intrinsic validity of their inherited way of life, but which cast doubt on the viability of that way of life in terms of the future, and in terms, therefore, of that most important aspect of Greek life, the children.

As time goes on this particular balance is likely to change more and more. The *émigré* of 1960 was impelled by hope of better things outside, rather than by disillusion from within. The *émigré* of 1970 goes because, 'This isn't a life' (δὲν εἶναι ζωὴ αὐτή). And yet this paradox, whereby the village survives in its own village-centred terms even while it fails completely in terms of the outside world, is never likely to be finally resolved, for the degree of emigration has by now taken the situation too far. In many of the

[1] See pp. 49–50.

larger or less remote towns and villages of Greece, the recent pattern has been one of increasing modernization whereby the world moves in before the inhabitants move out. This has not proved possible in Ambéli, and it is not going to be the infiltration of the modern middle-class ethos which will eradicate the traditional patterns still remaining to it, but final depopulation.

Of the earlier emigrations and the contact of village men with war and invasion, two general effects on village life may be isolated. One has been to highlight in many ways the traditional polarity of male and female roles, among the older married couples, by deepening the discrepancy between the experience of the men and that of their wives. The other has been to provide a basis for the older generations from which they can understand and sympathize with the younger ones who want to leave the village and make a new life for themselves elsewhere. Experimentalism and ambition, in terms of the ability to adventure into completely new worlds, are characteristics not foreign to the people of Ambéli. The result of this is that the village as a whole helps its sons to emigrate, its daughters to marry out, and in the most practical terms understands, while it laments, the permanent departure of its children from the family hearth.

Apart from the emigration discussed above, the political events which had the greatest impact in recent times were the two outbreaks of civil war in 1944 and 1947, with the consequent evacuation of the whole village to Kateríni for one year, from November 1949 to November 1950.

The two great periods of civil war, when fighting was generalized throughout all Greece and extended even into the towns, were in 1943 until February 1945, and in 1947 to 1949. However, during the whole period from 1942 to 1950 there was a state of disturbance in various parts of Greece with guerrilla bands operating in the mountains. During the first period the fighting was relatively localized between rival Resistance bands all over the country, interspersed with actual Resistance activity. During the second period, however, the Communist guerrillas involved the villagers by both persuasion and terrorism and, especially after the American involvement in Greece in 1947, were themselves hunted by the National Army in the mountains.

The villagers' involvement in the civil war was, primarily,

caused by the position of their village in the wooded mountains which were to become ideal refuges for the Communist guerrilla fighters or *andártes* (ἀντάρτες)[1] as they came to be called. Before the war, political differences between Venizelist[2] and Royalist supporters had existed in Ambéli, but political consciousness in the village is said not to have been such as to cause violence or long-standing quarrels. With the development of the guerrilla movement, however, the village split naturally into Left and Right, with those of the Left helping the Communists out of sympathy, those of the Right out of fear—neither however, at any rate in the beginning, aware of the real political movements in which they were so disastrously taking part. The villagers were, as always, the victims of the struggles of others rather than the active element of the struggle itself.

It was not surprising that the villagers were at first in ignorance of the real issues of the conflict, for this ignorance was a state shared initially also by the Greek Government in exile, and by the Allies.[3] EAM/ELAS[4] was initially the Resistance group which provided most of the effective partisan opposition to the Germans, and as such was given aid by the Allies—money and arms. It came quite rapidly, however, under the control of the Greek Communist Party (KKE)[5] and thus became involved in a struggle with EDES,[6] a Resistance organization operating mainly in north-

---

[1] ἀντάρτης literally means rebel, or partisan, but it has come, because of its associations in the civil war, to be associated on the whole with Communist guerrillas rather than with partisan fighters in general. The ἀντάρτες here referred to are the guerrilla troops which were known by that name and which replaced the National Popular Liberation Army, or ELAS (see note 4), during the second part of the civil war.

[2] Eleftherios Venizelos, a Cretan, gave his name to the Liberal Party which he founded in 1910. He was Prime Minister of Greece from 1910 to 1920, and from 1928 to 1932, and died in 1936.

[3] For an account of the means by which the Communist nature of EAM/ELAS remained hidden both from the Allies and from the majority of the Greeks themselves, and for the reasons for the power of EAM/ELAS over both villagers and more sophisticated Greeks, see C. M. Woodhouse, *The Apple of Discord*, London, 1948, pp. 59 f.

[4] EAM (᾽Εθνικὸ ᾽Απελευθερωτικὸ Μέτωπο), the National Liberation Front, was the name of the political Resistance coalition which was set up at the beginning of the occupation, and is usually referred to in conjunction with ELAS (῾Ελληνικὸς Λαϊκὸς ᾽Απελευθερωτικὸς Στρατός), the National Popular Liberation Army which refers to the guerrilla bands which first began operations in the mountains in the summer of 1942.

[5] Κομμουνιστικὸ Κόμμα ῾Ελλάδος.

[6] ᾽Εθνικὸς Δημοκρατικὸς ῾Ελληνικὸς Στρατός, the National Democratic Greek

western Greece, which, originally Republican, became increasingly Rightist under the control of General Napoleon Zervas. Straight-forward opposition to the invaders was thus confused with the struggle for power between these two rival groups, and the villages all over Greece were involved in this confusion.[1]

There is no doubt that when Resistance groups all over the country were formed at the beginning of the occupation, they were formed in answer to an intense popular resolution to evict the Germans. However, from the way in which the villagers now remember those days, it seems that later events overwhelmed this initial fervour, and that EAM/ELAS came eventually to exercise a hold over village imaginations in the opportunity it offered for adventure and excitement, and as a catalyst for the villagers' own private passions or generalized political leanings, rather than as a revolutionary cause to which they were dedicated.[2] During the civil war which followed the evacuation of Greece by the Germans, several of the villagers actively enlisted with the *andártes*, some because they were forced to, others as a means of implementing private grudges, others as a result of an ill-timed spirit of heroism or a general sympathy with the Left. It is said that one man joined the

Army. It is unlikely that EDES ever operated in Euboea, but the effects of the struggle were felt all over Greece and were not confined to the physical clashes between the actual Resistance bands concerned.

[1] This understanding of the activities of the Resistance bands as concerned more with internal political division than with a united national front corresponds with Woodhouse's description of the purpose of ELAS units '. . . whose leaders did not regard the war as being fought between national groups but between rival ideologies, which cut across national groups and were called Progress and Reaction'. C. M. Woodhouse, op cit., p. 61.

[2] For a description of the effects of EAM/ELAS on the socio-political structure of village life, see Woodhouse, op. cit., pp. 146–7: 'Having acquired control of almost the whole country, except the principal communications used by the Germans, they had given it things that it had never known before. Communications in the mountains, by wireless, courier, and telephone, have never been so good before or since; even motor roads were mended and used by EAM/ELAS. . . . The benefits of civilization and culture trickled into the mountains for the first time. Schools, local government, lawcourts and public utilities, which the war had ended, worked again. Theatres, factories, parliamentary assemblies began for the first time. Communal life was organized in place of the traditional individualism of the Greek peasant. His child was dragooned into the EPON, his nest-egg levied into EA, his caique commandeered to equip ELAN . . . Followed at a distance by the minor organizations, the EAM/ELAS set the base in the creation of something that the governments of Greece had neglected: an organized State in the 'Greek mountains'. EPON—National Panhellenic Organization of Youth. EA—relief work. ELAN—EAM's Naval Army.

Communists with the express intention of killing a rival inheritor of his father's; there was a young boy who involved himself with the first outbreak of civil war and then found himself too deeply involved to draw back. There was a boy of thirteen who was taken from his home at night by the *andártes* and retrieved only at the last moment by his mother who pleaded with the leader that her son was too young to be of any use to them. Yet another family who had a son in the National Army relate how they only resisted continual pressure to get him to desert and come to join the *andártes* by pretending that they had no idea where he was stationed.

The nature of the movement first began to reveal itself in Ambéli when speakers for the Communist Party had come round the villages exhorting disbelief in the Church and proclaiming the joys of communal living. A fat woman speaker, who scratched her behind as she was talking, made a particular impression on the villagers, ever, as is their nature, ready for a joke; and there was a man who appalled them by cutting tobacco on an icon in demonstration of the hollowness of faith. Still clearer to them were the political implications of the open fighting which broke out in the streets of Athens between ELAS and the liberating British troops in December 1944; but by that time those who had involved themselves with the *andártes* found it too late to withdraw.

The *andártes* only stationed themselves permanently in the village after it was evacuated in 1949, but before that they made periodic swoops for food, for conscription, or for revenge. It was a time of terror for all, both Left and Right, for betrayal was rife, and death was threatened from the *andártes* for opposition or refusal to help, while severe beatings were courted by villagers who came under suspicion of the Government troops. The slower-minded villager ran the risk of being beaten up by both parties for not being quick enough to evade accusation; the cunning one had a soft answer ready at all times. One old man told me how he used to watch his sheep on the mountain sides, and from time to time unidentifiable groups of men would approach him and ask roughly, 'What are you?' 'I'm a shepherd,' he would insist, feigning ignorance of the real implications of the question, 'I'm a shepherd'; while to me he said, 'How did I know what to say? You couldn't tell who they were, and if you said the wrong thing you might have got killed. That was how I escaped.' In the village at night the same thing would happen. A family sitting at its evening meal would be terrified by a thunderous knocking at the door. Trembling, the head of the house would open it, 'Welcome!' he would say. To me he explained, 'To the *andártes*, "You're welcome!" To the Government troops, "You're welcome!" What could we do? We wanted to live.' One woman told me how, when she was a girl, the *andártes* came to her house:

Masses and masses of men came, it was dark and I didn't know who they were. Then one of them said to me, 'Good evening, comrade.' When I heard the 'comrade' I was terrified, and went to my uncle's house, and I fell on to the floor and cried with terror and said that they must go to my house and protect my mother. They said not to be afraid, but after a little while I thought that I couldn't sit there in safety while they killed my mother, and so I decided, if they kill my mother, they will kill me too; if they leave her, they will leave me too. That is to say I came to a decision; and I set out. The house was full of *andártes*, there was mud everywhere, people's voices, and the tramping of feet. We had corn in the house, the *andártes* took it, I don't know how many loads. We had oil, they took it. We had rugs and blankets—I was a girl then and had a dowry made—they took them. They told us to leave the house and not to come back until ten o'clock the next morning, and we went to my uncle's house, and trembled and shook, like this [she folded her hands and shook her whole body convulsively to and fro]. We couldn't stop. I said to my mother, 'What on earth is this? I can't stop shaking.' And she was the same. And so we sat the whole night, and then went back to our house, shaking so much we could hardly walk.

Another time, when the *andártes* had not been to the village for six months, a girl visiting from Kateríni happened to come on the same night as the *andártes*. Hearing that they were looking for her, she spent the night hidden in a corn bin, and in the morning was away down to Kateríni like the wind.

The frequent presence of the *andártes* in the village made an impression on other aspects of life also, and, filthy from their hardships in the mountains, they would come to the village not only for food, but to clean and refresh themselves. One woman laughed as she remembered how they looked, sitting and hunting on their bodies for lice. 'That was when we all became lice-ridden', she said; '*Τότες ψειροβόλησε ὁ τόπος.*'

In Ambéli there were six deaths during that time. Four of these were young men who had joined the *andártes* and were shot by the army at varying times; the other two were inhabitants of the village, Royalists, who were killed by the Communists. The first was, it is said, popular with nobody, for he was a bully and also—a thing insupportable in such a period and never at any time considered admirable—a betrayer of people in the village to those outside. The *andártes* came for him one night early in the civil war, bound his hands, took him, chalk-white and trembling, from the village, and later killed him on the mountain slopes. They took his wife a few nights later, but released her when, as they say, the entire village rushed after them begging for her life and for those of her four children whom they were thus making destitute. The second of these men, however, was universally popular, and nobody could believe that the man with whom they had laughed a moment before, as he made jokes with them outside the church, had been taken and shot where he stood. At the same time as this was happening, other *andártes* were at work setting fire to his widow's house and burning in it everything she possessed. People still remember how the oxen bellowed from within the conflagration, and how the widow and her five children, all under the age of eight, left the next day for Kateríni with nothing but the clothes they wore. It was in the autumn of 1949 that this occurred, and the barbarity of this act is explained by the villagers as being the result of the long years of fighting and suffering, the increase of passion, and the deepening of bitterness.

Immediately following this event, the order went out that the entire village should be evacuated, and within a week this was done, carried out by the army with mules and men temporarily conscripted from the surrounding villages, and the villagers lodged in Kateríni in rooms commandeered from local families. It was a hard time, for although they had brought with them enough wheat to give them bread for that year and into the subsequent year to last them until the harvest, they were not able to bring down the straw which was then vital to the animals, and many of the villagers returned to Ambéli in November of 1950 with their flocks depleted by half. However, this year was noticeable in a positive sense for one thing, in that it 'woke up'—to use their own terminology—the villagers to an awareness of a standard of living and a range of ambitions of which they had until then been hardly aware. This new awareness coincided, after the return to the village, with a period of national economic expansion, and from that date is observable a noticeable degree of social change. In response to any question referring to the beginnings of new ways of thought and new customs in the village, the answer is almost invariably—'After we returned from Kateríni'.

In the old days, the people of Ambéli had been primarily shepherds, and 2,000 to 2,500 head of sheep and goats are reported to have grazed on their mountains before 1955, eating the evergreen bushes that grow in the forests, and the prickly shrubs on the mountain sides. With such a density of animals and no separate feeding stuffs, the animals were barely kept alive in winter, and even migration with the flocks to the nearby plains, leaving the women and children in the village, failed to save more than a quarter of the lambs and kids born, if the winter was a severe one. Agriculture was practised intensively, with up to twelve or thirteen acres of wheat being sown per family, which would provide, at a rough calculation, a family of eight with bread for nine months. For the remaining three months the family would eat bread from maize flour (μπομπότα), although many families ate maize bread for more of the year since they could sell their wheat at a good price and maize was relatively cheap. The use of oxen for ploughing, together with the area put under wheat, meant that the ploughing season could last from October until late April, for oxen are twice as slow as mules, accomplishing only a quarter of an acre in a long day, and the rains that fall in the autumn coupled with snow in winter meant that ploughing was impossible for much of this period.

Owing to the number of grazing animals and the fact that almost all the villagers owned at least a few animals and some as many as 200, the sowing had to be organized on a community basis in special areas set aside for certain crops. In the soil of Ambéli wheat could not, without fertilizer, be grown in the same field for two seasons running. Thus a system of leaving areas for the animals to graze (βοϊδολείβαδο, lit. ox-meadows) coincided with the interests of both shepherding and farming, for it stipulated that all the crops sown in the autumn should be collected in one area from which beasts were prohibited until the harvest from mid-June to July, and all those sown in the summer in another, where animals were allowed until planting began of the maize and chickpeas in

8. Lambing Time

May. The following year the order was reversed. Thus from the harvest time until May of the following year there was always a large area where the flock owners could take their herds unhindered, and without fear of straying animals doing damage. The vital interests of the community therefore coincided on the central point of farm management, and a high (though by no means total) degree of co-operation achieved.

The normal houses included, in the days before 1940, the joint family, which would split up either on the death of the father, or on the development of quarrels or the birth of more children than the house could adequately contain. A common size for such families is said to have been eight. Therefore to the high degree of integration created by the communal co-operation over the land was added the more particularized focus of smaller groups, integrated through kinship and common interest, and related outwards to the community by their various affinal links.

These large families provided the manpower to make complete exploitation of the properties possible, and consequently the land had a value immediately realizable in economic terms. Small children would herd the goats and sheep and watch the cows, one or two men would go to the forest, the remaining members of the family would go to the fields or do any other necessary tasks. There was therefore great competition over land, considerable variation of wealth within the village, and a hierarchy of prestige according to the pre-eminence of a few families.

There was frequent emigration from the village as pressure on the land forced some of the sons away, either to set up a business elsewhere, or more usually to marry uxorilocally as *esógambroi* into one of the neighbouring villages. Land was always at a premium, exchange or sale of land frequent, the value of money was high, and while those who were rich tended to get richer, the poor ones had to struggle even to keep their property. The variation in wealth encouraged a system of patronage, with a few families able to afford workers and to give loans, and the population at the lower end of the scale getting ever more heavily in debt, sometimes so heavily that they were forced to mortgage their properties or, unable to pay their taxes, to surrender land or equipment to the tax-collectors.

The use of oxen for ploughing meant that the working day was very much longer than it is now, and during the periods of most intensive ploughing the families used to return to the village at 11 o'clock at night and set out in the dark at 4 o'clock in the morning, lighting their way with torches of pinewood. At harvest time they would sleep by their fields, start work before dawn, and continue long after sunset by the light of the moon. In addition, however, to gruelling work in the fields, the girls found occasions for gathering together and dancing on the threshing-floors and working the rich embroideries on their costumes, and the young men for going in groups round all the houses on the name-days, omitting, it is said, none, not even those with whom they were on bad terms. And the music and dancing on occasions such as weddings and festivals were such, as they say, 'to stagger the universe' (σήκωσε τὸ σύμπαν).

The standard of living is said to have been the same for both rich and poor. All families would work equally hard, wear the same sort of clothes, eat the same sort of food. But the rich families had more prestige, more gold coins tucked away in their wooden chests, could afford to give their daughters good dowries, to pay workmen, have more animals, and perhaps more yards of material in the sleeves and skirts of the men's dress, and finer trimmings on the women's best clothes, while a man from a very rich family might have a gold coin sewn on to the front of his shoes. These, however, were possessions kept for festivals and Sundays; on working days all the villagers would normally go barefoot and all would dress alike. Not all the men had underclothes, and none of the women, and although shoes could be made out of pig-skin, or more rarely out of certain parts of a mule's hide, these became too stiff in the summer to be worn, and even in winter they would go into holes after a month or two if they were worn every day. No family therefore could afford to provide every member of the family permanently with such shoes, and the villagers' long tradition of self-sufficiency was such as to make it inconceivable for even the richest of them to buy shoes from the towns. On winter days when the snow lay thick on the ground they would wrap their feet with old strips of cloth and come in blue with cold with legs scratched and bleeding where the crusted ice had cut them; and a recurrent disability was a sore place on the sole of the foot which they called λιθοπάτ' (lit. 'hitting by stones') when pus collected deep under the layers of horny skin causing acute pain until it was ripe enough to be lanced with a razor. All the villagers slept in the same way, rolled up in rugs in rows upon the floor, and each family ate in the same way from one big dish set on a rug in front of the hearth, while the pig had to be driven away again and again, and the cocks crowed from the beams above.

The world depression of the 1930s hit Greece hard, and with the fall in agricultural prices the situation for many of the villagers by 1936, when Metaxas came to power, was grim. However, his remission of one-third of all the debts incurred by villagers to the State, the lease of the forest to a local timber merchant, and the high price for resin of 9 to 11 drs. per kilo in the years before the Second World War, set the community on its feet again, and by the time of the outbreak of war with Italy in 1940 the village as a whole is said to have had five million drachmas in the bank. This money, however, was nearly all lost when the drachma was catastrophically devalued at the beginning of the occupation, and everyone was reduced to the same economic level with only the possession of land differentiating the rich from the poor. One man who had come back to Greece from America a few years previously with enough money saved to live in comfort all his life, had only spent a little of it on a house when devaluation deprived him of all the rest. He wept 'black tears', and went back to America for good.

The German conquest of mainland Greece in April 1941, the stoppage of imported wheat, and the appropriation of the existing stocks by the invaders, had by the winter time brought famine to much of Greece. In Athens there was a period when hundreds of people a day died of starvation, the bodies being collected by carts which went round scouring the streets, and all over the land the townspeople flocked to the country offering jewellery, clothes, anything they had, for bread. The people of Ambéli, though better off than those of other villages owning less land, found their bare subsistence livelihood threatened, and from February until the harvest in June 1942 they eked out their meagre stocks of wheat and maize with roasted roots, and ate wild greens till their stomachs revolted at them. During that time there was one death of starvation in the village, a little boy whose mother had been widowed and had married again, and whose step-father and step-sisters edged him out of the house.

The ten years from 1940 to 1950 marked a serious run-down of social and economic activity. Marriages were reduced to a minimum and the resin trade stopped totally until 1945, although the people of the villages were able after 1943 slowly to begin saving a little money here and there by trading locally and by intensive cultivation of their land. Otherwise their lives were concerned chiefly with the perils and tensions of the Italian and later the German occupying troops, and the *andártes*. These empty years formed a break between the old world and the new, and this period can be seen now as the turning-point from which the Greek community as a whole departed from a way of life which accorded coherently with itself and with the system of values it embodied and by which it was organized, to one which, in adjusting to new economic and social conditions, was forced into tension and paradox and the abdication from the totality of many of the former beliefs.

After 1950 everything was to change. The previous living standards had not been due to lack of money only, but also to lack of knowledge, and after personal experience in Kateríni of living in separate rooms, of sleeping in beds, of wearing shoes and socks regularly to work, the villagers decided that they would continue in this way. They began to partition their houses to keep the animals in one half and themselves in the other; to buy clothes and household implements that they had previously done without; they began to use paraffin lamps instead of oil wicks, and to have coffee, sugar, and tinned milk as everyday necessities instead of rare luxuries. At the same time as these household improvements were going on, farming methods were also changing. Tin cups for collecting the resin became more popular, and replaced the wasteful scrapes in the ground at the foot of the trees. Instead of the wooden ploughs tipped with iron, which frequently broke, iron ploughs began to be used, and instead of oxen, horses and mules began to be bought—these last being valuable not only because of the speed at which they walk and because they may be left tethered and not, as do the cows, have to be left to graze and therefore to be watched; but also because they are able to carry heavy loads. The advent of fertilizer revolutionized the wheat farming and by 1956 all the villagers were using fertilizer in both the autumn and the spring and had quadrupled their crop.

After 1950 the claims of the school for the attendance of the children became more stringent, and families found that they increasingly lost their children as goat-, sheep-, and cow-herds to the demands of education. There had, since the school was started at the turn of the century, been a law that all boys should attend, and in 1916 school was made compulsory for girls as well. But parents needed the children to guard the herds, the children did not enjoy school anyway, the community was poor, and the teachers sympathetic. During the troubled times from 1940 to 1950 the school functioned only sporadically, and this accounts for the illiteracy of three inhabitants of the village who were in 1968 relatively young—aged between 34 and 39. But after 1950 the rule governing school attendance became more strict, and this was later matched by the parents' own wish that their children should, unlike so many of themselves, be literate.

The loss of the children to the school, of the growing daughters to the marriages which blossomed in the years of release after 1950, and, after 1960, of the men to the ships and countries abroad, coincided with the easier farming conditions as a result of fertilizer and resulted in the gradual selling, chiefly from 1958 until 1963, of the flocks of sheep and goats, until only two flocks were left. Resin gathering, however, still continued, and in 1965 the stabilizing of the resin prices at 4 drs. a kilo by government subsidy ensured a regular cash income for all those who owned forests and were able, or willing, to work them.

As a consequence of all this, the standard of living within the village and expectations from the outside world began to change, and instead of extreme physical hardship and a high degree of self-sufficiency, people began to reduce their hours of toil in the fields, to live more comfortably in their homes, and to develop a way of life involving increasing dependence on more modernized communities and a gradual acquaintance with urban ways of life.

One of the most significant features to arise from this change was an altered form of self-interest, and a very radical shift in the balance of forces which kept the community together. Ironically, with the entry into village life of material improvements and wider ambitions, the whole structure of the community life began to disintegrate, and inroads began to be made into the traditional pattern which were to result eventually in emigration and depopulation.

Before the war the necessity for reciprocity over the fields and animals, and for a high degree of interdependence in the internal affairs of the village because of the lack of amenities, meant that the interests of the village as a whole forced upon its inhabitants a certain degree of mutual co-operation. Self-interest in a narrow sense had to give way to the good of the community, and within the joint family individualism had to be strictly suppressed for the group as a whole to be able to function. As late as 1967, when the spiritual kinsman of a man with few resources at harvest time was helping him with his threshing, he commented: 'What can we do? We have to help one another since we find ourselves in such a useless place.' In his own understanding, the more 'useless' the place, the more its inhabitants have to depend on each other. This sentiment is borne out by the facts.

In the old days, groups of women had to collect for ten hours, two or three together in rotation, to beat a thick woollen cloth in water with their hands to felt it; now they go for all their clothes and even some of their traditional dowry articles to the shops in Kateríni or to the little weaving factory, and when I asked if the same degree of co-operation could be found now as had existed in earlier times, I was told, 'What, find so many women on good enough terms with each other to get together *now* . . .?' In the days before World War II there were several doctors in the area who would come up to the village in an emergency, but lack of any regular system of medical aid meant that the community had to be largely self-reliant and to depend on those of its own members who knew spells and herbs, and were healers or midwives. Today the community has little need of its local healers, for people go regularly down to the doctor in Kateríni, and since 1964 all the village women have had their babies in the clinic in Kateríni or in Chalkís.

Before 1950, joint families and a system of patronage linked the family groups to the outside community by relationships of marriage and obligation; the pre-eminence of the kindred, marriage into a hierarchy of prestige and wealth associated with possession of the land, the unquestioning acceptance of the agricultural and pastoral life and of the related values of independence and honour, were all values which kept the community solidly rooted in itself and in its environment; and these factors resulted in a total system in which the interests of the various families and those of the community coincided to a very great degree. Today the reverse applies, and the increasing reliance on the outside world, the diversification of ambitions, the decreasing value of the land

and the increasing dependence on cash, the fragmentation of the family group, the dispersal of the flocks and the incomplete exploitation of the farms, the rise of individualism and the weakening of traditional ties between the family, its kin, and its land, all involve the different families of the community in interests which basically diverge from those of their neighbours. The same force, that of self-interest in terms of the survival of the family, still persists; but the changed economic and social scene now provides an environment in which the impulses of generation and survival no longer act towards the exclusiveness and solidarity of the community, but flow outwards to cause village society to identify itself more and more with the nearby towns. Thus, along with a higher standard of living, a divergence of aims and a latitude for the individual are being brought into village life that act against a united social organization, and towards the breakdown of many of the traditional curbs on hostility and quarrelling.

The villagers' unanimous verdict on the worsening of social relations in recent years has been referred to earlier, and expressed in the phrase, 'The community has fallen into a state of hatred' (ὁ κόσμος ἔχει πέσει σὲ μῖσος). Two other phrases express the same idea. In the older days, the villagers say, 'People were on good terms with one another' (ἦταν ἀγαπημένος ὁ κόσμος), whereas now, 'Hatred exists' (ὑπάρχει μῖσος). Undoubtedly such sentiments are the result partly of nostalgia for the old days and the villagers' perennial longing for an unattainable state of concord, but nevertheless there appears in the present structure of village life as compared to that of pre-1955 much to indicate that these generalizations rest on a basis of truth.

One cause for this change from, as the villagers put it, love to hatred, or, as it may otherwise be put, from social solidarity to fragmentation, lies in the altered form of self-interest already discussed. Another lies in the altered value now given to the concept of 'advancement' or 'progress', for because of the increasing attraction of the way of life presented by the outside world, the terms in which progress are defined now relate exclusively to that outside world. While in the old days progress could be realized within the terms of village life, it can now be realized only by leaving that life for good. Thus the only really prestigious individual is one who has left the village, and so by the time he has gained, in village eyes, this prestige, he has left the sphere in which this type of evaluation operates. Prestige, therefore, is virtually unattainable within the terms of village life.

While, however, the means of achieving an unambiguous prestige within the village has largely disappeared, the struggle for pre-eminence has retained its momentum, and the only change in this respect between past and present is in the form in which this struggle now manifests itself. In former times the opposition of families was given particular scope in the continual struggle for physical existence, because there was in the most literal sense not enough to go round. Now that the whole traditional way of life has been devalued, envy continues to work and competition is as fierce as ever, but failing any outlet in a struggle for the effective attainment and retention of wealth and prestige, it is forced to express itself increasingly in words and actions which result in gossip and quarrels. At the same time there exists to a much lesser extent the traditional bar to unlimited quarrelling which was in earlier times provided by the villagers' need of one another. It is partly as a result of this that the word used to describe relationships within the village in the present day is not 'love' but 'hatred', and it is possible too that this, so to speak, negative way of competing—by denigration rather than by emulation—should have the effect of making this competition cumulatively more damaging than it used to be.

A further effect of the focusing of ambitions in terms realizable outside the village rather than within it, coupled with the inability of the villagers to exploit their properties fully and the levelling out of financial inequality in the crisis of 1940, is a radical change in the values attributed to the land. Land, it is frequently said, is immortal—it cannot die, it is always a secure investment; the man of property will live in the knowledge of the acres he has behind him, with their potential productivity and their possible monetary value should the wheel of fortune turn and Ambéli become accessible to timber merchants or building prospectors. Yet as he finds himself in the reality of the present economic moment the villager realizes that he is in possession of a commodity which he is not able to sell or fully to exploit, and which has no value as a dowry for his daughters or a legacy for his sons. Thus although people are still thought of as rich or poor in accordance with the property they own, this is an assessment gauged in unreal terms according to past standards of prestige which are not applicable to the present day. This situation illustrates one instance of the ambivalence of the mental conception the villager has of himself, both as an individual and as a member of the community. According to one standard of reference he is a landowner, and, depending on how much land he owns, a prestigious and independent member of society, backed by a property the value of which has been attested to by generations of his forebears, commanding the respect both of his fellow villagers and of the community at large. On the other hand he is a poor man in a dwindling community, a member of that despised race, the farmer, having to struggle hard merely to keep abreast of the minimal requirements of the modern world, and to save enough money to launch his children out into the world of technical and educated people that lies outside his village. One of the poles between which the villager alternates from a solid self-respect to a sort of despair is that which used to be the axis of financial stability and social worth—the possession of land.

While, therefore, it is in theory thought to be desirable to have a large property, in fact even a family owning relatively little land lacks the working force to cultivate it all, and is therefore, in terms of actual productivity, no worse off than the large landowner who is in the same position, and simply has more land to leave uncultivated. As a result of this, no one can by sheer possession of property gain anything amounting to a reputation for prestige—even though such possession may in certain contexts be a mark in his favour.

Thus the present situation is one in which not only is farming a trade that, compared with others of the modern world, carries very little renown; the farmer himself within the village is unable even to gain a relative prestige from his fellow villagers. There does still exist in Ambéli a kind of social ranking according to which one particular family may be known to be more successful than others, and others—such as the family in which nearly everyone is insane —which are not. However, the changing criteria of prestige have had the effect of making such recognition increasingly hard to attain, and on the whole it is true to say that there is no longer within the village an effective social ranking; there is not even one family which represents either to itself or to anyone else the fulfilment of village ambition; there is only a series of families all struggling (with the exception of the old) to get away. While, therefore, there are 'good' families, and those that are less 'good', these are on the whole placed according to individual preference and loyalty and individual application of community values, and therefore form a hierarchy which is infinitely variable, altering from day to day and even from house to house.

The alteration in the value placed on land is not the only factor which has affected this change in prestige values, although it is an important one. The break-up of the family through emigration and marriage out of the village has resulted in prestige being centred not in the good name of the house but in individual achievement, while the low esteem in which the village is held means that prestige through the marriage alliance is no longer achieved through the linking of the honour and wealth of two families, but by casting off for ever the bonds of village life. In this situation the part played by cash becomes increasingly important, for land can no longer be given in dowries and the 'good' bridegroom of a village in the plains is not normally content with a bride who brings with her less than 60,000 drs. At the same time, the cost of food, clothes, schoolbooks, and the extra expenses involved in higher education (which is becoming a necessity for girls as well as for boys and is another way in which the traditional dowry is being replaced) takes up a very large proportion of family incomes. Thus although the economic situation in Greece began to improve dramatically in the mid-1950s and has retained the same momentum until the present day, the expectations of the villagers are, as time passes, overreaching more and more their actual financial capabilities. In comparison with the past they are, materially speaking, infinitely better off. In comparison with the modern competitive world they are barely holding their own, and their self-respect suffers accordingly. If poverty may be judged by the discrepancy between what people have and what they want, the villagers of Ambéli today are probably poorer than they have ever been.

The present situation is, however, not only the result of wider ambitions, but also of a geographical position which has denied the villager of Ambéli the possibility of realizing any but a few of these ambitions within the confines of his village; and if any one factor is to be isolated as overwhelmingly responsible for the present state of depopulation in Ambéli—taken as given the initial movement towards change in the general shift of values from 1950 onwards—it could be said to be the lack of a road. This lack had, in 1966 when I first went to the village, bitten so deeply into the villagers' consciousness that any description of their village invariably ended with the words, 'It hasn't got a road.'

The contrast between Ambéli and the surrounding villages did not come about simply by virtue of the fact that Ambéli had no road while the plains had one, for the contrast is comparatively recent, whereas there has been a road in the plains, of a sort, since 1905, and a rudimentary bus service since 1917. The change came about after the Second World War, when machines were introduced into village life for which a road was indispensable, and when as a result of this certain villages became, at least in part, mechanized, while others did not. By 1966 things had reached such a pass that while in all the villages of the area the harvest was threshed by combine harvesters and transported by lorries, only in Ambéli was it not only cut by hand, but threshed by the animals and winnowed by hand as well. Every kilo of resin had to be taken by mule to Kateríni on Sundays and, in the autumn, every sack of fertilizer brought up the same way.

The good life, now seen almost entirely in terms realizable by living in a semi-urbanized environment, is thus inaccessible to the villager of Ambéli who has no way in which he can live like his civilized counterpart in Kateríni. The latter can dress up and sit in a café 'like a human being' (σὰν ἄνθρωπος), go to a cinema, eat a cake in a sugar shop, and on Saturday evenings go for a leisurely stroll down the street with his friends, both gazed upon and gazing; he can even, if he is reasonably prosperous, take a taxi to Athens for a day or two's sightseeing, and have three suits— one for weekdays, one for Sundays, and one for holidays. But to the villager of Ambéli all these longed-for activities are denied, and he is, in addition to this, forced to carry on his farming under conditions now almost totally outmoded in all the surrounding area. No electricity and no running water add to the physical hardship of his life, and it has been said to me more than once, 'Is this a life? We live like animals.'

This is the situation which has brought about the recent emigration, and the emigration itself affects the situation, making the lot of those who remain still harder—for an absolute value in the village (as in Greece as a whole) is the existence of *Kósmos* (κόσμος), people, a world in itself. Lack of easy communications with the outside world means not only that the villagers only get out with difficulty, but that the outside world never comes in in any numbers except, as was mentioned earlier, for the annual festival. And within the village, year by year, the tempo of life slows as the young people leave and the hope for the future languishes still more. In 1968 one of the main factors deciding emigration was the lack of population itself, for once the population falls below a certain optimum level it ceases to have regenerative faculties within itself and so cannot survive.

The Greek family is structured round its children, and all its physical, economic, and moral resources go into the shaping of these children and into caring for their future well-being. Thus the ambitions of parents for their children, and the way in which they accept their children's ambitions, is a sure index of the values they hold with regard to the modern world. Every villager has an explicit ambition for his children to live better than he did, and this better life is seen exclusively in terms of a more urbanized and literate existence. However, these values have been reached as the result of a drastic period of social change and are still not completely assimilated into the total value system, for this still holds very large traditional elements which conflict with the conscious adulation of and desire for the modern world.

This, as has been discussed earlier, involves them in a duality which they often do not admit and are certainly unable to resolve, for while they are completely committed to the break-away from the traditional forms of village life, they see many of the implications of such a disruption as contrary to much of what they have, until now, held to be good: as leading to the proliferation of hatreds and quarrels, to the unwillingness of one person to help another, to the changing customs for engagements and the increasing abandonment of traditional standards of feminine honour, to growing neglect of the land, to the loss of the old knowledge, resourcefulness, independence, and gaiety, to the break-up of the family group and to an increasing secularization of standards in every sense. So while every member of the community accepts without reserve on its own level the statement that the community is working towards a better life, and mobilizes all his resources towards ensuring that his children have a part in that life, and while this overriding value may cause him to accept verbally all the attributes of the modern world, he still keeps—even if in a contradictory and fragmented form—many of his traditional attitudes.

Although therefore, statistically speaking, the population has voted overwhelmingly for participation in the modern world and for approval of its values, this must be understood as one aspect only of a very complex way of thought and system of values which has been only partially modified by confrontation with new criteria for progress and prestige, and which still exists as a body of beliefs and ideas which in many respects conflict profoundly with the more modern ideology. The degree to which the population is still held by traditional beliefs is determined largely by age and education, and in Ambéli there is still to be found every range of belief from the old woman who knows, and trusts, charms and spells, and who despises doctors as charlatans who simply 'make things worse', to the young woman whose one ambition is to marry a civil servant and live in a town with shops and a cinema. But the older way of thought is not in fact retained exclusively by the old, for the sheer geographical position, the remoteness, and the type of occupations carried on in Ambéli, all render it inevitable that the traditional mentality continues strongly in all who are married and settled in the village, and thus committed still to that way of life. By empathy, and to a certain degree by actual experience of the modern world, a desire for a deeper participation in the advantages of urban civilization has become universal in Ambéli; but while empathy can produce a kind of mental identification with its object, it cannot produce the deep transformation of values which would create a consistent set of beliefs developed out of the old value system in accordance with new social realities.

The result for the villager is that he lives for a large part of the time in two ideological worlds at once. It is this that enables him to have a certain pride in himself and in the integrity of his work, while at the same time looking on his life as the meanest in creation. It is this that at the same time as causing such depopulation, allows the remaining villagers a vitality and a sense of life which does not accord with the sort of despair shown by the population index, and which prompted one woman of 56 to argue quite seriously against the emigration of the last members of a family— 'What will become of the vineyard?' The vineyard was half an acre.

The very desire of young people to emigrate, and the sympathy of their parents with this desire, presuppose the existence of a way of life from which they want to escape; but escape from many of the values held by that life is only possible once the life itself has been shaken off. This in itself is one of the main factors which causes the survival of traditional values in such a situation, and which re-creates and sustains a community even in the very throes of final depopulation.

EPILOGUE

THE structure which has been examined in this book represents on the whole a static pattern which is based on respect for traditional knowledge and an unquestioning acceptance of the social forms in which this knowledge was preserved. The unquestioning nature of this acceptance has until very recently been the strength of the village way of life, for the simple answer to any question, 'That's how we learned it and that's how we leave it' (῎Ετσι τὰ μάθαμε καὶ ἔτσι τὰ ἀφίνουμε), was proof against doubt and change. However, recent times have brought a threat to the security of traditional thinking to which such sheer conviction is, on its own, no answer, and all the various pressures and attractions of the modern world have combined to undermine the villager at what is now his weakest point—his lack of understanding of why he has traditionally followed the pattern of life that he has.

This pattern, derived from the dicta of a theocratic society which now no longer exists, has over the generations steadily been losing contact with the cosmology, or cosmologies, that first gave it birth, and the result is the present situation in which the beliefs and customs which it involved have survived as forms only, of which the intellectual content has largely been lost. This by no means implies that these forms are no longer significant, for sheer adherence to a particular ritual is able, even while lacking in conscious understanding, to evoke in the performer something of what it represents. Nevertheless, preservation without understanding produces a precarious equilibrium which is easily upset when violently challenged by an opposing system, and is liable to two dangers. One is that an inflexibility, leading to ignorance and even to barbarism, should develop through a lack of enlightenment from within; the other that the inherited conviction of the validity of these forms should succumb easily to a philosophy with a more readily comprehensible rationale. The particular savagery with which feminine honour, for instance, has traditionally been defended and lack of it punished, particularly in places like Crete or the Mani, or among the Sarakatsani, illustrates an instance of the former danger, when what should be an icon has become an idol. The latter is in constant evidence all over Greece today as the old symbolic patterns of life are being eroded by a new and basically secular idea of man, and as the people's understanding, insufficiently fed by their own tradition, is persuaded easily into abandonment of customs which suddenly appear to them to have no meaning. Ways of mourning, rejoicing, fasting, feasting, and a hundred and one other customs which all add up to a sense of life both intricate and profound, are more and more being relegated to the so-called *koutsohoriá* (κουτσοχωριά)—the 'backward' or 'primitive villages', as they are contemptuously named—of which Ambéli is one; while those who can leave such villages, together with those who have already left, do their best for themselves and their families according to a way of life which provides them not only with a higher standard of living but also with the logical, if limited, system of thought that goes with it.

It may be too late for the Greek villagers to be able to regain any lasting sense of the validity of their traditional way of life— though there are still, in villages less depopulated than Ambéli and possessing more modern conveniences, those who wish to go on being farmers. But whatever the fate of this society, and whatever may have been its limitations and its defects, there is no doubt that when it was integrated to a living tradition it gave to life both dignity and meaning—qualities which are conspicuously lacking in the type of society that threatens to succeed it.

APPENDICES

APPENDIX I
EMIGRATION AND DEMOGRAPHY

IMPOSSIBILITY of access to the demographic records of the community—such as they are—has forced me to extract what conclusions I could from various rather inadequate sources. Written sources are the forestry books for 1941 and 1945,[1] and the Census of 1961. Figures given from my own knowledge of the community are also exact, but they cover only a very limited period, from July 1966 to July 1968. These figures, therefore, taken together with a description of life in the old days as told me by the villagers, can do no more than give a rough sketch of population from 1853 until the present day, although the trends indicated may be taken to be accurate.

It is known from the number of properties, or *zevgária* as they are called,[2] into which the territory of Ambéli was first divided that there were at that time, in 1853, nineteen property owners. It is likely that this figure does not indicate the number of elementary families, since the custom at that time was for the married sons to live, at any rate for some years, with their parents. With the nineteen householders, therefore, there were certainly in many cases several families living under the same roof. In 1941, the date of the first forestry book, the village is described as having forty 'inhabitants' (κατοίκους), which must be taken to mean, again, heads of houses. By 1945 this number had risen to forty-four. In 1957 when the first attempt was made at a systematic listing of all the inhabitants of the village, the number is said to have been around 180 persons. In 1961 this figure had fallen to 171;[3] and by 1966 when I went to the village there were 144 inhabitants, a figure which had fallen by the same month two years later to 132—diminished by thirteen people due to death, emigration, and marriage out, and increased by the birth of one.

The figures given in the following charts are for the resident population only, which is, from the point of view of the viability of the village, the section of the community that has to be taken into account. Absent from the village abroad were 29 young men, divided among various countries in the following proportions: Germany 8; Belgium 6; Canada 6; Australia 1; South Africa 1. Seven men were, in 1966–8, in the

---

[1] *K. B. Δαμιανοῦ* (1941) and (1947).
[2] *Ζευγάρια*. For an explanation of this term see p. 37, n. 1, and Appendix II on Land Tenure.
[3] Population Census for 1961.

Merchant Navy. These men ranged between the ages of 15 and 42, by far the larger proportion being those between 26 and 34, i.e. born between 1930 and 1938. This exodus began in 1961 and has continued to the present day.

Included in the reckoning of the resident population are three people, one married man and one married couple, working in Germany but keeping their children and, in the case of the former, his wife also, in the village, and sending money regularly for their upkeep. But excluded from the count was one man who was at Athens University and who was to be a grammar-school teacher, and one who had become an

Table I
Demographic situation in July 1966
compared with that of July 1968
July 1966

A Married couples, widows, widowers	B Aged over 13 years. Unmarried (born before 1953)	C Aged between 6 and 12 years, i.e. attending the Demotic school (born between 1953 and 1960)	D Aged birth to 6 years	Total
80 M / \ F 39 41	22 M / \ F $(\frac{8}{7}2)\ (\frac{14}{4})^{*}$ 6 10	19 M / \ F 11 8	23 M / \ F 11 12	144

July 1968
The change in population is assessed in terms of the above categories, treating them as static

			+1 girl, born 1967	
−2 −3 37 38 M \ / F 75	−3 −5 3 5 M \ / F (+2) (+4) 14	11 8 M \ / F 19	11 13 M \ / F 24	132

* In terms of the assessment of the reproductive capacities of this group, six people, two men and four women, must be omitted. Three of these are crippled through, variously, polio, meningitis, and laming through an unknown disease; two through severe mental illness; one through the necessity for her to look after her old parents and mentally ill siblings. The youngest member of this sub-group is 37. The number of people of marriageable status, therefore, as opposed to marriageable age, is reduced to six men and ten women.

electrician in Chalkis, because they are only in the village occasionally and cannot be considered a regular part of village life. It should be pointed out also that these figures are not static but vary from month to month—one man, included among the numbers of those who have emigrated, returned to the village for over a year after being expelled from the host country for having remained there without a residence

Table II
Changing categories of villagers
between July 1966 and July 1968

A Married couples, widows, widowers	B Aged over 13 years. Un-married (born before 1953)	C Aged between 6 and 12 years, i.e. attending the Demotic school (born between c. 1953 and 1960)	D Aged birth to 6 years	Total
80 M/\F 39 41	22 M/\F 8 14 (—2) (—4) 6 10	19 M/\F 11 8	23 M/\F 11 12	144
Married couples, widows, widowers	Aged over 13 years, Unmarried (born before 1955)	Aged between 6 and 12 years, i.e. attending the Demotic school (born between c. 1955 and 1962)	Aged birth to 6 years	
—2 —3 37 38 M\/F 75	—3 —5 +3 +1 6 6 M\/F (+2)(+4) 18	—3 —1 +6 +5 14 12 M\/F 26	—6 —5 (birth)+1 5 8 M\/F 13	132

permit. This is often done by those who first join the Merchant Navy, work their way to a chosen country on a ship, and then stay there without labour permits trusting to friends to shelter them. Another man came back briefly from the ships to be with his family when they married their last daughter, and stayed on for a period to help with the farm. This type of resident, however, who is only temporarily in the village, survives there merely by enduring it, waiting only for the time when he can return to urban life, whether in Greece or abroad. These people therefore, while they make life more pleasant for their families and swell the population of the village while they are in it, cannot be considered as altering the population index in any significant way.

The most striking feature of these figures is an emigration rate, among the important category of those who are of marriageable age and status, which is almost total. The two years between 1966 and 1968 saw almost all the members of this group B effectively lost to the village; five women and two men married away, and one boy, aged 16, went into the Merchant Navy. Of the three males left, two were away doing their National Service and did not return to the village when they had completed it, and one was at the Kateríni grammar school and is naturally not expected to return to the village when he has finished his studies. Of the five girls left in this category, one was away at the grammar school, three were of marriageable age (19, 20, and 26 years old), and one was 15. All these girls were adamant in their intention to marry away from the village, and the three families of the eldest girls were all in the process of trying to arrange a marriage for them. This group therefore had by 1968 largely dispersed, or was shortly to do so, leaving only the hard core of six who were not able to marry or have children.

Of course the population of the village was still high enough in 1968 to sustain this depletion of a certain category, in the sense that there were at that moment enough children of a lower age group to fill the ranks of the older one as it dispersed, and it may be seen from Table II that the relative composition of group B, after two years had passed and eight members had left, was down only by four. But to compensate for even this small benefit was the fact that all the four new entrants to this group on leaving the elementary school in the village were continuing their studies at the grammar school in Kateríni, and were therefore lost to the village for two-thirds of the year. Also, more vitally, there had been no marriages in the village since 1964, and no children born since 1967, so that as the infants and the school-children reached more mature ages, no new generations were born to replace them. With the cessation of marriages from 1965 onwards, together with the current trend to limit families to an average of two or at the most three children, it seems that the replenishment of the community from new births will almost entirely cease, and a steady decline of population from emigration, marriage out of the village, and death is inevitable.

APPENDIX II
LAND TENURE

O F the 12,500 *strémmata*[1] bought by the inhabitants, only 6,000 *str.* were originally divided up officially amongst them. This was because the partition of the property was a long and expensive operation carried out by a professional surveyor, and the village could not afford to pay the fees necessary for a total survey of the whole area. The best land therefore, forest and field, was allotted to inhabitants individually, while the more precipitous or infertile ground was left undivided as common land. In this way the nineteen householders, plus the Church as additional property owner, each came into possession of what was known as one *zevgári*, amounting to 300 *str.*

A *zevgári* is the word used for a pair of anything and in farming refers without further description to the pair of animals used in ploughing. In the area of Ambéli it is also used as a term of measurement which is standard in any one village, but which varies in its application from village to village. One *zevgári* in Ambéli equals approximately 300 *str.*, but in Kateríni, where 25,000 *str.* were divided into eighty-nine portions, one *zevgári* equals approximately 282 *str.* The word *zevgári* therefore includes both the notion of property as well as that of extent.

As well as being sub-dividable into *strémmata*, the *zevgári* may also be reckoned in terms of a different form of measurement, the *dhrámi* (δράμι pl. δράμια).

A *dhrámi* is a concrete measurement in that 400 *dhrámia* = 1 *zevgári*, 300 *dhrámia* = ¾ *zevgári*, and so on, and, being more easily sub-dividable than a *zevgári*, is the measurement used officially for the landholdings of Ambéli. Each inheritance or sale is officially recorded, and the requisite amount of *dhrámia* added to or subtracted from the individual's list of holdings. However, although *dhrámia* is a term used to refer to a total property including forest and arable land, agricultural land as such is in fact invariably reckoned in *strémmata*, and it is only the forests that are administered in *dhrámia*. The result of this—since forest can be evaluated both by the number of trees in a particular area, and by the spatial extent of the area—is that the *dhrámi*, being applied particularly to forest, becomes a unit which is applied not only to extent but also to number. It is when it is applied to the latter that its exact value varies according to the type of forest it designates. If, for instance,

[1] As noted earlier, 1 *strémma* = 0·2471 acres.

a piece of land of 80 *dhrámia* has 320 trees in it, 1 *dhrámi* = 4 trees; in a piece of land the same size but with 400 trees, 1 *dhrámi* = 5 trees.

This double concept held in the notion of *dhrámia*—that of extent and of number—is responsible for the villagers' description of this form of measurement as 'indefinite' (ἀόριστο); and for a certain confusion in the way in which they think of their *dhrámia*. For although total properties are assessed by *dhrámia*, the arable part of these is for practical purposes converted into *strémmata* as the situation requires. Thus when a man gives away some fields, he does not think of giving the *dhrámia* but of giving the *strémmata* belonging to the *dhrámia*. This is because while the allocation of trees within an extent of land needs a flexible method of assessment to which the *dhrámi*, linked as it is to the proportional nature of the *zevgári*, is admirably suited, land is a constant factor and has in the *strémma* a unit of measurement which is also constant.

The concept of *dhrámia*, then, is used in general as an over-all way of assessing relative wealth in terms of property as a whole, and, in specific, to refer to stretches of the forest, or to specific numbers of trees within that forest. Being a variable unit of measurement in the way mentioned above, it is particularly useful for proportional distribution of forest areas where boundaries are uncertain, or are being reorganized.

The surveyor who carried out the original division of the property recorded it in a document known as the *Mánna* (Μάννα), of which there is one copy, which is the joint record of the whole of the original partition in the form of several pages of maps. It is a beautifully constructed document meticulously drawn up, with the land assessed in quality according to five categories. It was attempted from the beginning to effect a fair division, and because of the uneven nature of the land this was possible only by dint of dividing up the properties into a number of different sections so that everyone got the same proportion of good and indifferent land. As a result of this there is evident in this original map a high degree of fragmentation as people were allotted pieces from every category of the land spreading over a wide part of the area. Each *zevgári* was given a number, from 1 to 20, and in the *Mánna* the boundaries are drawn in with exact measurements; within each plot of ground the number of the *zevgári* is given on a line over the number of *strémmata*, e.g. $\frac{3}{1 \cdot 75 \ str.}$, and the name of the owner is added.

On every page the compass points are drawn in, north and south, and the completely infertile and rocky regions are drawn in with little patches of shading.

Unfortunately, although this document is known by the villagers as the *Mánna*, it is not in fact legally one at all, for a proper *Mánna* or

Index of Landholdings (*Πίναξ Κτηματολογικός*) is an index which has been ratified both by the Ministry of Agriculture in Athens, and by the local Public Records Office. This type of document is a legal record and is altered over the years as property is transferred. The document of Ambéli, not having been submitted on completion to any authority for reasons, the villagers say, of economy, has no such standing and cannot be used in a court of law. Over the years it found its way into the keeping of a certain family whose members have continually been involved in quarrels over land and who are reported by the villagers to have torn out or defaced any pages which give evidence contradicting their claims. Various separate pages are in the keeping of individual families who have somehow or other acquired them in the past.[1]

Apart from the *Mánna* there is another type of document available, known as a Land Register (*Κτηματολόγιον*). There are several of these, each one consisting of an individual record of the fields belonging to any one *zevgári* or part of a *zevgári*. It is likely that these Land Registers were drawn up at a date later than that of the *Mánna*, after the original *zevgária* had become to a certain extent sub-divided, for none of the Land Registers that I have seen lists properties as large as the 300 *str.* which is given as the size of the original holdings. These records are in the form of books having on the cover the number of the particular *zevgári* and the name of the original landowner. These landowners were the grandfathers of the present holders. Inside on the first page they list in *strémmata* the total of fields, sub-divided into four categories, and the total of forest, with finally the combined total of all the *strémmata* possessed. The following pages list every individual plot of land in the property, with the name of the particular locality in which it is found; the measurements of the boundaries are given, the category of land in which it occurs, and the names of the owners of adjoining plots. These books are, as far as they go, clear records, but they have not been altered since they were first drawn up, almost certainly some time late in the last century, and so are imperfect testimonies as to ownership of land in the present day. Several families have in fact no Land Registers and no record of their landholdings at all. Some have lost theirs, others have never gained possession of one, it having previously passed into the hands of a co-inheritor. The example of the first page of a Land Register which I give below is inaccurate for instance, in that $66\frac{1}{2}$ *dhrámia* of the total are due to a man now living in Kateríni who had a right to it before the remainder was sold to the present owner's father.

A	B	C	D	Fields	Forest	Total
6·800	26·600	52·200	42·300	127·900	45·00	172·900

[1] I did not gain access to the main folio, but I did see one sheet.

Inside were several pages of the type previously described, listing in all 42 different plots, and in some cases marking a shared ownership.

A third type of document, occasionally used in past times, though increasingly relied upon since 1950, is the Contract (*Συμβόλαιο*), a document written out by the public notary regarding inheritance, dowry, or sale, and filed in the Public Records Office. However, although they provide an accurate record of the *dhrámia* owned by any individual, they cannot be relied upon to settle an argument about the possession of a particular plot of land, because they designate the land not by exact boundaries and location, but simply by stating the number of the *zevgári* from which the land was bought, the amount bought, and the composition of the *dhrámia* as regards the size and number of (a) fields and (b) forest departments (*τεμάχια*).

This system of records therefore is inadequate to settle quarrels over ownership of land legally and without injustice. The *Mánna*, invalid in a court of law, is used only as a private guide in the rare instances that the interested party can get a glimpse of the relevant sheet; the Land Registers, written out about seventy years ago, provide an accurate description of the boundary division in any *zevgári*, but designate ownership as it was in the present villages' grandfathers' generation rather than in the present day; the Contracts, more accurate than the two foregoing records, necessarily have an indicative rather than a definitive function owing to the way in which they are drawn up. The historical situation, the nature of the topography under partition, the economic necessity for every householder to be a farmer and the consequent extreme fragmentation of the land, all combine to make the inadequacy of these documents inevitable. The nature of the original division, allocating land more by boundaries than by invariable and canonical extent, has been carried on into the present day, and has resulted in a situation in which the working of the law must rely chiefly upon witnesses and only tangentially upon documents. The demands in the lawcourts are not for written proof of a situation, but such questions as, 'Who tapped this tree five years ago?' 'What do you remember your father saying of this particular boundary?' A subjective system based on witnesses and personal memory as to boundaries and ownership, rather than objective appeal to legal documents, is therefore basic to the structure of the law with regard to land tenure. As the activities of witnesses are closely related to kinship, and to concepts such as self-interest and obligation, this creates a situation which is continually in flux, and always potentially combustible.

The dowry and inheritance systems have added to the difficulties of the situation in fragmenting still further the already fragmented land, in proliferating ownership, and in increasing dissension. This situation is still further complicated by the original Land Registers necessarily remaining in the hands of one family only, who therefore have (and often use) the power to refuse access to it by any relatives with whom they are not on good terms.

The history of the common land, which was at the time of the original partition not shared out, is also a source of considerable hostility among the present villagers. This land was kept as common land until *c.* 1955, and any letting of the common forest to timber merchants by the village was undertaken jointly, and the money paid was shared among the landowners in proportion to the *dhrámia* they possessed. Over the years, however, and increasingly after 1955, certain villagers had been extending their cultivation of fields or the tapping of trees into this common ground. Sometimes these operations were noticed but not complained about by others, sometimes there were fights 'with axes' for the right to claim a particular area. In 1960 all the people who had appropriated bits of the community forest, or who had hired the trees and then claimed them for their own, went to the lawcourts and were given possession. Common land thus disappeared from the community, and the Church *zevgári* with it. Those who added to their estates were satisfied; those who had not, referred to it, and still do, as 'stolen' land. The way in which this land was allotted to the present owners was not as permanent deed of transfer, but as a means whereby the original owners (in this case the community and the Church) retained legal ownership, but lost the right to the usufruct of the land which passed into the hands of the new cultivators. The only way in which the community can reassert its claim to the land is by accepting one of the two present schemes for land consolidation.

This allocation of land to someone other than the legal owner, on the grounds of his cultivation of the land over a certain period, was based on a law known locally as the Law of Possession (*Νόμος Κατοχῆς*), passed in 1946.[1] This law was designed to regulate the continually varying situation as regards the possession of land in Greece, and decreed that if a certain man cultivates for twenty years a field which is not his, and no complaint is lodged against him within that period, he is awarded possession. On the basis of this law the local lawcourt in Kateríni developed the custom of settling disputes over land on the principle of awarding the usufruct of any land to the person who has for the preceding year worked that land unchallenged. This is a simple mechanism for a quick settlement of a confused situation, which the owner can reverse by appeal to a higher court (*Πρωτοδικεῖον*), if he can produce sufficient proof as to his true ownership. However, many people in the past have for various reasons not progressed to the higher

---

[1] *Ἑλληνικὸς Ἀστικὸς Κῶδιξ* (Greek Civil Code), 23 February 1946.

court, and have lost their land; and according to the opinion of certain
people it is from the date of the introduction of this law that the
hostility which now exists within the village took root. Before that date,
people took land from one another by force, but the evicted owner was
only temporarily, not permanently, victimized. After 1946, this type of
theft became consolidated, and one frequent result was that a man
renting some land from another man would then cultivate it for a year
or two, go to a court of law and deny paying for it, and then be awarded
its use. However the known list of landholdings in Ambéli (over page) is
reckoned in *dhrámia* with any additions to or subtractions from the
holdings duly entered, and land acquired from individuals for usufruct
only and that acquired under the 1960 appropriation of common ground
is not considered legally owned and is not included.

There is therefore a considerable deviation in the practice of land
tenure in Ambéli from the theory, for the law itself has been forced, in
local practice and in the 1960 distribution, to accommodate itself to the
practice of theft and the impossibility of accurately verifying ownership,
while recognizing that this is merely a settlement of a situation rather
than being an application of justice. A man may in fact have claims
over a great deal more land than he appears to own, or, conversely, a
certain amount less. However, the manpower situation in the village,
the use of fertilizer, the size of families, and the rate of emigration all
coincide to produce a situation in which only one family wants or is able
to cultivate more than its legal holdings. The fact that everyone has
enough for their capacity to work has not lessened the degree of quarrelling over land, since quarrels generally occur not over necessities but
over rights. But it does result in the wealth of each family being
assessed by the villagers themselves in the terms represented by the size
of their landholdings, so these may be taken as indicating an important
aspect of relative wealth in Ambéli.

It is hard to assess, from the information available, the exact degree
of fragmentation of these properties, but it is likely that the figures
given in the Land Register quoted above are representative of the over-
all general condition. In this record, the largest single area of unafforested
land was 29·6 *str.* of which 15·6 *str.* were in category C and 14·4 in
category D. This field was shared with another owner, thus reducing
the largest undivided plot of ground to 15 *str.* The smallest plot was
half a *strémma*, and the categories of land in which the smallest number
of *strémmata* were listed were in the ones denoting the highest quality.
An area of just under half a *zevgári* consisted of 42 different plots.

The largest single pieces of property in Ambéli never exceed approximately 70 *str.*, and these pieces are always forest land and occur only in
the holdings of the largest property owners—those owning 1 *zevgari*
and more. The largest plot of arable land very rarely exceeds 10 *str.*,

TABLE III

LIST OF LANDHOLDINGS IN AMBELI

	dhrámia of land
Dhimos Pappandhoniou	600
Thanassi Mikros	600
Theodhoros Kalfos	508
Ioanni Pappadhopoulos	440
Dimitrios Georgiadhis	408
Dhimos Karas	375
Maria Iannara	250
Christos Milos	250
Ioannis Pagonis	240
Kostis Lavakis	240
Dhimos Christodhoulou	240
Mitzos Pappas	227
Georgos Pappas	200
Stamos Chariatis	200
Mitzos Karamaniolis	200
Zoi Frangopoulos	200
Thomas Planas	200
Georgi Milios	200
Stephanos Melidhis	175
Chrysoula Georgiadhou	175
Thanassi Roussos	160
Petros Frangoulis	160
Kostis Panagos	150
Petros Lekas	133
Nikos Georgiou	130
Aris Belos	130
Ioannis Skordhas	130
Pandelis Christodhoulou	100
Eleni Pallis + HH (absent)	67

Absent owners

Charis Dhimitriou	(Plataniá)	200
Georgos Skordhas	(Yeropótamo)	137
Panagiotis Skordhas	(Pýrgos)	60
Shared out between approx. 10 inheritors		50
Meni Georgiou	(Kalýva)	40
Eleni Pagonis	(Kalýva)	25

		7,600

19 *zevgária* = 7,600 *dhrámia*. Therefore the church *zevgári* and the originally unpartitioned land are not included in this list of holdings. This list was given to me by a villager, from memory.

if it is to be at all fertile, while the most usual size for a field is between 2 and 4 *str*. The better the field the more likely it is to be on the small side. The proportion of fields to trees per *zevgári* is not invariable, but the proportion given in the page quoted is thought by a consensus of opinion not to be indicative of the over-all situation in which the normal number of fields to be expected in any one *zevgári* is about 150 *str*.

The fact that the land was sub-divided right from the days of its original partition in the last century, together with the nature of the dowry and inheritance systems practised after that, has been responsible for this fragmentation; but working as a cohesive force in the opposite direction, and counteracting a degree of fragmentation which would have rendered the farms of Ambéli unworkable, has been emigration, for this has eased pressure on the land, and enabled the few remaining men in the village to buy out their absent co-inheritors and thus to inherit the entire family estate.

The chief element in the dowry and inheritance systems which causes them to be such powerful factors in land fragmentation is the fact that under Greek law all children must be equal inheritors of their parents' property, and although provision is made in the law for disinheriting a son or a daughter, such a child can, except in very extreme circumstances, lay claim to at least half his proper share.

It was plainly in an effort to avoid too great fragmentation that the older custom in the village used to be to give dowries to the girls in the form of money, a few *strémmata*—i.e. fields—and some animals, and thus preserve the majority of the fields and all the forest for the sons. In a large family sons of the sons would marry out of the village as *esógambroi* for the same reason. It was unlikely that the rule of equal division of the estate was observed in this arrangement for the daughters, but it is said that they were satisfied to receive as much as they did receive, and that the law was satisfied by the specification in a legal document, drawn up at the time the property was made over, that such-and-such a daughter had received her 'share' of the inheritance and was entitled to no more. Still, an insistent suitor could force his prospective in-laws into allotting a reasonable amount to his fiancée, and also to be taken into account by parents was the possibility that, in the event of an extremely inequitable distribution, the deprived child could on her parents' death bring a lawsuit and attempt to overthrow the will.

Even though, because of this custom of passing a larger part of the land down through the male line, fragmentation was to a certain extent inhibited, a considerable degree of fragmentation was nevertheless unavoidable, and this was increased by the efforts of both parents and children to avoid quarrels by ensuring a fair division of property which included very varying types of land. Because of this, individual fields in a single property were often divided up among the inheritors—the eastern part, for instance, being given to one son, and the western part to another.

The situation was still further exacerbated by the fact that the old people used their property to exact good behaviour from their children —'They manipulate affairs' (παίζουν πολιτική) as it is still said—and to this end they often refrained from making a will until it was absolutely necessary. Of course in many cases they left it too late, and there are many cases in Ambéli of parents who have died intestate, and thus laid their estate open to equal partition between all their children, including any who may in fact have already been given their fair share. It is said that such a child who thus falls heir to property in addition to what he or she has already received does not give it up.

Even if the parents do make their wills, or make their property over to their children before they die, the custom of retaining a part of the property (of the order, usually, of 10 *str.* or so) as what is known as the 'old people's portion' can cause further fragmentation still. This 'old people's portion' is said to be instrumental in ensuring, in cases where the children's affection is in doubt, a certain amount of 'respect and fear' (σεβασμὸς καὶ φόβος), and it also serves as a reward for the son who remains in his parents' house and cares for them in their old age.

APPENDIX III

TABLE IV THE ECOLOGICAL YEAR

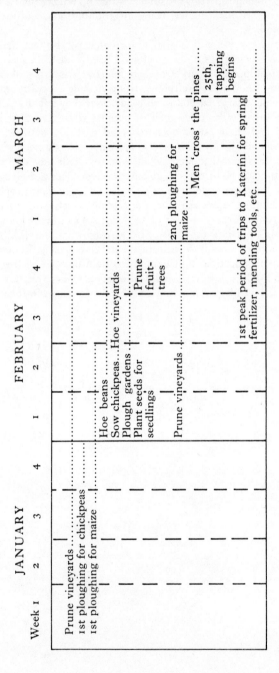

	APRIL				MAY				JUNE			
Week 1	2	3	4	1	2	3	4	1	2	3	4

Weeding corn and lentils............................10th

Spraying apples, corn, etc.

20th, sowing maize...

Planting out seedlings..............................

10th, weeding chickpeas.
10–15th, cleaning shoots from vines, and hoe vineyards for second time.
15th, pesticides on vines.
20th, cut green oats

Harvest oats for seeds, vetch for seeds, beans and lentils, thresh and winnow .↓.............

Harvest barley and thresh
Last day of June earth is built up round maize stalks

Water gardens twice a week from now on...
Cut vetch
Carry vetch and oats.........10th
Hoe maize

Trips to Katerini (general)

All sowing involves a further ploughing at which the seed is dropped or scattered. Thus maize ideally should be ploughed for three times, other crops twice.

	JULY				AUGUST				SEPTEMBER			
	Week 1	2	3	4	1	2	3	4	1	2	3	4

Wheat harvest....

Threshing......

Winnowing......

25th, harvest chickpeas......

Pruning and cleaning maize

20th, harvest maize, thresh it......

Women make tomato paste, trachana, dry figs, etc.

Collect fallen olives ....

Clearing and burning off fields

1st ploughing ......

Harvest the grapes

2nd peak period trips to Katerini with resin and for autumn fertilizer ....

Start collecting wood for winter ....

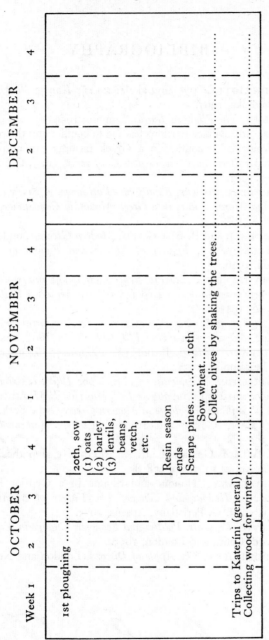

BIBLIOGRAPHY

N. P. ANDHRIOTI, *Ἐτυμολογικὸ Λεξικὸ τῆς Κοινῆς Νεοελληνικῆς*, Thessalonika, 1967.

K. ANDREWS, *The Flight of Ikaros*, London, 1959.

P. BIALOR, 'Intravillage tensions leading to conflict and the resolution and avoidance of conflict in a Greek farming community', *Acts of the Mediterranean Sociological Conference*, ed. J. G. Peristiany, Athens, 1963.

J. K. CAMPBELL, *Honour, Family and Patronage. A Study of Institutions and Moral Values in a Greek Mountain Community*, Oxford, 1964.

J. K. CAMPBELL and P. SHERRARD, *Modern Greece*, London, 1968.

A. COOMARASWAMY, *Figures of Speech and Figures of Thought*, London, 1946.

K. B. DHAMIANOU, *Ἔκθεσις περὶ προσωρινῆς διαχειρίσεως τοῦ συνιδιοκτήτου δάσους —, Εὐβοίας, διὰ τὴν περίοδον 1940–41 ἕως 1944–45*, 1941.

—— *Περὶ προσωρινῆς διαχειρίσεως τοῦ συνιδιοκτήτου δάσους —, Εὐβοίας, διὰ τὴν πενταετίαν 1/9/1947–31/8/1952*, 1947.

D. DHIMITRAKOU, *Μέγα Λεξικὸν τῆς Ἑλληνικῆς Γλώσσης*, Athens and Thessalonika, 1951.

Ἐθνικὴ Στατιστικὴ Ὑπηρεσία τῆς Ἑλλάδος 1962. Πληθυσμὸς τῆς Ἑλλάδος κατὰ τὴν ἀπογραφὴν 19ης Μαρτίου 1961, Athens, 1962.

E. FRIEDL, *Vasilika: A Village in Modern Greece*, New York, 1962.

M. GLUCKMAN, 'Gossip and Scandal', *Current Anthropology*, IV, 1963, 307–16.

R. PAINE, 'What is Gossip About? An Alternative Hypothesis', *Man*, Vol. II, No. 2, 1967, pp. 278–85.

J. G. PERISTIANY, 'Honour and Shame in a Cypriot Highland Village', in *Honour and Shame. The Values of Mediterranean Society*, ed. J. G. Peristiany, Athens, 1965.

J. TOMAŠEVIĆ, *Peasants, Politics and Economic Change in Yugoslavia*, Stanford, Calif., and London, 1955.

C. M. WOODHOUSE, *The Apple of Discord*, London and New York, 1948.

INDEX

Abduction, 93, 224
Abuse (including insult, 'words')
  as cause of quarrels, 202–3
  destructive power of, 73, 196
  in gossip, 201
  of men and women, 221
  types of, in women's quarrels, 222–3, 229
Accusation
  at end of friendship, 213
  in quarrels, 227
  in self-defence, 192
  in women's quarrels, 223
  of unchastity, 96, 195
  with reference to ideal values, 173
Adam, 101
  analogy of man with, 104
  Christ as second —; destiny of man in, 53
  cursing of, 102
  sin of, 54
Affines
  attitudes to sex regarding, 118, 161–2
  marriage between, 146–7
  relationships between, 148–50, 154–155
  terminology relating to, 98, 147–9
Albanian Campaign, 233
Ambitions
  community of, in house, 22
  for 'better' life, 6
  for road, 5, 253
  for urban life, 50, 252–6
  in abandonment of fields for forest, 38
America, 233, 234, 236
Andártes, 246
  definition of, 237
  involvement of villagers with, 238–241
Andhrioti, N. P., 201
Animals
  as part of family, 16–18, 89–90
  former accommodation of, 15, 245
  loss of, after evacuation, 241
  numbers owned, 242

  trespass of, 76, 175, 178, 181, 220, 223
  villagers' relationships with, 86–90
Apology
  absence of, 228
  avoidance of, 196
Asia Minor, 42, 233
Athens, 93, 178, 223, 239, 245, 253, 260, 266
Aunts, 144, 150
Australia, 234
Autumn, 15, 27, 30, 32, 208

Balkan Wars, 233
Baptism
  choice of godparents in, 164–5
  relationships created through, 162–163
  rules of, relating to concept of *katameriá*, 166
  significance of, 163–5
Belgium, 234
Belief
  attempt by *andártes* to undermine, 239
  insularity of, 42
  reality of, 61, 62
  regulation of social life by, 41
  solidarity created through, 50–1, 57–9, 211
  village unanimity in, 47, 57
Betrayal
  avoidance of, by lying, 199
  by kinsmen, 153, 156, 189
  by second cousins, 150
  fear of, limiting gossip, 210
  of friends, 190, 198, 200, 213
  reasons for, 196, 209–10
  to *andártes*, 239, 241
Bialor, P., 227
Birth, 82
Blood
  concept of relationship through, 132, 142, 144, 153
  'return' of, 147
Blood-tie, as ballast to relationships, 168